I0889798

Notes to Make the Sound Come Right

Notes to Make the Sound Come Right

FOUR INNOVATORS OF JAZZ POETRY

T. J. Anderson III

The University of Arkansas Press
Fayetteville
2004

Copyright © 2004 by The University of Arkansas Press

All rights reserved
Manufactured in the United States of America

08 07 06 05 04 5 4 3 2 1

Designed by Ellen Beeler

♾ The paper used in this publication meets the minimum requirements of the American National Standard for Permanence of Paper for Printed Library Materials Z39.48-1984.

Library of Congress Cataloging-in-Publication Data

Anderson, T. J., 1958–
Notes to make the sound come right : four innovators of jazz poetry / T. J. Anderson III.
p. cm.
Includes bibliographical references and index.
ISBN 1-55728-769-4 (pbk. : alk. paper)
1. American poetry—20th century—History and criticism. 2. Jazz in literature. 3. Mackey, Nathaniel, 1947-—Criticism and interpretation. 4. Music and literature—History—20th century. 5. Cortez, Jayne—Criticism and interpretation. 6. Jonas, Stephen. Exercises for ear. 7. Kaufman, Bob. Golden sardine. I. Title.
PS310.J39A53 2004
811'.509357—dc22

2004001819

For Yasmine and Céline, the music, the poetry, the future.

Contents

Acknowledgments

All love and gratitude to my companion and fellow poet, Pauline Kaldas, who has read this book more times than anybody I know.

Thanks to my parents, T. J. and Lois Anderson, and all the members of my family who continue to be inspirational and supportive through all of my endeavors.

I am grateful for the guidance of Professor Isidore Okpewho of SUNY-Binghamton, who saw this manuscript in its infancy and encouraged its growth.

This book would not be in your hands were it not for the support of Professors Jeffner Allen and Fred Garber of SUNY-Binghamton.

I offer this in loving memory of Professor Milton Kessler.

I am grateful for the encouragement and support I have received from Provost Wayne Markert, the members of the English and Creative Writing Department, and all my other colleagues at Hollins University.

Thank you to Chiji Akoma, Alyssa Antonelli, Amiri Baraka, Jayne Cortez, Paul Dean, Marcia Douglas, Thomas Sayers Ellis, Clayton Eshleman, Sascha Feinstein, Michael Gettings, Jeff Goodman, Ted Joans, Eileen Kaufman, Sunni Kessler, Nathaniel Mackey, Harryette Mullen, Dan Murphy, Aldon Lynn Nielsen, Maha El Said, Sonia Sanchez, Tony Seymour, and Joseph Torra.

I appreciate the patience and support of Larry Malley, director of the University of Arkansas Press, and the persistence of Angie Maxwell and Archie Schaffer IV, also at the Press.

This manuscript brought me in touch with a numerous group of supportive people, and though their names are too many to mention here, I appreciate all they have done to get this book to you. As Duke Ellington would say, "I love you madly!"

Grateful acknowledgment is made for permission to reprint substantial portions of the following poems:

"Afro American Talking Drum," from *Funk Lore: New Poems,* by Amiri Baraka. Copyright 1996. Reprinted by permission of the author.

"In the Tradition," "Wise 1," from *Transbluesency: Selected Poems,* by Amiri Baraka. Copyright 1995. Reprinted by permission of the author.

"Listening to Sonny Rollins at the Five-Spot," from *The Collected Poems of Paul Blackburn.* Copyright 1955, 1960, 1961, 1966, 1967, 1968, 1969, 1970, 1971, 1972, 1975, 1978, 1980, 1983, 1985 by Joan Blackburn. Reprinted by permission of Persea Books (New York).

"Backyards and Deviations," from *Blowing Mouth: The Jazz Poems, 1958–1970,* by Ray Bremser. Copyright 1978. Published by Cherry Valley Editions. Used by permission of Jeffrey Weinberg, Literary Executor for the Estate of Ray Bremser.

"Cabaret," from *The Collected Poems of Sterling A., Brown,* edited by Michael S. Harper. Copyright 1980 by Sterling A. Brown. Reprinted by permission of HarperCollins Publishers.

"Lonely, Woman," from *Pisstained Stairs and the Monkey Man's Wares,* by Jayne Cortez. Copyright 1969. Reprinted by permission of the author.

"Rose Solitude," from *Coagulations: New and Selected Poems,* by Jayne Cortez. Copyright 1984. Reprinted by permission of the author.

"Solo Finger Solo," from *Firespitter,* by Jayne Cortez. Copyright 1978. Reprinted by permission of the author.

"Why Not," from *Somewhere in Advance of Nowhere,* by Jayne Cortez. Copyright 1996. Reprinted by permission of the author.

"Dear John, Dear Coltrane," from *Songlines in Michaeltree: New and Collected Poems,* by Michael S. Harper. Copyright 2000. Used with permission of the author and the University of Illinois Press.

"Hey," "Negro Dancers," "Jazzonia," from *The Collected Poems of Langston Hughes,* by Langston Hughes. Copyright 1994 by the Estate of Langston Hughes. Used by permission of Alfred A. Knopf, a division of Random House.

"Jazz Is My Religion," from *Black Pow-Wow: Jazz Poems,* by Ted Joans. Copyright 1969. Reprinted by permission of the author.

"For Leroi Jones," "CXXXVII," "CXVIII," "XXXVI," "XCIV," "CXVII," "XVI," "LXI," "LXV," "XXVI," "XXXV," "CLV," from *Stephen Jonas: Selected Poems,* by Stephen Jonas. Copyright 1994. Reprinted by permission of Gerrit Lansing, Literary Executor for the Estate of Stephen Jonas.

"Mingus," from *Solitudes Crowded with Loneliness,* by Bob Kaufman. Copyright 1965. Reprinted by permission of Eileen Kaufman and Coffee House Press.

"HEATHER BELL," "Cocoa Morning," "Round About Midnight,"

"Jazz Chick," "Tequila Jazz," "His Horn," "Crootey Songo," "O-JAZZ-O," from *Cranial Guitar: Selected Poems,* by Bob Kaufman. Copyright 1996. Reprinted by permission of Eileen Kaufman and Coffee House Press.

"8th Chorus," from *San Francisco Blues,* by Jack Kerouac. Copyright 1959. Published by Grove Weidenfeld. Reprinted by permission of Sterling Lord Literistic.

"and when the Moon struck," "John Coltrane Arrived with an Egyptian Lady," "Capricorn Rising," "Ghost of a Chance," from *Eroding Witness,* by Nathaniel Mackey. Copyright 1985. Reprinted by permission of the author.

"For John Coltrane," "Black Music, a Beginning . . . ," from *Don't Cry, Scream,* by Haki R. Madhubuti. Copyright 1969. Reprinted by permission of Third World Press.

Section from *Muse and Drudge,* by Harryette Mullen. Copyright 1995. Reprinted by permission of the author.

"Words and Music in America," from *Moment's Notice: Jazz in Poetry and Prose,* edited by Art Lange and Nathaniel Mackey, poem by Kofi Natambu. Copyright 1993. Reprinted by permission of the author.

"Jazzoetry," from *Vibes from the Scribes: The Last Poets,* by Jalal Nuriddin. Copyright 1992. Reprinted by permission of the author.

"The Day Lady Died," from *Lunch Poems,* by Frank O'Hara. Copyright 1964. Reprinted by permission of City Lights Books.

"Thelonius," from *Ecstasy Is a Number,* by Margaret Randall. Copyright 1960. Reprinted by permission of the author.

"Old Words," from *I've Been a Woman: New and Selected Poems,* by Sonia Sanchez. Copyright 1978. Reprinted by permission of the author.

"Garden," by Cecil Taylor, from *Moment' Notice: Jazz in Poetry and Prose,* edited by Art Lange and Nathaniel Mackey. Copyright 1993. Reprinted by permission of the author.

"Mu," "Lamda," from *Harlem Gallery, Book I, The Curator,* by Melvin B. Tolson. Copyright 1965. Reprinted by permission of Melvin B. Tolson Jr., Literary Executor of the Estate of Melvin B. Tolson.

CHAPTER 1

The Jazz Impulse in Poetry

Wise 1

WHYS (Nobody Knows
The Trouble I Seen)
Trad.

If you ever find
yourself, some where
lost and surrounded
by enemies
who won't let you
speak in your own language
who destroy your statues
& instruments, who ban
your omm bomm ba boom
then you are in trouble
deep trouble
they ban your
own boom ba boom
you in deep deep
trouble

humph!

probably take you several hundred years
to get
out!

—*Amiri Baraka*

The term "jazz" has always been controversial when used to describe the music created by African Americans around the turn of the twentieth century that blended European and African musical traditions into a distinctly unique aesthetic rooted in the blues. Jazz has become a way of not only revising old musical forms, such as the spiritual, work song, and others, but also examining and signifying the intricacies of the African American social and cultural milieu. Thus, jazz is an extemporaneous means of cultural critique. The continual development and transformation of the music articulates an ongoing commentary on the complexities of African American history in the United States. It also becomes a way of transferring the visual to the aural, a way of interpreting the world through the agency of sound and musical symbol. The jazz musician evokes a mood and weaves a tale, as does the poet. "Swing—From Verb to Noun" is one of the chapter titles in Amiri Baraka's *Blues People,* a seminal study on the social roots of African American music emphasizing the mobility of the form. His focus on the movement, and subsequent reinterpretation of African American music, is not unlike the transformation that has occurred in Western poetry, where the genre moved from a predominately oral art form to one that places more emphasis on the printed text.

This book examines the work of four African American poets—Bob Kaufman, Stephen Jonas, Jayne Cortez, and Nathaniel Mackey—whose poetry is strongly informed by a jazz aesthetic. Its purpose is to examine the way jazz has been expressed in the poetry of these writers and to critique the jazz poem's role in the transmission of African American culture. These particular poets have been instrumental in terms of bringing new and innovative methods to the creative and performative aspects of the "jazz poem," and they are especially significant because their work spans a period (1960–90) during which jazz was undergoing tremendous changes. From bebop to free jazz to fusion, Kaufman, Jonas, Cortez, and Mackey all manage to skillfully create poetry rooted in an African American aesthetic that mirrors and responds to the challenges and subsequent changes that have occurred in the music. By choosing to focus on African American poets, I have been able to emphasize the link between uses of distinctly African rhythms to diasporic discourse, particularly apparent when the texts move toward social and political commentary critiquing issues of race and identity. To deny that race has been a factor in the development of jazz and African American poetry is to overlook an extremely important and complex issue that has contributed highly to the development of both forms of African American cultural expression.

In the past two decades there has been a resurgence of interest in jazz poetry. Writers like Michael Harper, George Elliott Clarke, Ted Joans, Hayden Carruth, Amiri Baraka, and Clark Coolidge have published several individual collections of jazz poetry employing a wide range of stylistic devices. Contemporary writers such as Jayne Cortez, Joy Harjo, Quincy Troupe, Yusef Komunyakaa, and Ntozake Shange, have made new recordings of jazz-influenced poetry. There have also been several reissued recordings by Langston Hughes, Jack Kerouac, The Watts Prophets, Kenneth Rexroth, The Last Poets, Gil Scott Heron, and others, thus significantly adding to the developing canon of recorded jazz poetry. Also important is the reemergence of the coffeehouse in the 1980s as a locale for the public performance of jazz poetry. This renewed trend obviously has its antecedents not only in the beat movement of the 1950s but also in the black arts movement of the 1960s and 1970s. Young recording artists like United Future Organization, Digable Planets, Us3, and Groove Collective have successfully merged hip-hop poetry and jazz, thus further acknowledging popular music's debt to African American cultural traditions.

In the early nineties, the new interest in jazz poetry resulted in the publication of several anthologies that sought to introduce the diverse ways in which jazz-inspired literature has been handled. Prose anthologies such as Richard N. Albert's *From Blues to Bop: A Collection of Jazz Fiction* and Marcela Breton's *Hot and Cool: Jazz Short Stories* have sparked renewed interest in the literature by becoming popular texts in college and university courses. *Seeing Jazz: Artists and Writers on Jazz,* edited by Elizabeth Goldson, captures the moods and rhythms of jazz as it has been expressed by poets, writers, painters, sculptors, and photographers. Sascha Feinstein and Yusef Komunyakaa's *The Jazz Poetry Anthology* and *The Second Set* include the work of several modern and contemporary American poets. *Moment's Notice: Jazz in Poetry and Prose,* edited by Art Lange and Nathaniel Mackey, was the first major collection to include both jazz-influenced poetry and prose.

Both *The Jazz Poetry Anthology* and *Moment's Notice* attempt to define a text that is written in the jazz idiom. Various issues arise when an editor goes about the task of defining and locating points of fusion between two transitional art forms like jazz and poetry. Several criteria come to mind when considering the acceptable boundaries that each anthology establishes. The notion of musical and literary boundaries poses a complex dilemma. Is the work selected because of its reference to a musician's life or a particular performance/event? Or is it because the actual language/syntax employed in the text manages to capture the multitudinous musical constructions and nuances of jazz? Sascha Feinstein discusses the controversy in his critical book *Jazz Poetry:*

> Some writers feel passionately that a jazz poem must in some way emulate the rhythmic pulse of the music; others claim that "jazziness" is an arbitrary term at best and that allusions to jazz musicians might be the only sure way to know whether the poem has been influenced by jazz. Proponents of the first approach criticize the other, particularly the work by West Coast writers and performances artists, for not substantiating the poetry as strong verse. Those in the other camp, however, strongly criticize narrative presentation for avoiding the essence of jazz—or, to use a more colloquial phrase, for being square. (2)

Unfortunately, too often, in most anthologies, subject matter, rather than a more experimental use of the poetic form adapted to a jazz aesthetic, becomes the main criterion for selection. However Feinstein and Komunyakaa's anthology strikes a fair balance between subject matter and experimentation. Although the majority of poems included are fairly conventional in their treatment of jazz, the anthology is international in its focus, giving readers the opportunity to examine how poets of various cultures have applied jazz music to their aesthetic process.

One of the interesting aspects of the Feinstein and Komunyakaa anthology is the manner in which the poems are presented. The editors place these poems alphabetically by the poets' last names as opposed to a chronological or thematic order. Such an organization may inadvertently lead to a comparison and judgment of diverse poetic materials and techniques. One could place work written in the 1940s that responds to bebop next to a work that takes its influences from free jazz. Would it be fair to compare an Art Tatum solo to a Cecil Taylor composition? Some would argue "yes," noting that the value of comparison enables the reader/listener to see how far the form has developed. However, the benefit of placing poets in chronological order reveals the way in which artists work with the materials of their times and can be just as enlightening. Fortunately, Feinstein and Komunyakaa have included "Statements of Poetics" by the various contributors and a music appendix that lists a general grouping of the poems according to musician or musical period. These provide a broader range in which the texts can be viewed. Feinstein and Komunyakaa characterize the jazz poem in their introduction to the anthology.

> In part, the act of visualizing jazz accounts for the range of poets engaged in the music's elusive accessibility: young black writers steeped in the tradition of black music, using poetry in part to achieve a political voice; older white poets attracted to the spirit of syncopated rhythms; some writers who feel bebop ruined the spirit of jazz; others who see modernism as surpassing all previous forms of the music; men pining over the women they wanted to love; women lamenting over the men who have done them wrong; people transported by the live drama on the bandstand; others, years later, transported still by memories and recordings; poets interested mainly in a detailed narrative; poets trying to break apart the language to imitate sound; friends of jazz musicians eager to keep their spirits alive on the page; jazz appreciators engaged in the spirit of an era; and all those who have tried to capture the swing, the sex, the dance, the violence, the laughter, the brutal rhythms and the tender sway of jazz. (xx)

As detailed as this description is, I quote the passage in full to call attention to the conspicuous absence of any references to political action that is propelled by the voice and subsequently transforms form. There is no reference to anarchism or surrealism as being one of the poetic responses to the free jazz movement, which certainly had a profound impact on the creation of jazz poetry.

Art Lange and Nathaniel Mackey's anthology, *Moment's Notice,* places the work in chronological order and is slightly more eclectic in its approach. The poetry and prose texts Mackey and Lange include are representative of a wide landscape of style and artistry, paying particular attention to the experimental end of the literary spectrum. With the inclusion of such culturally and aesthetically diverse writers as Lorenzo Thomas, Kamau Brathwaite, Melvin Tolson, Jack Spicer, Jayne Cortez, Clayton Eshleman, and Lawson Fusao Inada, several of whom appear in Feinstein and Komunyakaa as well, there are many examples of texts that are engaged in a variety of literary and musical possibilities. Particularly important is the inclusion of poems by musicians like Cecil Taylor and Abdullah Ibrahim. Thus, one is able to examine the similarities and differences between the musician and the writer in the use of voice. Although excerpted, the use of prose that responds to jazz presents a dynamic contrast when compared to the poetry. The reader is only able to read excerpts without the benefit of seeing the entire novel. These passages, then, can be seen as moments of improvisation or samples from a broader work, whereas the poems are more self-contained.

In addition to these two important anthologies, several academic publications have emerged, critiquing the various literary and cultural aspects of the music itself. For example, in 1991 the literary journal *Conjunctions* devoted an entire issue to American music, including significant essays on black music by Gerald Early, Amiri Baraka, Albert Murray, and Quincy Troupe. During that same year, *The Black American Literature Forum* published a special issue focusing mainly on jazz, including a noteworthy essay by critic Barry Wallenstein on the historical development of jazz poetry. More recently, *Callaloo* devoted an entire issue to jazz poetics that included a special section devoted to the work of poet Bob Kaufman. *Reading Jazz,* edited by David Meltzer and published in 1993, was a significant anthology of jazz literature in that it presented ways in which the music has been "mythologized, colonialized, demonized, defended, and ultimately neutralized" by European and white American critics (4). By choosing to focus exclusively on white criticism, Meltzer's anthology is a significant contribution to the discourse in that it examines the way that whites have perceived the roots and future of jazz, as well as its influence on varying forms of cultural expression. In 1995, Krin Gabbard edited two noteworthy volumes of jazz cultural criticism. *Representing Jazz* and *Jazz among the Discourses* examined the influence of jazz among other disciplines in the humanities, thus broadening the scope of the music's influence on modernist and postmodernist discourse. Robert G. O'Meally's impressive *The Jazz Cadence of American Culture* offers an even further critical discussion of the music by including a broader academic perspective from an interdisciplinary range of cultural critics who examine the effects of jazz on various elements of American culture.

Sascha Feinstein's critical work, *Jazz Poetry: From the 1920s to the Present,* published in 1997, marks the first time a fairly extensive historical survey on jazz poetry has been undertaken. His book discusses the connection between the musical development of jazz and its relation to poetry. Using a multicultural approach to the study of jazz poetry, Feinstein initiates his study by examining the connection between the early development of jazz and its influence on cadences of the poetic line as employed by early populist poets like Carl Sandburg and Vachel Lindsay. Feinstein, a musician as well as a poet, is also the founding editor of *Brilliant Corners,* one of the only academic journals devoted entirely to jazz literature.

Although such recent criticism has brought attention to the importance of jazz and its connection to poetry, academic inquiry often leads to categorization. Due to the highly charged issue of identity politics, there has always been a desire to compartmentalize, to place things in a particular order so they conform to our notion of empirical evidence. Most modern art forms such as jazz, film, and photography often incorporate other more established forms, thus it becomes difficult to isolate and decipher how one particular medium influences another. Mainly, though not exclusively, rooted in spontaneous improvisation, jazz music is more concerned with presenting various musical ideas and possibilities through the agency of sound and gesture. The physicality of the musician, whether on the bandstand or off, plays a key role, for jazz becomes an attitude, a way in which one defies conformity and creates new ways of presenting oneself to the world. Although certain elements in a musical performance may be similar, no solo is played the same way twice. There are always nuances, sometimes subtle, sometimes prominent. Even a listener can distort the sound of a jazz recording by simply adjusting the volume or manipulating the equalizer to affect modulations in the sound. Although the notes may be the same, the change in timber can result in a different emotional response on each listening, therefore implying that no musical number can be heard or played the same way twice. Jazz is a music that "embraces the chaos," as the novelist Leon Forrest says. It is through that embrace that the musician is able to relate the story not only of the individual but also of the diasporic community, and it is through this individual voice that the community receives its empowerment. In jazz there is a blending of the religious and the secular where the performer "testifies" and fellow musicians and audience members provide affirmation. Certainly, jazz is a simultaneously communal and individualistic art form.

Poetry that is informed by a jazz aesthetic attempts the same gesture. The poet is the soloist, providing a testimonial that employs a different medium but achieves a similar sense of audience intimacy whether the text is read aloud in a public venue or by a lone reader. The various ideas that inform a poet's individual jazz-influenced poetics often break from the constraints of traditionally structured verse. In jazz poetry, the tonal quality of the individual word is given special emphasis, and the manner in which the word is placed within the text is integral to how the entire poem sounds. Since sound is such a crucial element, the listener or critic is often unable to adequately articulate the ethereal connection between tone and meaning. This "inability" to provide a succinct textual analysis of a composition or performance is a legitimate response to the music as well. In *Black Music,* Amiri Baraka writes about the futility of jazz criticism as a means to delineate the complexities of a jazz solo. He astutely points out that it is impossible to fully capture the nuances of a blues or jazz solo by using notation and further adds that the music itself cannot be completely understood without examining the attitudes that produced it. Baraka argues that musical scores and transcribed solos by jazz musicians are inadequate, as they merely serve to speak to the "futility of formal musicology when dealing with jazz," and that something entirely different is implied via the jazz solo. Whatever it is, Baraka writes that it lies outside the realm of musical notation, "the notes of a jazz solo, as they are coming into existence, exist as they do for reasons that are only concomitantly musical" (15).

The use of jazz as it is applied in the creation of poetry can be viewed in a similar manner. Although the actual printed text is important and can easily lend itself to the often rigid criteria of formal criticism, how the work sounds when it is read aloud is also crucial. A poet can use his or her voice as a musical instrument, changing the pitch or cadence of a single word to create myriad images and sounds. The spatial relationship between words, what is silent or unsaid, is equally important. Thus, the poet straddles his or her role as musician and writer falling prey to the "impossibility" of criticism. This is similar to the role of the jazz performer/composer in which the music creates spaces of ambiguity that are uneasily decipherable. It's an echo of that famous question put to Louis Armstrong, "What is jazz?" and Armstrong's response, "If you have to ask you'll never know." The same question has been asked of all modernist and postmodernist art and particularly of poetry. Perhaps one of the most salient qualities this art shares is its ability to slip through any definitive answer and continue to promote and provoke critical debate.

One problem that often occurs in some texts of music criticism is the assumption that any African American musician and composer who utilizes the tools of improvisation are performing in the jazz idiom.

Composers and performers as diverse as Charles Mingus, Max Roach, Duke Ellington, and Anthony Braxton have preferred to define their music as black classical, American music, or simply "the music," vying for a more open-ended definition that encompasses cross-cultural musical influences. Overall, musical "specialization" is a label that has been imposed by the record companies in an attempt to market music toward particular ethnic or economic demographics. Such labeling produces a myopic sense of music. Whether the music is known by jazz or any other name, there will always be musicians who seek to expand existing definitions or belie any definitive categorization, thus making music a more organic enterprise.

When I was young, the noted pianist and ragtime composer Eubie Blake came to visit my family's Atlanta home. He played several compositions on the family upright piano, among them Scott Joplin's "Maple Leaf Rag" and his own "I'm Just Wild About Harry," a hit from his 1920 groundbreaking musical with Nobel Sissle, *Shuffle Along*. Blake was over seventy years old, and I recall how his long wrinkled fingers and hands skillfully traversed the keyboard. Since my father is a composer, the conversation naturally centered on music. We were entertained with stories of the early days of the black musical and the struggle to popularize a legitimate black theatrical tradition during an era of minstrelsy and Jim Crow. At one point in the conversation, Blake remarked that there was one word that he would not say in front of ladies. On a piece of paper, he quickly wrote the word "jazz." Although there has been wide speculation concerning jazz's etymology, Blake was obviously sensitive to its brothel origins. He had played the clubs of New Orleans's famed Storyville district when jazz was in its infancy. In jook joints, flophouses, and speakeasies, the music has often been associated with booze and good times. In those days, many a churchgoer, black and white, would rally against the dangers of the "primitive" secular song and its sexual candor. Such an attitude certainly maligned any serious considerations of the creative and sophisticated pulse that drove the music. Even Sterling Brown, the great poet and scholar, had difficulty introducing any kind of academic inquiry into jazz music at historically black Howard University in the 1930s because of its negative connotations.

It was the spontaneity of the music, the ejaculation of sound that, according to its detractors, could lead to sexual promiscuity. "Jazz," in several minds, was a corruption of the word "jissom" (sperm). It is interesting to note that the sexual meaning of the word also fits into the musical context and reflects the energy that occurs during an improvisation as a spontaneous and unrehearsed combustion of music. Famed pianist Jelly Roll Morton claimed to have "invented" jazz while playing for brothel customers in Louisiana and informed ethnomusicologist Alan Lomax that the music was a particular favorite among the "whores of Bourbon Street." However, the word "jazz" has other origins. In *Juba to Jive,* Clarence Major's etymological dictionary of the black vernacular, the word's origins are traced to the African Bantu *jaja,* meaning to dance and make music (255). Thus, the use of the term "jazz" as a means to label the music takes on even more significance in that it stretches and goes beyond the African musical conventions of sound, timber, and pitch by employing an African linguistic component as well.

The Europeans who brought Africans to the Americas attempted to eradicate all traces of African indigenous culture. Ethnic and linguistic groups were separated in an attempt to subvert notions of rebellion. What was African became forbidden and any manifestation of native cultural tropes was suppressed. This was particularly indicative in music and dance. It was feared, and reasonably so, that the practice of cultural traditions from the homeland would lead toward rebellion. There were several instances in which African practices were expressly forbidden and punishable by law. In 1739, after the Stono rebellion in the colony of North Carolina, laws against music and literacy were enacted.

> And for that as it is absolutely necessary to the safety of this Province, that all due care be taken to restrain the wanderings and meetings of negroes and other slaves, at all times, and more especially on Saturday nights, Sundays and other holidays, and their using and carrying wooden swords, and other mischievous and dangerous weapons, or *using or keeping of drums, horns, or other loud instruments, which may call together or give sign or notice to one another of their wicked designs and purposes* . . . And whatsoever master, owner or overseer shall permit or suffer his or their negro or other slave or slaves, at any time hereafter, or *beat drums, blow horns, or use other loud instruments,* or whosoever shall suffer and countenance any public meetings or seatings or strange negroes or slaves in their plantations, shall forfeit 10 current money, for every such offense.

(Gates and McKay, *Norton Anthology of African American Literature* xxix; emphasis added.)

It is interesting to note that the particular instruments named in this prohibition have been very crucial to the development of jazz music. It is the drum that often communicates cadence within a musical performance, forming cohesiveness between individual and communal statements. Oftentimes, the drummer responds directly to a soloist, providing a supportive musical dialogue. As an instrument of communication, the drum can be played in a variety of ways, creating a mosaic of timber and sound that mirrors the human voice and thus continues to evoke an African aesthetic and cultural memory. In *Blues People,* Amiri Baraka cites the importance of the drum in Africa and by inference in African American music by writing that the drum was not a "kind of primitive Morse code," but a "phonetic reproduction of the words themselves," the result of which is a highly "developed and extremely fine" and "complex rhythmical sense" which is "unusually responsive to timbral subtleties" (26).

I remember seeing the percussionist Michael Olatunji in concert. He played two large conga drums that he personified by referring to them as "sister speakers." He demonstrated the connection between the human voice and the percussive instrument by saying a phrase in Yoruba and repeating it on the drums. The pronunciation was astoundingly similar. I introduce this story in order to illustrate the manner in which the drum becomes a means of appropriating the human voice and how this appropriation acts as an alternative means of communicating, thus placing the function of the instrument in a non-Western aesthetic concept.[1]

The trope of assigning a specific gender to the drum, as expressed through Olatunji's reference to sister speakers, has been carried over in jazz. For example, Duke Ellington's 1957 album *A Drum Is a Woman* tells the story of jazz through the character of a dancer named Madame Zajj. The use of dance as a means to relay the historical development of jazz is crucial because the movement of the female body accompanied by music acts as a kind of text in which both visual and sound imagery encode elements of African American culture.[2]

In citing the Stono proclamation of 1739, it is noteworthy to emphasize the days in which the practice of African American cultural traditions were said to have occurred. These "cultural performances" happened on "Saturday nights, Sundays and Holidays." The prohibition probably cites these specific days because these were the only days when slaves were allowed some "relaxation" from physical labor. Coming together on these festive occasions gave people the opportunity to communicate and pass on longstanding cultural traditions. These days also enabled musical apprenticeship to flourish and, although slave owners attempted to disassemble the various ethnic languages by insisting that all communication be spoken in English, music became a way of reconnecting strands, a way of voicing and "recording" the collective concerns of the diaspora. In *Stomping the Blues*, a study of the blues and its effects on American culture, Albert Murray questions why, of all the places in the diaspora where the slave trade was so integral, it was only in the United States that blues and subsequently jazz developed. I agree with Murray's contention that music became an essential means of communication among Africans in the United States because of the linguistic barriers that were imposed by those who sought to uphold slavery. The various African ethnic groups that were subjugated to slavery in Central and South America were not separated on the same scale as they were in the United States. For example, there were larger plantations in the Caribbean, whereas in the United States small farmers were slave owners as well. Thus, ethnic groups were separated in an attempt to suppress any form of communication that would subsequently lead to rebellion. It has been well documented that such a policy was doomed to failure. It is ironic that in most instances it was the spread of Catholicism in South America and the West Indies and its reconfiguration into Voudoun and Santeria that managed to maintain the African cultural continuum.

Prohibitions were not only against music at Stono; they were also against literacy.

> And whereas the having of slaves taught to write, or suffering them to be employed in writing, may be attending with great inconveniences; Be it enacted, that all and every person and persons whatsoever, who shall hereafter teach, or cause any slave or slaves to be taught to write, or shall use or employ any slave as a scribe in any manner of writing whatsoever, hereafter taught to write; every such person or persons shall, for every offense, forfeit the sum of one hundred pounds current money. (Gates and McKay, *Norton Anthology of African American Literature* xxix)

The power of the written word, as a methodology of liberation, is a vital component of African American culture. Achieving literacy is a prominent trope in African American literature and often becomes a vehicle for a character or writer to become enlightened and aware of the world in a larger and often broader cultural context. Perhaps the best-known example of this occurrence is the incident in Frederick Douglass's autobiography when he is being taught to read by his mistress in Baltimore and the anger this provokes from his master. Despite Douglass's problematic construction of manhood, his introduction to literacy in the narrative marks a moment when he shows how a "slave becomes a man." Also familiar but somewhat lesser known is *A Narrative of the Most Remarkable Particulars in the Life of James Albert Ukawsaw Gronniosaw, An African Prince, As Related by Himself,* first published in 1770. In the narrative, Gronniosaw writes of observing the captain of a slave ship reading a passage from the Bible to his fellow crewmembers. Gronniosaw becomes aware of the reverence his captors have for those mysterious words. Later he sneaks into the captain's cabin, removes the Bible from its hiding place, and opens it. It was his expectation that he would have the same experience he noted in his captors. To his consternation, the book doesn't talk to him. He believes this is because he is black. This event marks a turning point in Gronniosaw's narrative because it instills in him the desire to read, write, and eventually create his own text that "talks" to his people.[3]

Just as the talking drum of several West African societies acts as a communicator and recorder of the cultural and historical continuum, the "talking book" in America is of equal importance and performs a similar function. In his theoretical study of African American literature, *The Signifying Monkey,* literary critic Henry Louis Gates writes about the trope of the talking book. He states that African American literature is a continuing dialogue among writers that traverses generational lines. Each book written by an African American author comments or "signifies" against a preceding text, engaging in a continual process of (re)vision. This is not unlike the practice of "call and response," which, although often cited as a practice within the black church, has its origins in African music. A literary work becomes what Gates refers to as a talking book, taking on ramifications that go beyond the general narrative and appearance of the text. This continual dialogue in African American letters becomes not only a way of preserving the culture but also a means of transformation and reconfiguration in order to respond to different historical epochs. The practice of signifying, particularly by employing the black vernacular tradition as a means of constructing a text, works to encode a complexity of readings that are firmly rooted in

African American discourse. This practice has relevance in jazz composition as well. Gates argues that fixed musical texts (standards like "April in Paris," "My Funny Valentine," and "My Favorite Things") usually provide examples in which signifying takes on more dramatic revisionist proportions. He writes that this "principle of repetition and difference, this practice of intertextuality, which has been so crucial to the black vernacular forms of Signifyin(g), jazz—and even its antecedents, the blues, the spirituals, and ragtime—is the source of my trope for black intertextuality in the Afro-American formal literary tradition" (Gates, *The Signifying Monkey* 64).

One of the first African American music critics to explore the complexities of jazz and its historical legacy is Amiri Baraka in *Blues People,* a landmark study of musical and social criticism. The book details the development of African American secular music, particularly the blues and jazz. Baraka examines how these types of music derive their aesthetic and formal characteristics directly from sacred music, such as African praise songs, spirituals, and secular music like work songs and country blues in a way that parallels the development of African American history and culture. Responding to the complexity of history as a catalyst for music, Baraka writes:

> Blues is the parent of all legitimate jazz, and it is impossible to say exactly how old the blues is—certainly no older than the presence of Negroes in the United States. It is a native American music, the product of the black man in this country; or to put it more exactly the way I have come to think about it, blues could not exist if the African captives had not become American captives. (17)

Baraka's historical and social approach to the creation of African American music demonstrates how the nonmaterial aspects of African culture managed to survive attempts at eradication by Euro-American culture. He astutely points out that the stanza format of the twelve-bar blues is encoded within the call-and-response form used in work songs and slave spirituals. In jazz, Baraka argues, the call-and-response form is grounded in individual and communal contact. In *Shadow and Act,* Ralph Ellison argues that jazz is an act of "individual assertion within and against the group" and that "improvisation represents an assertion of individuality in a collective context linked by the chain of tradition" (234). Thus, the musician or jazz poet who employs improvisatory gestures participates with the audience in the creation of the piece. This can be observed during performances when a musician connects with an audience's vocal or visual responses and the music reaches a new level of intensity. Poet Nathaniel Mackey writes that, in *Blues People,* Baraka "emphasizes nonconformity in his treatment of bebop, stressing what he terms its 'willfully harsh, anti-assimilationist sound'" (Mackey, "Other: From Noun to Verb" 87). This anti-assimilationist sound takes on particular significance in the jazz poetry that veers away from a linear narrative and predictable meter. This practice mirrors bebop in its offbeat musical ascents that play against an established nonjazz musical standard. When asked in an interview for the journal *Black Nation: Journal of African American Thought* about the relationship between poetry and music, Baraka responded:

> It's the same thing, poetry is a form of music, an early form of music . . . Poetry is the first music. I think the poet predicts music and I don't think you can disconnect poetry from music.—I think when poetry gets away from music, as is the case of academic poetry, it tends to be anti-musical, having more and more to do with rhetoric than it has with music. The more poetry gets disconnected from music, the less interesting it is and the less likely it is to live as poetry. (Lewis 78)

There is no general consensus as to what elements comprise a jazz poem. Since it has been so difficult to define the music, defining the literature continues to be a daunting task that is problematic as well. In his essay "Poetry and Jazz: A Twentieth-Century Wedding," Barry Wallenstein writes that there are three plausible ways to approach the connection between jazz and poetry. One way that Wallenstein suggests is to "search out traditional poetic definitions and values in jazz lyrics" (595). For example, one could examine the "poetic values" of Billie Holiday's rendition of "Strange Fruit," or even the vocalese improvisations of Eddie Jefferson. By examining jazz poetry in this fashion, one must certainly infer the importance of the aural sound over the written text. It is the nuance of the voice and how it reconstructs the cadence of the text that places particular emphasis on certain syllables and tones in order to convey poetic image and meaning. While critiquing poetry in this fashion would be useful, its scope would be extremely limited in terms of other poems that respond to different criteria. How would we categorize bebop vocalizations under such a definition? When musicians like Dizzy Gillespie, Betty Carter, Babs Gonzales, or Jon Hendricks sing scat, emphasizing sound as opposed to identifiable words, how would we classify their performance? When does one form become poetry and the other music? Of course, this has been an issue much under debate and, to some listeners, the difference would be miniscule or nonexistent.

Noting that the performance of jazz is not unlike the performing language of poetry, Wallenstein also suggests that one could study the structure of jazz composition, particularly improvised solos, and how they relate to the improvised gestures of free verse. There is a lot of validity in this approach. Several poets who write in the jazz idiom often use recognizable musical cadences, particularly solo improvisation from jazz performances, and try to replicate those sounds through both conventional and unconventional syntax. However, the problem with this approach is that some jazz poems are responses to the musicians' lives rather than responses to a particular piece. These poems can often take on a more linear format or can be open-ended, having little difference in language with a poem that does not employ jazz as its subject matter. Jazz poets write in different styles that often reflect a particular musical era. For example, poets enamored of the swing era may choose a more structured approach to their poetry as opposed to those who are influenced by the openness of free jazz.

Another difference that occurs between the improvisatory gestures within the music and those of the poems on the page is that during a jazz performance a particular kind of spontaneity is involved that the soloist would be unable to repeat. Jazz does not desire to replicate detail for detail what was done earlier. It is the point of the music to transform and change with each performance. This is not to say that poetry cannot achieve the same manner in performance, particularly when it is done "spontaneously" without a text or with a text that is used as a means of guiding the improvisation. However, this is seldom the case. Most jazz poets have prepared the text in advance. Another way to approach this study, Wallenstein suggests, is to observe how a "traditional-sounding first line won't necessarily be followed by regular rhyme, meter or rhythm" (595). This approach is problematic as well, because most postmodern verse tries to veer away from structured rhyme and meter and can equally be influenced by modern painting as opposed to any strict jazz aesthetic. Frank O'Hara's *Lunch Poems*, published in 1964, is a good example of work that is equally influenced by both forms of art.

In *Thinking in Jazz: The Infinite Art of Improvisation*, Paul Berliner discusses the dual connotations of the term "improvisation" among musicians. He notes that when musicians use the word as a noun to refer to improvisations as artistic products, they mainly concentrate on the improvisation's relationship to the original model of the musical performance. In describing the improvisatory techniques of saxophonist Lee Konitz, Berliner observers that Konitz views improvisation as the "most radical transfiguration of the melody" and that "altogether new ideas [come] from progressively subtler alterations falling within the realm of variation, embellishment, and interpretation" (221). Musicians who use improvisation during performances focus not only on the transformation of previous models, and subsequently the creation of new musical ideas, but also on the "dynamic conditions and precise processes underlying their transformation and creation." He further elaborates:

> Typically, [musicians] reserve the term for real-time composing—instantaneous decision making in applying and altering musical materials and conveying new ideas. Players distinguish such operations during solos from the recall and performance of precomposed ideas, those formulated outside the current event in the practice room or in a previous performance. From this standpoint, unique features of interpretation, embellishment, and variation, when conceived in performance, can also be regarded theoretically as improvised. (221–22)

The jazz artist's vocabulary is made up of a variety of influences, from swing figures and bebop licks to free jazz gestures, and that vocabulary can also extend to include quotations from popular songs, Western classical music, or songs from other traditions. Thus, the artist weaves a mosaic that simultaneously alludes to different musical traditions while at the same time developing a new one.

Jazz poetry can be viewed in a similar context in that the poet draws upon the various traditional/nontraditional (African and/or European) cultural elements and forges a unique expression of individual and racial or musical identity through his or her poetry. The jazz poem, although separated by the self-containment of individual form, is also part of a continuing collective dialogue that has its roots in West African oral tradition, as well as in the black American South, regardless of which ethnic group employs it. The use of various metrical devices in the formulation of a poem is linked to and often mirrors the innovative qualities of the music. In his study on the influence of blues in the poetry of Langston Hughes, Steven C. Tracy writes that even the jazz and blues musician's improvisations are not "spontaneous acts" but are circumscribed by a vocabulary (style, patterns, and techniques) that are the "accepted conventions of the specific genre." He notes that these "elements are at work even if they are being deliberately violated" (225). This reading of improvisational technique applies to jazz poetry and is perhaps one of the major commonalties that the two art forms share.

Also important to the jazz musician and the jazz poet is the ability to tell stories through their respective mediums. Against the backdrop of the collective musical dialogue that occurs between performers, the soloist initiates a tonal narrative that complements the established structure of the collective tale. For example, in Charles Mingus's moving elegy to tenor saxophonist Lester Young, "Goodbye Porkpie Hat," soloist Eric Dolphy movingly interprets Young's musical tone. Although Dolphy's voice is quite different from Young's, the tone of his musical phrasing evokes Young's ability to slur pitches and produce an unmistakably fluid sound. In examining the importance of mood within any jazz composition, Berliner writes that "the piece's precise mood has a powerful tempering effect on improvisers, guiding their personal feelings to blend with those appropriate for the performance" (203). A parallel event occurs during the creation of jazz poetry, particularly if the poet is responding to a piece of music. The rhythmic cadence often dictates the mood and timber of the text. For example, Paul Blackburn's "Listening to Sonny Rollins at the Five-Spot" captures the cadence of a Rollins improvisation of the standard "There Will Never Be Another You."

THERE WILL be many other nights like
be standing here with someone, some
  one
  someone
  some-one
  some
  some
  some
  some
  some
  some
  one
  there will be other songs
  a-nother fall, another-spring, but

there will never be a-noth, noth
anoth
noth
—anoth-er
noth-er
noth-er
                Other lips that I may kiss.
but they won't thrill me like
                        thrill me like
                                        like yours
used to
        dream a million dreams
but how can they come
when there
                    never be
a-noth

The poem manages to simultaneously evoke the original sentimentality of the song's lyrics and re-create the repetition of Rollins's tonal variations. Thus, by emphasizing sound through the placement of word fragments and single words on separate lines, Blackburn is able to construct a poetic narrative that achieves both performative and textual unity. Additionally, the nonlinear appearance of the poem, particularly in the final lines, creates a visual shape that replicates the fluidity and sensuality of Rollins's voicings.

In the groundbreaking book *Jazz Text,* a study of poetry and its connection to jazz, Charles Hartman astutely points out that the use of the term "voice" is of particular importance. Hartman writes that the tone of the spoken word can convey more than the written text, but that poets have methods for "recreating a tonal supplement" in a poem. Hartman implies that this "tonal supplement" becomes a means of defining the "voice" in a poem. "Going in the other direction," Hartman continues, "subtracting from the speaking voice the words and the information they convey—musicians can transfer the eloquent remainder to an instrument; so that we can also speak of the 'voice' of a musician who might be physically mute" (3).

Hartman further critiques the complexities of examining "voice" and the various extensions of the term, noting how the different modes of voice, such as singing, talking, and reciting, can be extended to include the printed poem, which can be viewed as an instrumental solo. Voice works as a way of attributing the text or sound to the artist who created it. Most listeners of jazz are usually able to point out whether a musician playing on a recording is John Coltrane or Dexter Gordon or Lester Young. This also goes beyond merely recognizing the identifiable musical signature of a particular performer. An astute listener can listen to a contemporary musician playing and say, "Hey, that's a Charlie Parker line," or "That's a Clifford Brown riff." Thus, the "sound" becomes a way of delineating and identifying voice. How musicians "sound," whether they are actually performing or someone else is appropriating an identifiable piece of their work, becomes their signature. These signatures are constantly being dissected and critiqued on the bandstand. Whenever, and wherever, a musician plays, some element of jazz history employed through the agency of sound plays an active role in the construction of a piece. Therefore, the voice takes on special significance in jazz and poetry because it is part of a continual dialogue that not only revoices or reinstates but also reworks and reinvents.

The use of voice in poetry functions in this manner. A reader can look at line placement, vocabulary, personal and social concerns, and other things and can identify the particular poet writing. For example, when students take the GRE subject exam in English literature, they are asked to identify the authors of selected passages. The choice a student makes depends upon his or her knowledge of a writer's style. The awareness of "voice" occurs in the "silent" medium of the printed page. Whether the printed text is read aloud or subvocalized, there is a certain tonal quality of which the reader becomes aware. The same is true for specific jazz cadences or time signatures. A poet who skillfully uses alliteration can certainly convey the tonal qualities of various instruments. Hartman correctly states that "voice seems to be not self but the going outward of the self, a going that can be indirect or redirected" (3). Surely that "going outward" is one of the prime motivations for the creation of some of the most innovative jazz-inspired poetry. It is a way of communicating through sound and image. This outward direction applied to jazz music occurs where the music's vocabulary can be viewed as a kind of lingua franca because it employs multiethnic musical traditions. Thus, the music and the poetry become two organic forms, constantly engaged in reaching out and expanding, becoming projective.

While Hartman acknowledges that the complexities of voice are a crucial element in both poetry and jazz, the use of image is just as important. The mood or emotional impulse behind a piece can evoke a particular set of images in the listener's mind. How can we not fall prey to the sensual imagery that Ellington creates in "Prelude to a Kiss?" Had we been unaware of the title, hearing the composition's instrumentation with the prominence of the saxophone over a muted trombone section, the sensual imagery evoked would still be easily conjured up in our imaginations.[4]

I have tried to emphasize how jazz poetry and music can be viewed in a similar light because the poet draws on various traditional/nontraditional (African and/or European) cultural elements and forges a unique expression of individual and community identity. Rather than constructing verse that uses European, or "formal," meter, jazz poetry makes use of improvisation in terms of how the sound of the logos is manipulated to convey the rhythmic qualities of the music. Since poetry is an art form that is closely aligned to music, devices such as tone and meter become crucial in the construction of texts. Therefore, there are moments in the poetry when "meaning" collapses and tonal and rhythmic qualities play a significant role in fashioning a successful text, as well as moments when the poetry has more formal literary constraints, such as closed verse, linear narrative, and a tightly structured meter. It is important to emphasize that jazz, in all its manifestations, plays an important role in terms of expanding the way poetry can be read or heard. As mentioned earlier, this book proposes to explore how the jazz form has been articulated in the poetry of four distinctly different African American writers whose innovations have made a significant impact on the direction of the form. The idea is not to arrive at a definitive conclusion as to what constitutes a jazz poem, but to examine some of the most groundbreaking and experimental strategies that have come close to replicating the music through text.

Chapter 2 provides a brief historical survey and a multicultural approach to jazz poetry, focusing on the main practitioners of the form and the significant/representative texts that were generated. Langston Hughes's *The Weary Blues* (1926), M. B. Tolson's *Harlem Gallery* (1930), Jack Kerouac's *Mexico City Blues* (1959) and innovative texts by Sterling Brown, Kenneth Rexroth, Paul Blackburn, Amiri Baraka, Frank O'Hara, and others will be briefly examined. The purpose of providing this loose chronological overview is to observe and critique how these innovations were later incorporated into the work of Bob Kaufman, Steven Jonas, Nathaniel Mackey, and Jayne Cortez.

Chapter 3 examines Bob Kaufman's 1967 book *Golden Sardine.* Kaufman (1925–86) is particularly known for his bebop-influenced work that uses the elements of jazz cadence to set the rhythm/tone of the poem. His work is crucial to our understanding of how the jazz poem works because he follows the tonal perimeters of the music, not unlike a scat or vocalese singer, thus emphasizing the integral connection between music and poetry. More important, Kaufman's texts are diverse. With a surrealist's sensibility he works with jazz on a variety of levels, from rhythmic and tonal sound, to biographical anecdote, to performance response. Several poets who fall under the various rubrics of literary "schools" (beat, Black Mountain, black arts, New York) and write jazz poems have named Kaufman as a primary influence on their work, and his contributions to the form are easily discernible.

Chapter 4 focuses on Stephen Jonas's *Exercises for Ear* (1968), published a year after Kaufman's *Golden Sardine.* Jonas (1925?–70) was a little-known Boston poet who employed jazz and European classical sound structures in his work. He was also a poet who made significant use of the African American vernacular, infusing in his work the musicality of everyday speech. *Exercises for Ear* is an important text to examine because of Jonas's attempt to write poetry that re-creates the aural quality of jazz music and occasionally lapses or sacrifices meaning. *Exercises* is a series of short notational and tonal poems in which Jonas experiments with various rhythmic textures in order to create shifts in intensity, pitch, and timber, slightly similar in construction to Frank O'Hara's *Lunch Poems* written four years earlier. Jonas wrote with an improviser's sensibility and an ear that was well tuned to music.

In chapter 5, I examine several jazz-inspired texts by Jayne Cortez (1936–). Cortez has performed her work with musical accompaniment since the 1960s and has made several recordings. Her ability to craft poems that not only recall the music's historical legacy and performative techniques but also express the brutality of the American judicial system are important to our understanding of how a jazz poem can work on a didactic level. I also look at poems performed with bassist Richard Davis on a 1974 recording *(Celebrations and Solitudes)* and examine the differences between the poem on the printed page and the poem heard. In this kind of duet performance, the single instrument mirrors the individual voice in a more apparent auditory fashion, where what occurs is the bass's translation of words into musical sound, thus a conversation and reconfiguring into another idiom emerges. Cortez often alludes specifically to jazz music in her work, and the timber and rhythm of her voice reflects a jazz-influenced delivery. She is a poet who is particularly skillful in appropriating the musician's method of restructuring a piece, making it slightly recognizable and then subverting its original meaning.

Chapter 6 focuses on the work of Nathaniel Mackey (1947–), specifically his continual series of poems, *Song of the Andoumboulou,* which have appeared in *Eroding Witness* (1985), *School of Udhra* (1993) and *Whatsaid Serif* (1998). *Song of the Andoumboulou* is an important text because of its episodic nature and scope. The poem recreates the African diasporic journey through a complex narrative weave that incorporates an erudite vocabulary. A CD recording (*Stick: Song of the Andoumboulou* 16–25) of Mackey reading the work with an ensemble of Western and traditional African instruments is particularly illuminating because the music functions as a companion to the vocal delivery of the text. Mackey's voice astutely weaves in and out of the music like an instrumentalist, not sacrificing "meaning" for sound.

In the coda, I reexamine Kaufman, Jonas, Cortez, and Mackey's innovative writing practices and discuss the effect those practices have had on new and emerging writers. Further attention is also paid to the continual development and redefinition of jazz poetry.

When the tall ships came to Boston in the 1970s, my family and I went to see one from the then Soviet Union. On the ship, a military band performed Kurt Weil's "Mack the Knife" from *The Three Penny Opera,* also made popular by Louis Armstrong. Overall, it was a straightforward performance with no improvisation. After the concert, my father, who does not speak Russian, went up to the lead trumpeter, who did not speak English, and pointed to the musical score. He hummed a few notes that opened up the possibility for improvisation. He pointed to a part of the score, and the Russian nodded his head in agreement. For my father's efforts, the Russian gave him a souvenir medal and the appreciation of adding something distinctly African American to a Russian performance, a jazz riff. Thus, a voice crossed over.

CHAPTER 2

Voices Crossing Over: A Historical Overview of Jazz Poetry

Words and Music in America

Jazz poetry was not discovered by
Allen Ginsberg or Jack Kerouac
let alone Kenny Rexroth
Nor was it a literary invention of the
Beat(up) school, the New York School or
any other official institution of 20th
century AVANT-learning
It started if you really wanna know
(and you damn well should) in a white
whorehouse in East St. Louis, Illinois
in August 1928 where a bunch of drunken
unemployed Negro poets were sitting around
trying to sound like LOUIS ARMSTRONG as a
rickety Victrola ground out 1900 choruses
of "Tight like That" in the early mourning
hours of Eddie Jefferson's 12th birthday
It was Eddie's father who told the other cats
present that they should donate their individual
stanzas to little Eddie as a birthday gift as Jefferson, Sr.
didn't have no money as usual to buy his wide-eyed son that
silver-grey saxophone he'd seen in the window of a weary
looking pawnshop called LIGHTS OUT in the "nigger section"
of town
The rest as they say is MYSTERY . . .

—*Kofi Natambu*

There has always been a preoccupation among music critics and scholars with ferreting out the historical lineage of jazz. Some researchers examine a variety of ethnomusic and, with pincerlike precision, pick up a musical strand that later may have made an appearance in a jazz performance or composition, all this in an effort to delineate jazz and its influence on or by diverse musical systems. However, several problems occur when one attempts to define the exact juncture when some forms of European music merged with African American musical traditions, such as blues, spirituals, and work songs, began to take on the unique improvisational qualities of jazz. Many of the early jazz musicians such as the legendary New Orleans trumpeter Buddy Bolden were unrecorded and thus only remembered for their live performances. Therefore, a significant amount of the music's early history has been handed down orally or through practical musical demonstrations by a generation of musicians who viewed the bandstand, and not necessarily formal music academies, as an environment for musical education and instruction. Typically, the African American inventors and innovators were given scant credit for their contribution toward defining American culture. It is interesting to note that a group of white musicians called the Original Dixieland Jazz Band (ODJB) billed themselves as "the creators of jazz" and made the first jazz recording in 1917. The name the group chose for itself is noteworthy because it marked an attempt to authenticate their interpretations of the music. Surely any other group, white or black, that emerged playing the same music would be viewed as imitators and therefore lack legitimacy. Although jazz was recognized by some as a distinctly black art form in the early 1900s, it took a group of white musicians to lay public claim in order for it to become palatable among white audiences and the black middle class.

The commercially successful ODJB's first recording made a wide impact on American popular culture. It has been the general consensus by several scholars that the recording ushered in the Jazz Age. Thus, jazz became the red hot music of the era because its brassy sound evoked the continual transition from a rural America toward a more urbanized locale with its steel mechanisms and skyscrapers, an America in which one could dance with wild abandon into the brave new world of the future. To date and place the beginning of the Jazz Age in connection with a recording from a group that were not the originators of the music is extremely problematic in terms of creating an accurate historical record on the development of jazz. However, it is noteworthy because it provides insight into the history of white appropriation of African American cultural forms. Grover Sales writes about the ODJB's influence on white culture in *Jazz: America's Classical Music.*

> The dizzying success of the ODJB was the start of another recurring phenomenon in American music, including rock 'n' roll: Each successive wave of Afro-American music, from the "Jazz Age" through the Rock era, made its first impact on white middle-class youths by way of white imitations of authentic black music. (According to legend, before the Victor Talking Machine Company gambled on the ODJB they offered black New Orleans trumpeter Freddie Keppard the chance to make the first jazz records, but Keppard refused because he "didn't want people stealing my stuff off records.") (93)

Keppard's refusal to be recorded is understandable when one considers the importance of a musician having a unique musical signature as a means of achieving an artistic and financial livelihood. Within two years of the first jazz recording, the concept of targeting racial groups and marketing particular kinds of music (race records) was introduced. One of the first recordings by an African American artist was "Crazy Blues" by Mamie Smith, which was followed by several other commercially successful recordings. Smith's recordings achieved widespread popularity but have often been ignored in historical accounts of jazz because of their blues label. Smith was more of a vaudevillian performer than a blues singer and did not have the popular appeal that Ma Rainey and Bessie Smith enjoyed. Her famous recording was actually a historical accident. Okeh records had planned on recording white singer Sophie Tucker, but she was unavailable. Smith's manager, Perry Bradford, persuaded the record company to let Mamie sing the blues with a black band as backup. "Crazy Blues" was recorded on August 10, 1920. It was a huge success, and the record sold more than one hundred thousand copies in the first month of its release.[1]

One should bear in mind that the blues form is a significant element in jazz and that the word "blues" as a designation of a musical form may have been employed in music labeling practices because of the negative connotations of the word "jazz," which was discussed earlier. The implications of this choice became very apparent when the ODJB chose to label their brand of music as Dixieland, which was more acceptable than the single identifying qualifier "jazz."

Although the first jazz recording was important in a broader cultural context, it had little effect on the musical techniques of the musicians who learned the craft by participating in or witnessing live performances. Writing about the effect of the jazz recording on jazz musicians and how it managed to change the paradigm, Martin Williams explains:

> The pioneer writers on jazz in the 1930s recognized that improvisational jazz was uniquely suited to the phonograph, which could preserve for posterity—in an ultimate twentieth-century American paradox—music, which was sometimes made up on the spur of the moment . . . Yet it was not necessary for the younger musicians of the 1920s—those to whom the leadership ultimately fell in the 1930s—to have heard Louis Armstrong live in order to have absorbed, used, made personal, or extended his remarkable innovations. Beginning in 1923, they heard him on recordings and learned him from recordings. (224)

Similar problems occur when attempts are made to historicize the jazz poem by placing its inception in relation to literary publication. In *Jazz Poetry: From the 1920s to the Present,* Sascha Feinstein makes the connection between the history of jazz music and the jazz poem. He observes that white populist poets like Carl Sandburg and Vachel Lindsay were the first to publish jazz-related poetry, while great African American innovators like Sterling Brown and Langston Hughes had a more integral approach and connection to the music and "did their best to promote a national respect for jazz and blues" (16). When referring to the current reception of the historical lineage of jazz poetry, Feinstein points out that there has been an "ironic yet appropriate reversal of emphasis" and that the achievements of Langston Hughes have "overshadowed" the jazz poetry of white writers. However, it should be remembered that Vachel Lindsay is often credited as the man who "discovered" Langston Hughes one year after his manuscript *The Weary Blues* had been accepted for publication by Knopf. Although it may be appropriate to acknowledge the contributions of white writers such as Lindsay and Sandburg, their use of a jazz-inspired cadence or imagery often serves to "minstrelize" the form and spoof the music, showing a profound ignorance regarding the complexities of African American culture. In 1922 Lindsay wrote a letter to Harriet Monroe, the poet and editor of *Poetry,* saying that he "abhorred the kind of Ball-Room dancing that goes with Jazz, and the blasphemy that Jazz has made of the beautiful slow whisper Negro Spirituals" (Feinstein 17). It is obvious that Lindsay's view of African American music was extremely myopic and that his naive attempts at jazz poetry were purely ornamental and meant to undermine the music's aesthetic importance. For Lindsay, jazz music was rebellious and cacophonous.

Although Lindsay wrote and published several poems that employed jazz as subject matter, such as "The Daniel Jazz," "The Jazz of This Hotel," and "A Curse for the Saxophone," he displayed considerable distaste for jazz as a musical form because it evoked for him the "savagery" or perhaps the "Africanness" of the black race. His famous poem, "The Congo: A Study of the Negro Race," written in 1913, expresses a stereotypical and uninformed view of African and African American culture. The poem is divided into three sections, "Their Basic Savagery," "Their Irrepressible High Spirits," and "The Hope of Their Religion." Lindsay places italicized instructions on how the text should be read, and on musical accompaniment, in the right-hand margins. Langston Hughes would later employ this treatment to greater effect in his collection, *Ask Your Mama: Twelve Moods for Jazz,* published in 1961. The opening of the poem establishes Lindsay's conception of African American rhythm.

> Fat black bucks in a wine-barrel room,
> Barrel-house kings, with feet unstable,
> Sagged and reeled and pounded on the *a deep rolling*
> table, *bass.*
> Pounded on the table, Beat an empty barrel with the handle of
> a broom,
> Hard as they were able,
> Boom, boom, Boom
> With a silk umbrella and the handle of a
> broom
> Boomlay, boomlay, boomlay, BOOM.
> THEN I had religion, THEN I had a vision.
> I could not turn their revel in derision *More*
> THEN I SAW THE CONGO, CREEPING THROUGH *deliberate*
> THE BLACK *Solemnly*
> *chanted.*
> (178–79)

Here Lindsay uses capitalization as a means to evoke a modulation in sound, as opposed to these words having any real literal significance beyond their stereotypical usage. One of the most important aspects, in terms of the rhythmic quality of jazz, is the placement of accents on the offbeat rather than the first beat of the measure. Lindsay obviously ignores this practice by placing stress on the opening word of each line. His use of assonance and alliteration to establish rhythm is fairly simplistic, repeating words that begin with the "B" consonant ("black bucks," "barrel-house," "beat," "boom") to accentuate sound and propel the movement of the poem. Additionally, it is noteworthy that he decides to allude to African American music by naming the ragtime derivative "Barrel-house" to describe the type of music the men are pounding out. It is his awareness of this "Boom" music that transports him to Africa and the root of black music.

Blatantly apparent is the poem's racist opening with "Fat black bucks." Although Lindsay is trying to write about music coming out of the black experience, he immediately places his subjects in a stereotypically sexual context. It is key in our assessment of this poem that we consider the issue of authoritative voice and its political implications. Here, it comes from someone who is apparently outside of African American culture and who is unable to see beyond racial stereotypes. Even in the final four lines of the strophe, when the poet receives black culture through the osmosis of music, it comes in as something sinister —that is, "CREEPING THROUGH / THE BLACK." Thus black music is evoked as a kind of sinister disease.[2]

Another attempt to articulate the power of black music is made in Carl Sandburg's poem "Singing Nigger."

> I know where your songs came from
> I know why God listens to your, "Walk All Over God's Heaven."
> I know you shooting craps, "My baby's going to have a new dress."
> I heard you in the cinders, "I'm going to live anyhow until I die."
> I saw five of you with a can of beer on a summer night and I
>   listened to the
> five of you harmonizing six ways to sing, "Way Down Yonder in
>   the Cornfield,"
> I went away asking where I come from. (108)

Although there is scant acknowledgment of the complexities of African American music, the images that Sandburg sets within the poem are mainly racial stereotypes, with the poet privileging himself, as does Lindsay, to the "inner workings" of black culture. But certainly it is African American culture that leads the poet in a search of self-discovery. This search of self-discovery via African American music would then propel writers like Jack Kerouac years later. Nevertheless, it was mainly Lindsay and Sandburg who defined for several Americans the "anarchism" of the age, not because their poems employed an authentic jazz or blues cadence, as the works of Langston Hughes and Sterling Brown would eventually do, but because they employed stereotypical imagery and made it palatable to a voyeuristic audience that had little to no contact with African American culture. Perhaps it can be surmised that Lindsay's and Sandburg's contribution to jazz poetry as an art form was that in choosing African American music as subject matter for their poems they "legitimized" it for a wider audience. Subsequently this opened up textual spaces, later allowing the acceptance of poets like Hughes and Brown, who were more adept in employing the use of a jazz aesthetic in poetry.

In his book *Playing the Changes: From Afro-Modernism to the Jazz Impulse,* Craig Hansen Werner describes the "differences" between African American and Euro-American poets in order to develop a cohesive theory of an African American aesthetic. Werner writes that African American poets employ materials mainly from folk artists and singers who have been generally ignored by Euro-Americans. He says that black artists "embrace a performance tradition that seeks to forge a communal response to assaults on black integrity" and that the performer derives aesthetic power through his or her ability to "elicit an affirmation from the audience," which assumes the role of collaborator in the performance (165). Werner explains that Euro-American modernist poets looked to Asia for poetic sources, and when they looked to Africa it was mainly to focus on the visual arts. Conversely, he says African American modernists used the polyrhythms of Africa, Louis Armstrong's improvisations, and Ellingtonian jazz suites to inform their poetics. Noteworthy as his definition is, it continues to be problematic when one begins to consider issues of text and readership. The importance of Werner's argument is that it accentuates the differences that occur when African American and European American modernists attempt to create a form that has shared conceptions with regards to its general design yet develops alternative perceptions informed by the particular stylistic considerations unique to each group. Generally speaking, it is when the jazz poem has been placed in the hands of African

American practitioners that the form achieves more parity with the music.[3]

One of the first major modernist American poets to successfully experiment with the musical elements of jazz and blues in poetry was Langston Hughes. He was particularly astute at appropriating and revisioning the blues lyric and placing it in a textual format. He worked with the basic musical pattern of the twelve-bar blues, a three-line form in which the first line states a situation, the second line restates the first line, and the final line functions as a commentary or expression. In his book *Langston Hughes and the Blues,* Steven C. Tracy writes that one of the primary elements found in blues music is its emotional content that reflects a particular lifestyle or situation, "something that has happened to the singer or someone else, or that has been imagined as possible, or that has been imagined to reflect a deeper truth about the life of the singer, though the situation is not literally possible" (84).

A Hughes poem that fairly typifies how he makes use of the blues form is the short poem,

"Hey!"

Sun's a settin',
This is what I'm gonna sing.
Sun's a settin',
This is what I'm gonna sing:
I feels de blues a comin',
Wonder what de blues'll bring? (112)

In the poem, Hughes uses such poetical devices as alliteration ("sun," "settin'," "sing") to accentuate the rhythmical qualities of the blues, and he manages to employ symbol and metaphor to convey mood. This practice of the subtlety of image is also mirrored in African American music performances, particularly slow tempo blues like Bessie Smith's rendition of "St. Louis Blues" or Sidney Bechet's moving "Blue Horizon." In addition, Hughes uses a vernacular influenced line that reflects the ethnicity of the speaker. The rhythmic stress that Hughes creates in the first four lines changes later in the closing couplet to indicate the uncertainty of the situation. "Hey!" the title of the poem, is also noteworthy because it implies a spontaneous moment of transience when the reader suddenly becomes privy to a comment perhaps heard in passing.

Hughes's poem "Negro Dancers"—first published in the influential Harlem Renaissance journal, *Crisis,* in 1925 and later in his first collection, *The Weary Blues*—is a significant poem because of its blues influences and its critique of the Charleston, a black-originated dance that achieved widespread popularity during the Jazz Age.

Negro Dancers

"Me an' ma baby's
Got two mo' ways,
Two mo' ways to do de Charleston!
   Da, da
   Da, da, da!
Two mo' ways to do de Charleston!"

Soft light on the tables,
Music gay,
Brown-skin steppers
In a cabaret.

White folks, laugh!
White folks, pray!

"Me an' ma baby's
   Got two mo' ways,
Two mo' ways to do de Charleston!" (44)

The opening two lines of the poem begin in the traditional blues format, with the third line simultaneously repeating the second line but adding a new idea by defining "two mo' ways." The stress that Hughes employs in the third line is additionally important because it mirrors the rhythmic accents within the dance step. The fourth and fifth lines mirror that rhythm as well. By using monosyllabic sounds, he further emphasizes the importance of cadence within the poem, particularly when referring to another art form. Performing in "two mo' ways" establishes the importance of improvisation. It demonstrates the black community's ability to retake a popular form and reconfigure it. Thus, it becomes a means of revitalizing and reclaiming what has been taken away. If one has "two mo' ways to do de Charleston," it would then seem not only that the process of invention and improvisation is ongoing, but also that the individual or couple is capable of creating their own unique signature and means of identification and that the process of inventing within an African American context is an ongoing practice.

The third strophe performs an interesting function as well, because Hughes appears to appropriate the stereotypical images of blacks as being highly religious or constantly in good humor and transfers them onto whites. Additionally, it can be surmised that whites are not dancing because the action in the poem is taking place in a racially segregated cabaret where blacks are the entertainment. Yet, the stanza break implies an ambiguity in reference to the "white folks," as there is the possibility that they may not even be in the cabaret at all. If so, this may indicate that within the black community, which the white gaze is not privy to, a slightly different aesthetic occurs. The poem ends, repeating the first three lines, enclosing the "secrecy" of the dance and echoing the mystery of improvisation.

In the poem "Jazzonia," Hughes captures the nuance of a Harlem cabaret in which jazz is being played. First published in 1923, the poem may possibly mark one of the first times a major African American poet used the word "jazz" to describe not only the music but also a level of existence.

Jazzonia

Oh, silver tree!
Oh, shining rivers of the soul!

In a Harlem cabaret
Six long-headed jazzers play.
A dancing girl whose eyes are bold
Lifts high a dress of silken gold.

Oh, singing tree!
Oh, shining rivers of the soul!

Were Eve's eyes
In the first garden
Just a bit too bold?
Was Cleopatra gorgeous
In a gown of gold?

Oh, shining tree!
Oh, silver rivers of the soul!

In a whirling cabaret
Six long-headed jazzers play. (34)

The poem begins with a blues lyric, which is repeated three times. The phrase is slightly varied the second time it is used, with Hughes replacing "silver" with "singing." This slight change demonstrates Hughes's subtle use of improvisation in which word substitution creates a new context while also alluding to a previously mentioned word. By using the "ing" suffix, the word becomes more tonally matched with "shining," thus accentuating the connection between the tree and the rivers as symbols of a shared historical legacy. Hughes's use of the exclamation "oh" in the poem's refrain also places importance on tone before meaning.

The manner in which Hughes uses language becomes more narrative in the second strophe and locates the action of the poem in a Harlem cabaret. His decision to not open the poem with this strophe is indicative of Hughes's feeling that the rhythmic qualities of the dance and the speaker were more crucial designators of atmosphere and place. The rhythmic structure of the poem changes as well, taking on a more conventional meter.

The use of repetition and improvisation also occurs in the second and sixth strophe. The lines, "In a Harlem cabaret/ Six long-headed jazzers play," are repeated in the two strophes. However, Hughes creates a variant reading by substituting the noun "Harlem" with the verb "whirling" in order to demonstrate the movement of the dancer and the music. Thus, as the poem progresses, one becomes caught up in the rapture of art, and locale becomes secondary. Although the meter and the end rhymes of the poem are fairly conventional, Hughes's language moves closer towards a jazz aesthetic that makes subtle use of improvisatory gestures as a key factor in fashioning the musical and emotional impact of the text.

Hughes's early blues poems were thematic in the sense that they contained a single and coherent theme or told a story. In later, more directly jazz-influenced works, he would experiment with various poetic devices, such as nonlinear line placement, typography, polyrhythmic meter, and varying stanza breaks to convey "both the spirit of the oral performance and the psychological or sociological complexity that stood up to such literary treatment on the page" (Tracy 144). *Montage of a Dream Deferred* (1951) is one of his most significant serial poems. It weaves various African American popular music sources along with a vernacular language and cadence in order to portray, according to Hughes, a community in transition. Hughes's description of the poem is startlingly similar to the manner in which jazz music has often been characterized as a music in transition, referring to the continual process of change the art form undergoes as it adapts to new musical influences. In the poem, Hughes takes advantage of the structural characteristics of bebop by "drastically reordering the traditional limitations imposed upon the poem" and by breaking down the barrier between the beginning and end of the "separate" poems that comprise the work, making the text open ended (Tracy 224). Thus, the title accurately describes the work as being a series of short poems or phrases that contribute to a unified text. In his introduction to the collection, Hughes emphasizes the use of music in the construction of his poetry.

> In terms of current Afro-American popular music and the sources from which it has progressed—jazz, ragtime, swing, blues, boogie-woogie, and be-bop—this poem on contemporary Harlem, like be-bop, is marked by conflicting changes, sudden nuances, sharp and impudent interjections, broken rhythms, and passages sometimes in the manner of the jam session, sometimes the popular song, punctuated by the riffs, runs, breaks, and distortions of the music of a community in transition. (387)

The opening poem of *Montage* demonstrates Hughes's virtuosity in jazz poetry experimentation:

Dream Boogie

Good morning, daddy!
Ain't you heard
The boogie-woogie rumble
Of a dream deferred?

Listen closely:
You'll hear their feet
Beating out and beating out a—
          You think
          It's a happy beat?

Listen to it closely:
Ain't you heard
something underneath
like a—

What did I say?
Sure,
I'm happy!
Take it away!
Hey, pop!
Re-bop!
Mop!

Y-e-a-h! (388)

Unmistakable is the rhythmic quality of the poem, capturing a bebop cadence as well as the implied message of sociopolitical discontent. Hughes's closing bebop riff becomes not only a weapon to articulate the "rumble" but also a passageway to the spiritual and redemptive quality of African American music.

In *Ask Your Mama,* Hughes introduces poems by using musical notations as a means of explaining how the work should be read. By doing this, Hughes emphasizes the importance of poetry's connection with music and its aural qualities. His instructions indicate how he imagines the poem should be performed/read. Between the musical notations for "Hesitation Blues" and "Shave and a Haircut," he writes in italics:

The traditional folk melody of the "Hesitation Blues"
is the leitmotif for this poem. In and around it,
along with the other recognizable melodies employed,
there is room for spontaneous jazz improvisation,
particularly between verses,
where the voice pauses.
The musical figurine indicated after each "Ask your mama" line
may incorporate the impudent little melody of the old break,
"Shave and a haircut, fifteen cents." (475)

Italic script is used throughout the poem to instruct the musicians as to how the work should be performed. However, it should be noted that

Ask Your Mama is a collection of poetry that is meant not only to be heard but also to be read. When a reader approaches the work, he or she notices the italic script and perhaps internally hears the musical emphasis Hughes intended. Hughes once remarked that the "poetry of sound . . . marks the beginning of a new era . . . of revolt against the trite outworn language of the understandable" (Rampersad 64). Hughes would also experiment further with our notions of a poetry text by including liner notes for "the poetically unhep," making this appear like the liner notes of a record album.

Hughes also worked with musicians to add a musical setting to his poems. Listening to his recordings, particularly those done with Charles Mingus, one recognizes and hears the lyrical and tonal quality of a text that takes its cues from black music.[4] In an interview with music critic Nat Hentoff, Hughes remarked that the music "should not only be background to the poetry but should comment on it." He said, "I listen to what they [musicians] say in their playing, and that affects my own rhythms when I read. We listen to each other" (Tracy 178). Indicative in Hughes's remarks is the musical significance of an oral performance in contrast to the "silence" of the printed text and the importance of a collaborative aesthetic that springs from the jazz tradition.

Another poet who worked with folk materials, including the blues form and subsequently jazz, was Sterling A. Brown. A contemporary of Hughes, Brown incorporated the speech patterns of southern rural and northern urban African Americans into his poetry. Like Hughes and the dialectical experimentation of Paul Laurence Dunbar, Brown manages to successfully capture the nuance of black speech as well as impart messages of black proletarian pride. In his introduction to Brown's collected poems, poet Michael S. Harper says that one of Brown's strengths was his ability to show the reader "how the suggestive powers of language can call reality into play with uncommon force, revealing terrible potential for turbulence beneath mirth that is in the final analysis no more than surface deep" (7). This "suggestive quality" that Harper refers to comes directly from the blues lyric and the work songs that Brown was skilled in recording and later incorporating into his own poetry. Brown's master poem "Strong Men" is a work that demonstrates his ability to place the work song into a poetic text. He experiments with the appearance and musicality of the poem by printing the majority of the text in italics. The beginning of each line is strongly stressed with personal pronouns, "They" and "You," obviously mirroring the rhythm of a work song. Brown's use of italic print serves to highlight the content of the text and emphasize the atrocities of the slave trade. Because of the curvature of letters in italic script, visually a more musical rendering is implied where the letters take on a quality not unlike the shape of musical notation.

> *They dragged you from homeland.*
> *They chained you in coffles.*
> *They huddled you spoon-fashion in filthy hatches,*
> *They sold you to give a few gentlemen ease.* (56)

The only time in the poem in which the italic text is not used is during the refrain "The strong men keep a-comin' on / The strong men get stronger." Stylizing the refrain in this manner creates a startling visual contrast to the italic litany of atrocities inflicted upon African Americans. The refrain provides an indication of black resilience and strength. It certainly fulfills several of Stephen Henderson's criteria for black poetry, particularly by evoking an "assumed emotional response." Thus, the poem becomes a receptacle in which the black struggle is stored and recounted in various stylistic methods. By using rhythmic cadences that are rooted within the black musical tradition, the encoding of culture is achieved. It is the change of the artistic medium from music to poetry that continues to record the African American legacy.

In the poem "Cabaret," Brown creates a narrative that describes the environment in a jazz club. Written in 1927, a few years after "Strong Men," the poem employs novel uses of line placement as well as short imagistic passages to convey atmosphere.

> The jazzband unleashes its frenzy.
>
> *Now, now*
> *To it, Roger; that's a nice doggie,*
> *Show your tricks to the gentlemen.*
>
> The trombone belches, and the saxophone
> Wails curdlingly, the cymbals clash,
> The drummer twitches in an epileptic fit
>
> Muddy water
> Round my feet
> Muddy water (111)

Unlike the steady rhythmic drive used in "Strong Men," "Cabaret" fluctuates between proselike description and blues and jazz phraseology. The above passage demonstrates Brown's skillful use of form to achieve fluidity of mood and place. As the poem continues, Brown uses italic print to create another text alluding to slavery's historical legacy while at the same time describing the entertainment in the cabaret. This method creates a visual separation that also comments back or signifies the normal print text, similar to the musical signification that occurs in jazz. The images Brown uses in the strophe recall the humiliation of the slave market, where blacks were forced to show their physical attributes (teeth, breasts, buttocks, etc.) to prospective buyers. By using these images, Brown also alludes to the inequity of black musicians in the white-owned entertainment industry. Thus, the atmosphere Brown describes is a club in which African Americans appear as entertainers, not as patrons. Sascha Feinstein argues that "Brown's understanding of this dispassionate performance helps to put in perspective the anxiety-ridden, jazz-related poetry by many of his white contemporaries. Aware of the many misconceptions about jazz, Brown intentionally degraded the musician in his poem by describing the jazz band as something animalistic that 'unleashes its frenzy'" (52). However, the jazz band's unleashed frenzy could be viewed as an antagonistic and rebellious response toward the audience. Perhaps the "belches" are examples of blacks signifying on white culture.

The poem also contains a few jazz riffs, not unlike those used by Hughes in *Montage,* to indicate the intensity and drive of the music. The use of this sort of phrasing apparently indicates moments in the text when "conventional" language fails to adequately capture or convey mood. Like Hughes in "Dream Boogie," Brown closes the poem with a rhythmical release "Dee da dee D A A A H." By emphasizing the rhythmic quality as opposed to using words with "meaning," Brown makes the poem "swing." In doing so, he recognizes the preeminent position rhythm occupies in jazz and subsequently in the production of poetry. In his book *The Swing Era,* Gunther Schuller writes that the rhythmic impulse is one of the primary elements of musical expression and it is as significant as pitch and timbre (8).

Melvin B. Tolson's unfinished epic poem, *Harlem Gallery,* first published in 1965, deals with musical sources in a slightly different way. Craig Hansen Werner writes that Tolson "acknowledges the existence of a community oriented oral aesthetic developed primarily by Afro-

American artists and an individually oriented visual aesthetic developed primarily by Euro-American modernists" (163). Framed by the Greek alphabet, *Harlem Gallery* is a complex text with references and allusions to pre-Christian history, African folktales, European history, and African American culture. The poem contains a combination of Hughes-like rhythmic impulses, as well as experimentation similar to those found in Ezra Pound's *Cantos*. It has often been said that Tolson's work is so esoterically dense that he "out pounds Pound." In addition, it is important to point out that the poem is set in a "Gallery," which also alludes to and signifies on the European museum or salons, with its emphasis on "high art." Significantly, it is Tolson's gallery that is egalitarian, refusing to participate in any sort of historical or cultural hierarchy.

Tolson experiments with print and line breaks in a manner that is rooted in the rhythmical practices of the black music tradition. The "Mu" section of the Gallery often appears in jazz poetry anthologies as representative of Tolson's handling of musical materials, and it displays the clash of two cultures (British and African American) and their aesthetic practices. One of the most intriguing strophes of that section is the closing, where Tolson combines Shakespearean references with descriptions of jazz performance.

The yanking fishing rod

of Hideho's voice
jerked me out of my bird's-foot violet romanticism.
He mixed Shakespeare's image with his own
and caricatured me:
"Yonder Curator has a lean and hungry look;
he thinks too much.
Such blackamoors are dangerous to
the Great White World!"

. . .

With a dissonance
from the Weird Sisters,
the jazz diablerie
boiled down and away
in the vacuum pan
of the Indigo Combo. (76)

In a manner similar to the way in which a jazz musician may mix musical quotations from other songs into a composition, Tolson mixes literary references, thus refashioning our reading of the literature. Here, Tolson places the African American musical tradition of spontaneous improvisation on equal footing with Shakespeare's *Hamlet* and *Macbeth*. Thus, Tolson acknowledges the shared legacies of Europe and Africa that are prevalent in American culture. What Tolson expresses here is certainly a debt to jazz in which a recognizable theme/melody is improvised on and "made new."

In the "Lambda" section that precedes "Mu," Tolson fits Henderson's criteria for black poetry by placing a musician as the poem's primary focal point (47). In the closing strophe of this section, he equates the playing of Louis Armstrong with that of the biblical figure Gabriel. The entire strophe appears in italics to indicate the potency of Armstrong's musical virtuosity.

Old Satchmo's
gravelly voice and tapping foot and crazy notes
set my soul on fire.
If I climbed
the seventy-seven steps of the Seventh
Heaven, Satchmo's high C would carry me higher!
Are you hip to this, Harlem? Are you hip?
On Judgment Day, Gabriel will say
after he blows his horn:
"I'd be the greatest trumpeter in the Universe
if old Satchmo had never been born!" (63)

Louis Armstrong's position as one of jazz's first major innovators is unquestionable. Obvious in "Lambda" is Tolson's feeling that the power of African American music transcends earthly possibilities. The celestial implications of black music is profound and the innovative prowess of a titan figure like Louis Armstrong is particularly immeasurable when one contemplates how jazz music created swinging devotees who traded the comfort of Victorian parlors for the speakeasies and dance floors. Tolson's far-ranging historical epic pays homage to the black music and its ability to weave and re-create world history.

Arguably one of the most influential poets of the twentieth century, William Carlos Williams advocated the use of common American speech in poetry. He attempts to make use of jazz music in his poem "Ol' Bunk's Band." The poem opens up with an arresting first line, "These are men!" The line is arresting because it follows the title of the poem in which "Ol'" becomes indicative of a kind of white familiarity and patronizing view of black culture. It reads as a kind of false term of endearment, reminiscent of such historically condescending forms of address as "Mammy," "Uncle," or "Boy" and recalls such Southern standards as "Ol' Folks" or "Ol' Black Joe." Williams wants to emphasize, within his already established trope, that these musicians are human —that is, "men." What is equally disturbing is that, although the poem is an attempt at homage to African American music, Williams expressed quite different feelings about that music in an interview with Walter Sutton. Although the interview was primarily about how the beat poets used jazz, Williams should be taken to task for his comments. Williams argues that the "Beat generation has nothing to do with beat, and they should if they're interested in jazz because jazz is always percussive. But in jazz music even the saxophone sounds are not advanced enough from the primitive to interest me at all. I don't like jazz. The artists in Paris rave about jazz but it's too tiresome, it's too much the same thing" (Meltzer 220). It is hard to imagine what type of jazz music he was referring to when he made this comment. Williams does use the "percussive" elements of jazz in his poem, but rhythmically his use of jazz is fairly redundant. Lines like "Drum, drum, drum, drum, drum / drum drum!" appear to echo the monotonous rhythmic structure of Vachel Lindsay's poem "The Congo" rather than indicating the often complex and polyrhythmic qualities of African American music. It would appear that Williams was so focused on what he saw as the "primitive" qualities of the music that he failed to notice its rhythmic sophistication. In lines like "These are men / beneath / whose force the melody limps," it is fairly obvious that under Williams's view of "primitive" lay a culture alienated from Western concepts of aestheticism. He refuses to acknowledge jazz's ability to transcend the melody, not weaken it. Hayden Carruth astutely recognizes the shortcomings of Williams's poem when he writes that Williams treats Johnson and his fellow musicians as "unintelligible anthropological specimens, people from a distant culture making noises for the mere hell of it or out of animal exuberance" (24). At the forefront of modernism, Williams's stereotypical view of black music remains problematic to say the least. It should be remembered that his view was shared to some extent with "well-meaning" and innovative comrades like Gertrude Stein, Pablo Picasso, and Carl Van Vechten, who in their desire to critique black sensibility and artistic standards fell prey to a new type of chauvinism.

In Ishmael Reed's highly acclaimed 1972 novel, *Mumbo Jumbo,* an antiplague called "Jes Grew" infects people by causing them to dance and step outside of the rigors of a puritanical American culture. Signifying on Topsy's remark about her origins in Harriet Beecher Stowe's novel *Uncle Tom's Cabin,* Reed's antiplague has no antecedents and no one is able to ascertain where it came from. In the novel, Reed satirizes literary critics who say that there is no origin/history behind the black aesthetic. In the course of the novel, the origins of Jes Grew are eventually explained and the long legacy of black writing and art is reestablished. It is significant that Reed set his novel in the 1900s during the era of the Harlem Renaissance, combating the notion that art simply springs out of nowhere.[5] This same idea of Jes Grew has been applied to the origins of jazz poetry. Most of the critical articles and books on the subject ignore the importance of orality in establishing the form and prefer to focus on the first appearance of the poem in text. However, a truly authentic jazz poem can be practiced in both textual and/or oral contexts.

The poem in this chapter's opening epigraph, Kofi Natambu's "Words and Music in America," is significant because Natambu recognizes the conditions for the development of a jazz poetics by acknowledging that historically the jazz poem was created beyond the perimeters of the printed page. There are several lines in the poem that enable us to question the manner and perspective in which this form has been historicized. The poem opens with two negating statements: "Jazz poetry was not discovered by" and "Nor was it an invention." Natambu's first few lines evoke the hegemonic implications that occur when one ethnic group assumes dominance over another culture by appropriating an already established form—that is, the Original Dixieland Jazz Band's claim to have invented jazz. His opening stanza establishes the view of many Eurocentric academics that believe that white writers were the important innovators of the jazz poem. The second stanza is displaced more to the right of the first stanza to demonstrate a separation not only of historical viewpoints but also of cultures. Natambu even offsets the environment in which jazz poems were developed. He moves from the "official institution" to the "white whorehouse," evoking the music's "brothel" origins. The form is initiated by an anonymous group of "drunken unemployed Negro poets" listening to a recording by Louis Armstrong. This image evokes the communal and collective origins that were central to the early development of the jazz poem and places it in the realm of folk art. By mentioning Louis Armstrong's recording, Natambu emphasizes the connection between music and poetry. In the final stanza, these poets "donate their individual stanzas" to young Eddie Jefferson, underlining the importance of a communal and shared aesthetic. Eddie Jefferson, a jazz singer, was one of the first innovators to use vocalese as a technique in which words are employed to mimic jazz instrumental improvisations. It is noteworthy that Natambu does not directly name Jefferson as the originator of jazz poetry. By taking stanzas from the other poets, Jefferson becomes a compiler. The final line of the poem, "the rest as they say is MYSTERY . . ." calls attention to the difficulty of pinning down any exact historical origins to the form. Similar to Reed's "Jes Grew," the ellipses used at the close of the poem make the text open ended, implying not only continuation of the form but also its fragmentary origins.

Although insufficiently labeled, so-called beat poets such as Kenneth Rexroth, Jack Kerouac, Kenneth Patchen, Ray Bremser, Robert Creeley, Ted Joans, Lawrence Ferlinghetti, Allen Ginsberg, and Bob Kaufman all made very innovative experiments with poetry and jazz music. West Coast poet Kenneth Rexroth, the oldest member of this group, was performing his poetry to music as early as 1940 (Hughes started in 1920) and later worked with such jazz innovators as Charles Mingus and Ornette Coleman and employed jazz as a supplemental rather than an integral part of poetry. Rexroth obviously did a great deal of thinking about the role of jazz in poetry. In an essay published in the March 29, 1958, issue of *The Nation,* Rexroth takes on the question, "What is jazz poetry?"

> It isn't anything very complicated to understand. It is the reciting of suitable poetry with the music of a jazz band, usually small and comparatively quiet. Most emphatically, it is not recitation with "background" music. The voice is integrally wedded to the music and, although it does not sing notes, is treated as another instrument, with its own solos and ensemble passages, and with solo and ensemble work by the band alone. It comes and goes, following the logic of the presentation, just like a saxophone or piano. Poetry with background music is

> very far from jazz. It is not uncommon, and it is, in my opinion, usually pretty corny. (27)

Although Rexroth did dabble a bit in jazz poetry prior to the 1940s, his essay was written out of a concern for the recent developments in jazz poetry, particularly the jazz and poetry collaborations by poets like Jack Spicer and Kenneth Patchen. It was Rexroth's contention that jazz poetry was becoming a fad and that poets were using jazz as an auxiliary enterprise in which music served a minor role. He felt that often the texts were inferior and not clearly linked to jazz's musical impulse. However, when one listens to Rexroth's recordings *Poetry and Jazz at the Blackhawk* (1957) and *Poetry Readings in the Cellar* (1958), it becomes painfully apparent that there is certain stiffness in his performance that belies the spontaneity of the music. Perhaps this is due in part to Rexroth's notion of a "comparatively quiet" jazz band in which the poet functions as the primary performer and not simply as another musician. Despite the shortcomings of Rexroth's performances and his occasional lack of musical timing, it is crucial to acknowledge that he was one of the first American poets to attempt to respectfully articulate the importance of jazz poetry as a new art form. Rightly so, he saw the connection between jazz poetry and the early recitations of the bardic tradition found in an ancient poet like Homer. What he failed to notice was the African precedent in the recitations of the griots. Rexroth's knowledge of the historical aspects of the music was certainly inspirational to poets like Jack Kerouac and Allen Ginsberg. Rexroth was primarily concerned with keeping jazz poetry as a popular and nonelitist art form. He wrote that it "is very important to get poetry out of the hands of the squares. If we can get poetry out into the life of the country, it can be creative. Homer, or the guy who recited Beowulf, was show business. We simply want to make poetry part of show business" (Cerulli, Korall, and Nasatir 117). Like Walt Whitman and William Carlos Williams, Rexroth sought to maintain and further strengthen poetry's tie to folk culture and common speech by believing that it was worthy of a wider public dissemination.

Beat icon Jack Kerouac was a writer whose linguistic improvisations in performance and text came significantly close to capturing a jazz aesthetic in literature. On recordings like *Blues and Haikus* (1958) with saxophonists Al Cohn and Zoot Sims and *Poetry for the Beat Generation* (1959) with pianist Steve Allen, Kerouac uses jazz music as a means of creating what he refers to as "spontaneous composition."

His use of jazz-inspired prose and poetry is tempered by the musical accompaniment. For example, in *Poetry for the Beat Generation,* Kerouac recites the closing chapter of his novel *On the Road* and attempts to improvise over the often pedestrian playing of Allen. The attempt is uninteresting because Kerouac's desire to get into the heart of improvisation is not reciprocated by Allen, who simply quotes or slightly embellishes popular melodies. Here music functions as auxiliary to the text. This is slightly different in *Blues and Haikus,* where Cohn and Sims engage in a call-and-response format. But no interesting or new musical ideas emerge between the collaborations, and the music functions merely as uninspired accompaniment, making the work tedious and predictable. It is curious that Kerouac did not use African American musicians in these recordings. Perhaps he was in awe of them. One observes that when Kerouac does refer to African American musicians in either his poetry or his fiction, they are often given divine attributes that occasionally verge on a form of cult worship that tends to belie their humanity. Jazz innovators like Charlie Parker are referred to as being Buddha-like and having some sort of elusive quality that negates the frailties of being human. The image of the jazz musician as being something more than human is a trope that transcends the race of the poet. Homages to musicians like Louis Armstrong, John Coltrane, Billie Holiday, and Thelonious Monk often portray them as tragic yet transcendent figures in most jazz-influenced poetry.

Kerouac viewed his poetry and prose alongside musical performance/composition. *San Francisco Blues,* written in 1954, was his first serial-length poem involving jazz influences, and it underscores the importance of jazz as an integral component in his creative process. He writes:

> In my system, the form of blues choruses is limited by the small page of the breast pocket notebook in which they are written, like the form of a set number of bars in a jazz blues chorus, and so sometimes the word-meaning can carry from one chorus into another, or not, just like the phrase-meaning can carry harmonically from one chorus to the other, or not, in jazz, so that, in these blues as in jazz, the form is determined by time, and by the musician's spontaneous phrasing & harmonizing with the beat of the time as it waves & waves on by in measured choruses. It's all gotta be non stop ad libbing within each chorus, or the gig is shot. (1)

In the poems, Kerouac experiments with line placement, idiomatic language, and bop phraseology, often at the risk of losing narrative coherency. In doing so, he focuses mainly on the poetry as an opportunity to imitate the sound of a musical text and capture the "spontaneity" of improvisation. The eighth chorus of *San Francisco Blues* provides an illustration of how Kerouac handles diverse poetic materials. It is obvious from this excerpted passage how meaning is sacrificed in order to place more emphasis on the musical tone of the text.

> Oi yall!
> She yaws to lall
>   La la
>   Me Loom
>   The weary gray hat
> Peacoat ex sailor
>   Marining meekly
> Hands a poop a pocket
> Face
> Lips
> Oh Mo Sea! (7)

But it is in the introductory note of *Mexico City Blues* that Kerouac clearly defines how he wants his work to be read. He writes, "I want to be considered a jazz poet blowing a long blues in an afternoon jam session on Sunday. I take 242 choruses; my ideas vary and sometimes roll from chorus to chorus or from halfway through a chorus to halfway into the next" (1). Thus, it is evident that Kerouac viewed music as an integral element in terms of how his work should be read and understood. His view certainly validated a return to the orality of the text and its longstanding historical connection to music for many beat writers.

Although there has not been much written on the influence of jazz in the poetry of women, for beat poets like Anne Waldman, Diane di Prima, Joanne Kyger, Barbara Guest, Margaret Randall, Rochelle Owens, ruth weiss, and several others, the music obviously made a profound impact on the manner in which these poets used rhythm and meter. Winner of the 1997 American Book Award, Brenda Knight's *Women of the Beat Generation: The Writers, Artists and Muses at the Heart of a Revolution* is to date the most comprehensive offering of innovative work from these writers.[6] Generally speaking, their jazz-inspired verse was often engaged with the "eccentricities" of musicians like Charlie Parker, Dizzy Gillespie, and Thelonious Monk rather than their actual musical contributions. This practice of focusing on the personality of the musician as opposed to the music is certainly not unusual for many writers of jazz poetry. Among these writers, there are several exceptions where both biographical portrait and music merge. For example, this poem by Margaret Randall concerns itself not only with the physicality of pianist Thelonious Monk, but with his musical characteristics as well.

Thelonious

Monk played with
his hat on—rest
that hat man! spilled
the liquid voice and
his sound comes slow

slow the blind
sure joy ha the
ha ha wail hard the
off-time play cool
it man cool

cool wail of
the hot beat
heavyjuice air and
Monk played with
his hat on, but he
got plenty of hair! (187)

Randall uses one-syllable words to evoke the elegant sparsity of Monk's playing. The repetition of the heavy accented "hat," "ha," "hair," "heavy," and "hot" evoke those off-beat musical surprises for which Monk was so famous. The poem captures the perceived simplicity of Monk's music, particularly with its repetition and often-singular focus on Monk's hat. However, the image becomes ironic when the poem ends "but he / got plenty of hair," thus, implying the complexity of his music.

Another beat poet who has worked extensively with poetry and jazz is ruth weiss. Weiss's jazz poetry made a particular impact on the North Beach scene when she performed her poetry in 1956 at The Cellar with musicians Sonny Nelson, Jack Minger, and Will Carlson. A well-respected performer and master of the haiku form and short lyric, weiss is a poet who does not need to directly reference the historical legacies or personalities of jazz to create a jazz text. Her use of orality has been a key factor in the successful merger of jazz and poetry. The poet Jack Hirschman accurately describes her importance as a jazz poet by saying that weiss's poems "are scores to be sounded with all her riffy ellipses and open-formed phrasing swarming the senses. Verbal motion becoming harmonious with a universe of rhythm is what her work essentializes. Others read *to* jazz or write *from* jazz. ruth weiss *writes* jazz in words" (Knight 247).

Two beat-influenced jazz poets who shared the dubious honor of being Charlie Parker's New York City roommates were Ray Bremser and Ted Joans. Both poets were active in the loft scenes in New York, where crucial avant-garde figures like Cecil Taylor and Ornette Coleman expanded the harmonic possibilities of the music. Being in such close contact with these innovative musicians informed the use of jazz music in their own work. Bremser, who was white, and Ted Joans, who was African American, used jazz extensively in their collections *Blowing Mouth* (1958–70) and *Black Pow Wow* (1969) respectively. Bremser's work is more personal and maintains a confessional quality. He often writes about familial relationships, alluding to the taboo subject of incest. Thus, he uses the jazz aesthetic of improvisation as a means to explore the internal self rather than to relay broad historical information, as in this excerpt from "Backyards and Deviations":

> my sister used to dress me up (I think)
> some kind of giddy kiddie anagram or
> entertainment game
> of bobbiesox & implethoric girlie girlie
> plum breast applica!
> but I was nervous, hungry,
> ate a plum & did the bit with
> half a laughed at chest of bubbling
> sans gruesome awesome plausible
> cupbola-boola breast! (7)

One would be hard pressed to link any of Bremser's poetry in terms of referencing a jazz musician or employing a recognizable jazz cadence in the construction of his text. However, Bremser's debt to jazz is in the spontaneity of the poem and the rhythmic staccato that can only be heard when the poem is read aloud. Bremser's creative process and final project reflect the spontaneity of an improvised performance. Lines like "implethoric girlie girlie / plum breast applica!" and "cupbola-boola breast!" indicate moments of improvisation within the poem when Bremser decided to follow his instincts for sound. In Bremser's case, the poem becomes an outlet for release, not unlike a jazz solo, quickly blown or spewed over the page. When one reads a Bremser text aloud, one becomes aware of the musical construction at work even though there is no direct reference to "jazz culture." In the contributor notes of Sascha Feinstein and Yusef Komunyakaa's anthology, Bremser is described as a "Jazz-ear Sound Poetry Genius, old Elvin Jones roommate, syncopating wow-sound word walloper; long ago jailbird, original NY late-1950s coffee shop Beat bard with Kerouac & Leroi Jones" (252). Thus, even the style of his contributor's notes reflects his debt to jazz and that his artistic lineage is musical as well as literary.

Ted Joans's poetry is more directly linked to jazz. Joans, a protégé of Langston Hughes and an extensive traveler who for years has made his home in both Mali and France, is known for his dynamic live and recorded performances rather than his publications. In his work, Joans takes on the role of griot in that he records the historical legacies of jazz music. Although Joans is extremely adept at incorporating a surrealist vocabulary with an African American vernacular, his most successful and apparent jazz poems take on a variety of forms—from a simple listing of musicians, somewhat in the celebratory spirit of African praise poetry, to complex metaphysical meditations, as in the poem "Jazz is . . . ," dedicated to pianist Cecil Taylor. Joans's well-known poem "Jazz Is My Religion" is a work that voices the importance and spiritual role of music to African American culture. As M. B. Tolson does with the "Lambda" poem in *Harlem Gallery,* Joans places the music on reverential footing.

> JAZZ is my religion   and it alone do I dig   the jazz clubs are
> my houses of worship   and sometimes the concert halls   but
> some holy places are too commercial (like churches)   so I dont
> dig the sermons there   I buy jazz sides to dig in solitude   Like

> man/Harlem, Harlem U.S.A. used to be a jazz heaven where most of the jazz sermons were preached but now-a-days due to chacha cha and rotten rock'n'roll alotta good jazzmen have sold their souls (49)

Reading Joans's poetry on the page, particularly his repetition of "jazz" and "dig," sometimes achieves the same redundancy as reading a musical notation on a Bird solo. Joans's use of hipster language and bebop phraseology marks a merger between the language of the street and the musical language of the bandstand. The poetry is meant to be heard, further emphasizing poetry's original link to the spoken word as opposed to the written. In a 1980 lecture on jazz poetry at the University of California at Berkeley, Joans indicated that sound and orality are the prime criteria for listening to jazz poetry and that the written text was not as instrumental—pun intended.

Often linked to the New York School of poetry, which was equally influenced by modern art as well as music, Frank O'Hara's *Lunch Poems* were constructed in a similar fashion to Kerouac's serial poems, where "meaning" is sometimes sacrificed for spontaneous improvisation. O'Hara spontaneously wrote the majority of his poems on a display model Olivetti typewriter during his lunch breaks, after walking around Manhattan. With little or no revision, several of the poems successfully capture the spontaneity of the time and the locale of their creation. "The Day Lady Died," a poem from the collection that is often anthologized, is held up as a work that successfully deals with jazz materials. The event of the poem is the speaker learning about the death of Billie Holiday. What is memorable about the poem's construction is its narrative of common events. The poem consists of five strophes. In four of them, the speaker recounts, with accurate specificity, the "mundane" events of the day: he takes the train to the city, buys a magazine, buys cigarettes, thinks about friends. In a moment of sudden epiphany, Billie Holiday's photograph appears in a copy of the *New York Post,* and the narrative is suddenly switched to a recalling of a Holiday performance. The shift in the poem occurs so abruptly that the importance of Holiday's life as well as her impact on the speaker and subsequently on the reader are unmistakable.

The passage below begins with the poem's fourth strophe to indicate the sudden change in mood that O'Hara skillfully achieves. Although the final strophe is linked to his continual run-on narrative, with its use of "and," O'Hara creates a slight tempo change by adding a smooth-flowing lyrical line, "while she whispered a song along the keyboard," that creates the anticipated excitement of a Holiday performance. By employing this method, he displaces the earlier established rhythm of the poem, creating what is known in jazz as a "change," thus upsetting the work's continuity. Barry Wallenstein says that the poem "allows the mourned figure to inform and color all observations" and that the text can be compared to an "improvised performance around a set theme, in which the personality of the poet (or musician) sets the mood" (597).

> and for Mike I just stroll into the PARK LANE
> Liquor Store and ask for a bottle of Strega and
> then go back where I came from to 6th Avenue
> and the tobacconist in the Ziegfield Theater and
> casually ask for a carton of Gauloises and a carton
> of Picayunes, and a NEW YORK POST with her face on it
>
> and I am sweating a lot by now and thinking of
> leaning on the john door in the 5 SPOT
> while she whispered a song along the keyboard
> to Mal Waldron and everyone and I stopped breathing (27)

* * *

In the 1970s, the critic Stephen Henderson edited the significant anthology *Understanding the New Black Poetry.* In his introduction to the book, Henderson attempts to articulate the various poetic elements that contribute to making a poem "black." A significant amount of his introduction focuses on the importance of black music and how it forms the basis of black poetry. Henderson lists ten types of "musical" usage:

1. The casual, generalized reference
2. The careful allusion to song titles
3. The quotations from a song
4. The adaptation of song forms
5. The use of tonal memory as poetic structure
6. The use of precise musical notation in the text
7. The use of an assumed emotional response incorporated into the poem: the subjective correlative

8. The musician as subject/poem/history/myth
9. The use of language from the jazz life
10. The poem as "score" or "chart" (47)

It can be argued that several white poets also fit within the confines of Henderson's criteria for a black poem as well. Further examination of Henderson's criteria demonstrates the connection between black poetry and jazz music and serves as a strong model in terms of defining a jazz poem. Keeping Henderson's criteria in mind, I will examine the manner in which the jazz form has been used specifically by African American poets during the 1960s and 1970s as a means of not only recording black cultural tropes but also transforming such distinctly black aesthetic practices as improvisation and polyrhythm from jazz music to poetic text.

It is interesting that Henderson does not directly mention improvisation in his outline. How a poet follows his instinct for sound is a crucial factor in the creation of jazz poetry. This practice is certainly a response to the more or less "rational" practices of Western culture and represents a type of rebellion that celebrates the primacy of emotion/feeling against logic/thought. The value of this recalls Leopold Senghor's hotly debated remark that "emotion" is African as "thought" is Greek. In *Saying Something: Jazz Improvisation and Interaction,* Ingrid Monson writes that improvisation often functions as a "metaphor for hybridity . . . and for liberation from the inhibiting confines of both hegemonic ideologies and structuralism" (214). In some instances of jazz poetry, improvisation works as a movement between the conscious and unconscious, with the poet weaving in and out through various layers of awareness. Therefore, what occurs is the abandonment of a "logical" cohesiveness, supplanted by emotional openness. It is this openness that connects the poetry to one of the key elements of jazz.

The prolific writer Amiri Baraka has been included in several jazz poetry anthologies. He is seen as being the quintessential jazz poet, particularly due to his skilled use of bebop phraseology, innovative form, and technique.[7] It is difficult and problematic to place Baraka in a particular literary movement because his writing has constantly undergone change due to his engagement with political and cultural issues. Several scholars have chronologically placed Baraka's work in the following periods: beat (1957–62), transitional (1963–65), black nationalist (1965–74), and Third World Marxist (1974–). In *The Poetry and Poetics of Amiri Baraka,* William J. Harris writes that Baraka's "transformations are not always neatly expressed in terms of symmetrical inversions; rather [like jazz] his creative destruction takes many forms: rejection, extremism/completion, violence, dismemberment, creative anger, and revolution" (18). Key here is Harris's assertion of jazz being defined as "creative destruction." Perhaps it is this very quality that enables Baraka to write such acerbic and polemically charged texts.

In his work with jazz, Baraka looks mainly to the innovative music of artists like John Coltrane, Thelonious Monk, Albert Ayler, and Sun Ra and views them as heroic figures who fought against conservative musical and political tastes. Charles Hartman reminds us, in his book on jazz texts, that Baraka's view of black music also comes from a specifically socialist perspective in which the music cannot be separated from economics, or the culture separated from the politics (148). This view is well articulated in Baraka's sociomusic critique of black culture, *Blues People,* and he has always been a consistent advocate for authentic black music and performance as a viable means of articulating the continual legacy of the African diaspora.

John Coltrane, one of the most significant artists to be involved in music as a means of "creative destruction," has been a particularly important inspirational figure for the formulation of Baraka's aesthetic. A good example of Coltrane's creative destruction, or creative deconstruction, is in his well-known 1961 rendition of Rodgers and Hammerstein's "My Favorite Things" from *The Sound of Music.* Rather than deliver the syrupy 1960 recording by Mary Martin, later "sweetened" even more by Julie Andrews in 1966, Coltrane signifies and deconstructs the piece, making it his own and expressing the complexity of individual and communal articulation. Harris describes how Baraka uses Coltrane's aesthetic:

> Like Coltrane, he transforms white forms and ideas into black ones through a jazz process; his poetry reveals his attraction to his white fathers' ideas, his battles with them, his rejection of them, and, finally, his transformation of them into his own rich and multifarious black art. (16)

Amiri Baraka's homage to composer Duke Ellington, "Afro American Talking Drum," is an excellent example of Baraka simultaneously alluding to the connection between African and African American musical traditions, particularly the talking drum as a disseminator of cultural history.

Duke

If you got real spooky
& became Duke Ellington
America wd deny it
just like they did
to the real Duke
Ellington

Ellingtonia

Duke
    speaks for everybody
& the Devil
    resents
      this!

It disturbed me
    so much

I was determined
    to ask him, the
                  Devil,
Why this was
So. Why did he resent

         Duke Ellington?

The Devil, not being a
         racist
         explained

    (& in a very convincing
              way)

    that he didn't mind
    Duke
    it was his
    music

that he
despised!

(Baraka, *Funk Lore* 100–101)

Central to our understanding of this poem is Baraka's awareness of the revolutionary qualities of jazz music. The poem challenges the "popular" historical record by raising the issue of white appropriation and the attempt to manipulate African American music. Even today it is still inconceivable that Duke Ellington never received a Pulitzer Prize or McArthur Award during his lifetime. Yet it is in the face of such adversity that the work ultimately triumphs.

In his poem "In the Tradition," Baraka displays his genius for appropriating the exploitative images of popular culture (1970s television shows like *The White Shadow* and *Starsky and Hutch*) and then weaves his immense knowledge of African American culture in as well, signifying within the text.[8] The poem explodes into a litany of voices "talkin', testifyin', and bearin' witness."

the president of all this
of the blues and slow sideways
horn. tradition of blue presidents
locked up in the brig for wearing zoot suit
army pants. tradition of monks & outside dudes

of marylous and notes hung vibrating blue just beyond just after

just before just faster just slowly twilight crazier that europe or its
racist children

bee-doo dee doop bee-doo dee dooo doop (Arthur
tradition
of shooters
& silver fast dribblers
of real fancy motherfuckers
fancy as birds flight, sunward/high
highhigh
sunward
arcs/swoops/spirals
in the tradition

(Baraka, *Transbluesency* 202)

In this section of the poem, Baraka refers to several musicians by either using their names or alluding to their musical attributes. The poem praises the innovations of musicians like Lester Young (presidents), Thelonious Monk (monks), Mary Lou Williams (marylous), Arthur Blythe (Arthur), Charlie Parker (birds), and Sun Ra and his Arkestra (sunward, arcs). It is interesting that he often uses the plural rather than the singular in his references, thus implying that there have been dozens of unknown musicians who have been part of the "tradition"—that is, the collective musical impulse that creates cohesion in the black community. Baraka merges the dominant tropes of African American culture and history and employs them as a means of reading the texts of white culture. His poem provides an interesting example as to how word and sound can be manipulated to read and comment on history. By creating a text that incorporates the complex rhythms of jazz, Baraka and other jazz poets manage to negotiate the various art forms, musical, written, and visual, in a manner that transcends the clichés found in most modernist American poetry.

Kimberly W. Benston correctly defines the black aesthetics/black arts movement in *Performing Blackness: Enactments of African-American Modernism* "not as creed or even as method, but rather as a continuously shifting field of struggle and revision in which the relations among politics, representation, history, and revolution are productively revalued" (3). The black arts movement of the 1960s and 1970s made a significant impact on the creation of jazz poetry as well. With ideas grounded in the work of musical innovators like Ornette Coleman, Sun Ra, Pharaoh Sanders, and John Coltrane, poets like Etheridge Knight, Carolyn M. Rodgers, Mari Evans, Haki Madhubuti (Don L. Lee), Amiri Baraka, Sonia Sanchez, Nikki Giovanni, and Jayne Cortez emphasized the connection between music and the vernacular. Additionally, the work of Larry Neal, Hoyt W. Fuller, Addison Gayle Jr., and Stephen Henderson generated several creative and theoretical concepts that opened up numerous "spaces" and influenced the direction of the genre.[9] The main theory centered around the black arts aesthetic was that art should be used as propaganda and that the literature of the movement should be written by, about, and for blacks. In one of the defining essays of the movement, Larry Neal writes that "the black artist's . . . primary duty is to speak to the spiritual and cultural needs of black people. Therefore, the main thrust of this new breed of contemporary writers is to confront the contradiction arising out of the black man's experience in the racist West" and to reevaluate "Western aesthetics, the traditional role of the writer, and the social function of art" (62–63). Neal envisions a propagandistic art that mirrors black political thought and is the "spiritual sister of the Black Power concept."

Sonia Sanchez is one of the most significant poets to come out of the black arts movement, and her work shows a debt to some of the most innovative qualities of jazz music. In these two strophes from the poem "Old Words," Sanchez manipulates line breaks to musically portray the contributions of Billie Holiday and Lester Young to African American music.

> sing it billie
>   baby.
> sing away that ill wind
> blowing you no good.
>   no good
> ill wind.
>   spread yo/strange
> fruit amid these
> stones. we all
> strangers here. sing.
>   i hear
> yo/words quivering with silks
>   i smell
> your black soul.
>   sweet.
> . . . .
>   go Prez.   go man.   move
> those plastic hands
> up and down that sax
> blow.   man.   blow.   ride
> yo/saxophone cross
> the stage and back again
> we all riders
> here. blow.
>   man.
> can't you see this
> transfixed audience
> staring at you while
> you bleed.
>   blow.
>   ride.
> bleed . . . blow. (44–45)

Sanchez liberally uses alliteration to emphasize the sound and rhythmic qualities of the music. Names and lyrics of songs are evoked ("Ill Wind" and "Strange Fruit") in order to further strengthen the musical allusion to the performer. In lines like "we all / strangers here" and "we all riders / here," Billie Holiday, Lester Young, Sanchez, and the reader of the poem all become part of the same African diaspora. The poem becomes a testament to the music's power to articulate the cohesiveness of African American culture and to express that the artist's musical aspirations are not separate from the aspirations of the community, thus affirming the link between politics and culture, a crucial criteria for black aesthetic writers.

Another poet who integrated jazz aesthetics and political comment is Haki Madhubuti (Don L. Lee). In 1969 he published *Don't Cry, Scream.* His title poem in that collection has this dedication: "for John Coltrane / from a black poet / in a basement apt. crying dry tears of you ain't gone." The poem attempts to capture the quality of Coltrane's sound.

> the blues exhibited illusions of manhood
> destroyed by you. Ascension into:
> scream-eeeeeeeeeee-ing   sing
> SCREAM-EEeeeeeeeee-ing   loud &
> SCREAM-EEEEEEEEEE-ing   long with
>   feeling (28)

The poem alludes to Coltrane's free jazz album *Ascension* with Madhubuti including performance instructions not unlike those pioneered by Langston Hughes. Typography used for lines like "screeeeeeeeeeCHHHHHHHH / creeEEEEE" have almost become a Coltrane cliché in several black arts poems.[10] In the poem "blackmusic / a beginnning," from the same collection, Madhubuti employs a different technique to express the rhythmic qualities of the music. This excerpt from the poem demonstrates the effectiveness of one-word lines to propel the rhythmic movement of the text.

> pharaoh sanders
> had
> finished
> playing
> &

the whi
te boy was to
go on next.

him didn't
him sd
that
his horn
was
broke.

they sat
there
dressed in
african garb
& dark sun glasses
listening to the brothers
play. (taking notes)
we
didn't realize
who they
were un
til their
next recording
had been
released: the beach boys play soulmusic.

real sorry about
the supremes
being dead,
heard some whi
te girls
the other day—
all wigged—down
with a mean tan—
soundin just like them,
sigin
rodgers & hart
& some country & western. (48–49)

Writing about the exploitation and appropriation of black music by white musicians, Madhubuti's "unconventional" use of spelling and punctuation serve to undermine the conservative poetic forms of the academy and deliver a rapid fire rhythm of political intent. It is also quite evident that the poem echoes similar issues raised in Sterling Brown's poem "Cabaret," written decades earlier.

The Last Poets are a group of poets who have been performing for over three decades. They have been admired mainly for their recorded performances, which later made a profound impact on several rap artists. Although the personnel from the group has changed over the years, the focus and content of their work remains the same. Influenced by the black arts movement, the poets were significant in that they were able to gain a popular footing among African American and, later, white listeners. First recorded in 1970, their work articulates the passion, anger, and irony of black America. It should also be noted that, although the bulk of the Last Poets' work focuses on racial injustice, they have also successfully written poems that critique the American economy and corporate destruction of the environment as well.

In recorded poems like "O.D.," "Jazzoetry," and "Bird's Word," the Last Poets celebrate the creators of jazz music by employing a highly stylized oral delivery that replicates the tone and timber of the music. Biographical and historical references are also a key component and attribute to the authenticity of the texts. Thus, the Last Poets function as "New World Griots" by continuing the historical legacy of black culture. Last Poet Jalal Nuriddin describes the aesthetic behind the poem "Jazzoetry": "We move on, like notes out of a horn, flooding the landscape with images from scenes of musical dreams reams and reams of soft loud screams interlocking the methodology of musicology. Each word fated to be interrelated. Jazzoetry is sound poetry" (Last Poets 19). This section of the poem demonstrates how Nuriddin has fashioned a text that combines the rhythmic elements of the genres of music and literature.

> Minor chords, soft keys, summer breeze, winter freeze, listen PLEASE Breakin' the rules, schooling the fools JAZZ is cool that's the truth dig my proof rhythm and swing doing your thing Abnormally, informally, Jazzoetry is poetry Poetic vibes, masculine bass Flute and drums pick up the pace Piano keys on a spiraling flight That's jazzoetry in black and white. (19)

Michael Harper's 1970 collection *Dear John Dear Coltrane* is mainly comprised of jazz poems. The work stands as a memorial to the musical and spiritual explorations of John Coltrane, a musician Harper particularly admires and had the opportunity to know. In an interview with Sascha Feinstein, Harper remarked that he had written the title poem "Dear John, Dear Coltrane" before Coltrane's death, saying that he "had a vision about this, and it was just a disturbing vision, so much so that [he] did not publish the poem" because he felt that "this was almost a sacrilege" (5).[11] The title of the collection is interesting on several levels. "Dear John," taken in its negative connotation, is a form of nonpersonal address. Among prostitutes, the word "John" refers to a customer. In popular culture, to write a "Dear John letter" is to break off a romantic relationship. When Harper chooses to personalize the method of address with Coltrane's name, he is attempting a more intimate embrace that looks beyond the public facade of the implied relationship. Thus, the title evokes a duality: first, an anonymous object and then a specific identity. By coupling the two phrases together, Harper places us in limbo. We are able to enjoy and love the artist, yet not quite understand the message and drive behind the music. In the title poem, Harper offers no theoretical explanations for Coltrane's personality or work, instead choosing to emphasize its rebellious nature. Thus, things are what they are.

> *Why you so black?*
> *cause I am*
> *why you so funky?*
> *cause I am*
> *why you so black?*
> *cause I am*
> *why you so sweet?*
> *why you so black?*
> *cause I am*
> *a love supreme, a love supreme* (26)

Kimberly W. Benston writes that "Harper locates Coltrane's being in a progressive series of hypostatized abstracts, wresting a *topos* of praise from the lexicons of racial abuse and identification" (183). In addition to "wresting a *topos* of praise," Harper's poem is akin to Coltrane's wresting of Western scales.

Harper's well-anthologized poem, "Brother John," recalls and signifies Williams's "Ol' Bunk Johnson," discussed earlier. The first strophe of the poem begins:

> Black man:
> I'm a black man;
> I'm black; I am—
> A black man; black—
> I'm a black man;
> I'm a black man;
> I'm a man; black—
> I am— (3)

The strophe captures an attribute of Coltrane's musical performance in which he constantly repeats or inverts musical phrases, causing some people to remark that he was practicing on stage. Coltrane's drummer, Rashid Ali, once asked him why he played with so many notes, and Coltrane remarked that he had a lot to say. Harper's text reads like a musical score in that it captures the spontaneity of performance. The repetition of "I am a black man" weaves throughout the poem as Harper feeds in various images of Coltrane's musical life. Opening the collection, this poem also captures the difficulty in getting a "letter" started that seeks to express Coltrane's artistic impact. Harper chooses to emphasize the turbulence of Coltrane's music and, by extension, black identity, through the repetition of language rather than through breaking away from linear form. His continual adherence to linear form and tight narrative structures occurs in several of his jazz-inspired poems, particularly in the collection *Healing Songs of the Inner Ear* (1985).

Among the several jazz musicians like Cecil Taylor, Charles Mingus, Sun Ra, and Archie Shepp who have written poetry to accompany their musical explorations, Cecil Taylor seems the most interesting in terms of using one art form to mirror another.[12] His poem "Garden" cascades into an exploration of the complexities of the African American cultural tradition and locates the poem as a place for fertile creativity. It is the same tradition that he draws from his keyboard. As in his music, Taylor incorporates a cinematographic view of history propelled by the syntactical movement of the text, and the result is astounding.

> Can you dig the recognition performance
> preparation organism energies of fusion
> the placing experiences metamorphosized
> human exchange toward complete submission
> to the spirits conscious digestive response
> the sulting process many level'd hitting
> various constructs:
>   Group sound
>   speech transported
>   muscles are taut
>   relax'd talons
>   deifying purpose
> wait above all functioning, building
>   Joy to
>   exhaulted elevation
>   ascending life . . .
>
> (Lange and Mackey 116)

The section from the opening of the poem certainly captures the dynamics of a Taylor performance. The manner in which the lines are constructed are of particular importance. The opening lines are dense, as if they are stream-of-consciousness. This technique could imply a quick cadence or a rapid delivery of the text. However, Taylor uses words that have the same suffix ending and creates a lingering tone—"recognition," "preparation," "submission"—similar to the type of tonal resonance that can also be heard in his musical performances. The lines that are indented to the right of the margin imply the staccato effect of Taylor's playing. In a 1994 interview with Chris Funkhouser for *Hambone,* he discussed his aesthetic process.

> What I am doing is creating a language. A different American language. I feel that . . . I don't make a separation between intellect and emotion. I think with the great artists that I love there was the same thing. By that I mean they had a structure, technique, and the thing that made the technique and the structure move was their passion . . . Obviously, I'm fascinated with words. And without thinking of rhythm in language, but knowing that it's there, and reading a lot of different people, finally what happens is the same thing that happens when we are involved in music. (24)

Taylor's remarks obviously articulate the importance of music and emotion as a means of informing a creative process that leads to the poem.

It is impossible to discuss all the poets who have made use of jazz music as the aesthetic focal point of their work, but it is indeed crucial that we view jazz as an art form that has enabled cross-cultural pollination and maintains integral roots within the African American tradition. The use of tools such as polyrhythm, improvisation, and various tonal modes unique to jazz allows the musical pallet and vocabulary to expand. Jazz poetry has employed these same techniques and, like the music, it becomes an expression of a self, both individual and communal, that voices itself against the will to destroy it. By speaking its own language, jazz poetry moves in its own sphere and asserts its ability to critique and subsequently transform American culture.

CHAPTER 3

Body and Soul: Bob Kaufman's Golden Sardine

> *My head is a bony guitar, strung with tongues, plucked by fingers & nails . . .*
>
> —*Bob Kaufman*

One day in February 1926, musicians Lil Hardin, Kid Ory, Johnny Dodds, Johnny St. Cyr, and a young trumpet player from New Orleans prepared to make their second recording for Okeh Records. The young trumpeter had received quite a bit of notoriety as a protégé of King Oliver and had acquired the reputation of being one of the exciting innovators of this new, hot music called "jazz." The group was performing a song called "Heebie Jeebies." But something went wrong during the recording process, and Louis Armstrong leaned into the microphone and began singing a series of nonsensical syllables, slightly mimicking the tone and timber of his horn. This new sound was to create a vocal sensation called "scat," placing emphasis on the human voice as an additionally important component in jazz music. Armstrong's recording of "Heebie Jeebies" was the Hot Five's first hit record and transformed the direction of jazz. During that same year, Langston Hughes's jazz influenced collection of poems, *The Weary Blues,* was published. And, somewhere in New Orleans, two-year-old Bob Kaufman was probably uttering his first full sentence.

Louis Armstrong's experimentation during that 1926 recording made a major impact, not only on jazz singing, but on poetry as well. In his excellent book on African American music, *The Power of Black Music,* Samuel A. Floyd Jr. quotes a 1955 study in which Willis Lawrence James provides insightful speculation on the folk origins of scat singing in the vocals of Armstrong and Cab Calloway.

> Somehow, Armstrong and Calloway found the trick of using old folk cry principles to supplement the normal means of singing . . . Being gifted in voice projection, Calloway invented or adopted a series of nonsense syllables and fitted them into his songs. When this was done, people realized the thing as a part of themselves, but they did not know why. They did not realize that they were listening to the cries of their vegetable man, their train caller, their charcoal vendor, their primitive ancestors, heated in the hot crucible of jazz, by the folk genius of Calloway and Armstrong until they ran into a new American alloy. It is possible that neither Calloway nor Armstrong realized what took place. If so, the more remarkable. The response of the orchestra itself in imitating the cries of Armstrong and Calloway carried the cry into the orchestra itself. (Floyd 117)

It should be remembered that several African American poets made similar use of such materials in their desire to craft a poetry firmly rooted in the black oral tradition. James's observations can obviously be extended to apply to other African American "nonmusical" art forms as well. Several poets, from Langston Hughes to Amiri Baraka, have made use of scat singing by placing runs of nonsensical syllables at crucial moments within the text when "logical language" seems to collapse. In jazz poetry, scat phrasing acts as a kind of verbal release that alludes to the instrumental quality of the human voice, as opposed to conveying any formal sense of meaning. Its use is significant because it transcends our conventional notions of "meaning" and emphasizes the importance of music as a key ingredient of the text. Armstrong's scat singing also influenced the singing technique of bebop innovator Dizzy Gillespie, who first began recording bebop in 1944 with saxophonist Charlie Parker. Both Armstrong and Gillespie used scat singing because it could expand the musical ideas they expressed through their horns. Although their scat vocabularies were often unintelligible, they had in them a rebellious quality that defied the musical status quo. Gillespie expressed the connection between bebop and language in his autobiography, *To Be or Not to Bop*, remarking that bebop endeavored to retain the cadence of the African American vernacular and that musical notes, like words, were bent "into new and different meanings that constantly changed" (181). Thus, Gillespie's observation explicitly implies that language like music is in the constant process of transition.

In *The Dark End of the Street: Margins in American Vanguard Poetry,* Maria Damon offers an interesting insight into bebop and its relationship to the body. Damon writes that "bebop got down, into the rhythm of the organs and the blood, making the body conscious of its internal movement and the eruptions, eliminations and ejaculations by which it expresses itself and shatters decorum: Oo-Pop-A-Da!—orgasm, defecation, flatulation, oral exclamation, and belch" (71). Insightful as her comments are, there is yet another way in which bebop, particularly its vocal form, can be critiqued. Perhaps, as Gillespie implies, the bebop vocal is an attempt at fashioning a new language that not only responds to the musical tones of the instruments but also attempts, imaginatively, to call back and reclaim the various African languages lost in the diaspora.

Bebop was created for economic reasons as well. During the swing, or big band, era, large ensembles usually performed jazz music. The financial expenses for managing such large enterprises was daunting, particularly for the African American musicians, who were typically paid well below their white counterparts. Due to the instability of the U.S. economy, during the depression and the war years several bands were forced to cut back on their personnel. Thus, small ensembles with multi-instrumentalists capable of creating the illusion of the big band sound emerged. The subsequent evolution of swing to bebop was in part due to the desire of African American musicians to create a music that would be difficult for whites to copy and receive financial reward. It must be remembered that prior to the advent of bebop, white musicians such as Paul Whiteman, Benny Goodman, and The Dorseys had achieved public notoriety and financial gains often by using arrangements by African American musicians like Fletcher Henderson, Jimmie Lunceford, and Chick Webb, while several African American composers and performers were exploited.[1] In *Jazz: America's Classical Music,* Grover Sales supports this view, writing that the "black musicians who created bebop felt . . . they were concocting a style so involved and demanding that, for once, 'the white man couldn't rip it off and get rich off it' . . . Jazz artists had bitterly seen white imitations of black music far outsell the originals . . . Bebop was a natural byproduct of this smoldering resentment against white copycats getting rich off black music" (131). Thus bebop, and later free jazz, was developed, in part, to keep musical innovation away from Euro-based interpretations and in the hands of its African American inventors. Although bebop generally makes use of the changes or chord progressions found in several Tin Pan Alley–type standards, the discordant cadence of bebop stands antithetical to the formal neatness of Western musical structures. Bebop becomes a way of not only asserting difference but also presenting a uniqueness outside the linear margins of popular music. In understanding jazz poetry, it is important to observe how artists like Kaufman, Jack Kerouac, Ted Joans, and other writers who were part of the beat orbit, managed to apply the rhythmic and tonal techniques of bebop in order to achieve their aesthetic purposes. Their use of bebop propelled the cadence and often the subject matter of the poem. Kaufman and other like-minded poets viewed jazz musicians like Charlie "Bird" Parker as the quintessential American artist who pushed his artistic explorations to a fever pitch, often resorting to drugs and other assaults to the mind and body. However, despite the use of drugs or, some would argue, because of the use of drugs, these artists explored the boundaries of human consciousness and created several prodigious compositions. The triumph of musicians like Charlie Parker and his fellow beboppers was that they were able to create a musical style that articulated an alternative vision to 1950s American paranoia and conservatism.

Scat, to some extent, and vocalese played an important role in influencing the poetry of Kaufman and his contemporaries. Critic Barry Keith Grant defines vocalese as "the setting/singing of lyrics (almost always composed rather than improvised) to jazz instruments, both melody and solo parts, arrangements and solos, note for note . . . It relies on language rather than simply sound" (287). Grant's definition implies that scat singing is more directly connected to musical improvisation than vocalese. The distinction he makes between scat and vocalese is significant, particularly because Kaufman's jazz poetry often ignores the differences between these two vocal forms and writes texts that demonstrate an ability to blend and blur their demarcations. He also emphasizes the "music" of silence, the rhythms that occur outside our concepts of conventional music. In a letter to the *San Francisco Chronicle* that is included in his poetry collection, *Golden Sardine,* he writes about the "silent beat in between the drums."

> That silent beat makes the drumbeat, it makes the drum, it makes the beat. Without it there is no drum, no beat. It is not the beat played by who is beating the drum. His is a noisy loud one, the silent beat is beaten by who is not beating on the

> drum, his silent beat drowns out all the noise, it comes before and after every beat, you hear it in between, its sound is. (81)

Note the repetition of "beat" in this passage. It occurs eleven times in its various forms. In doing so, Kaufman emphasizes the rhythmic qualities of the prose passage and establishes our recognition of the "silent beat" that coveys an opposite and concurring rhythm as well. This emphasis is additionally important in terms of reading a rhythmically defined art form such as poetry, indicating that the space between words is of equal importance. As a poet, Kaufman managed to successfully convey the importance of poetry as an aural as well as a written creation. Kaufman seldom wrote down his poetry, preferring to recite his poems spontaneously on the street or in bars and cafes, often changing the words and cadences to whatever the situation or atmosphere called for.

In order to gain insight into Kaufman's appropriation of jazz materials, it is essential that we examine his biographical data and the particular manner in which he chose to present himself. Kaufman was born into a middle-class family in New Orleans on April 18, 1925. His mother, a schoolteacher, emphasized reading and had an extensive personal library. She encouraged her thirteen children to read the works of Whitman, Proust, James, and Flaubert. Kaufman's eclectic reading would later inform certain experimental qualities in his poetry. His father was a Pullman porter who died of a heart attack when he was nine, although Kaufman would later inform biographers that his father drowned and was lost at sea. He was very close to his maternal great-grandmother, who came over from Africa on a slave ship, and it was through her that he learned his appreciation for nature, which became an important element in his work.

The mixture of African, European, and Caribbean cultures that feed into the Louisiana tradition of aesthetic improvisation found its way not only into Kaufman's poetry but also into his description of his ancestors. Although both of his parents were African American, he would constantly invent biographical data that transcended strict racial classification.[2] In contributor's notes to various anthologies in which his work appeared, he would write that his father was a "German Orthodox Jew" and his mother was a "voodoo Martinican Roman Catholic." Even authoritative reference sources like *Contemporary Authors: New Revision Series* emphasize his Jewish and Catholic upbringing, often using it as a means to gloss his poetry. Maria Damon, who devotes a chapter to Kaufman in her book, interviewed several members of Kaufman's family and provides convincing evidence to refute Kaufman's biographical claims. He once remarked, "One thing for certain I am not white. Thank God for that. It makes everything else bearable." By refusing to specify his race and by having a recognizably Jewish last name, Kaufman became the quintessential American outsider. Maria Damon speculates the reasons why Kaufman fashioned his ancestry. She keenly observers that the "power of the half-Black and half-Jewish myth may have arisen, in the war years and afterward, from a sense of solidarity with suffering and the desire to appropriate a doubly marginal status, which might have appealed to a Beat sensibility, as would the idea of a powerful but unorthodox and variegated spiritual heritage" (34). By choosing to emphasize origins (Voodoo, Judaism) "outside" Christianity, Kaufman created a mystique that would transcend any form of religious or racial categorization. Like the jazz musician who utilizes a variety of sources to create one cohesive piece of music, Kaufman created a complex persona that would dictate the manner in which he lived his life, as well as the manner in which critics responded to his poetry. Sascha Feinstein remarks that Kaufman lived his life "much like the stereotypical jazz musician of the time: addicted to nightlife, to drugs, and to the avowedly non-academic, non-self-promoting world of the arts" (104). In the preface to his collection *The Ancient Rain: Poems, 1956–1978,* he wrote, "I want to be anonymous. I don't know how you get involved with uninvolvement, but I don't want to be involved. My ambition is to be completely forgotten" (ii). He therefore chose to turn his back on literary accolades and financial gain in order to create a body of work that was unconventional and transcended the staid standards of conventional verse. Kaufman had a prodigious memory and the bulk of his work was never written down in journals. Rather, his words were composed aloud or written down on assorted scraps of paper and later typed or recorded by his friends. The fact that Kaufman rarely bothered to write down his works can be viewed as part of his desire for anonymity. Since most of his work was performed orally, Kaufman sought to return poetry back to its original roots as an oral art form first and foremost, anticipating the concerns of Beat writers like Jack Kerouac, Allen Ginsberg, Gary Snyder, and Ted Joans.

Although Kaufman cultivated the outsider persona, he was not oblivious to the failings of American democracy, and he took perilous personal risks as an advocate for racial and social justice. As a result, he experienced all the violence and antagonism that America had to offer. When he was thirteen, a lynch mob hung him in an icehouse all night by his thumbs. At the age of eighteen, he joined the merchant marines and became an active member of the National Maritime Union as well as a communist labor organizer in the South. This was quite dangerous in McCarthy-era America. He was constantly being brutalized by the police and was arrested more than thirty times during a two-year period. In 1963 he was arrested for walking on the grass in New York City's Washington Square Park, taken to the Tombs, transferred to Rikers Island, and then sent to Bellevue Hospital, where he received more than fifty involuntary shock treatments.

In the early 1940s, Kaufman moved to New York to study literature at the New School for Social Research. While there he met poet Allen Ginsberg and novelist William S. Burroughs. The three traveled to San Francisco and became part of the literary scene. While in San Francisco, he met and later married Eileen Singe and had one child, whom they named Parker, after Charlie Parker. San Francisco's North Beach area had several jazz clubs and coffee houses that became favored hangouts for emerging avant-garde writers. From 1958 to 1959, Kaufman booked musicians at the Jazz Workshop on Broadway and North Beach because the owner did not know anything about jazz (Eileen Kaufman, interview, September 2000). It was in these clubs that Kaufman experimented with the complex rhythms of bebop. He often recited his spontaneous compositions on the streets, earning "The Original Bebop Man" as a nickname. At clubs like The Place, he and fellow beat poets Jack Kerouac and Ted Joans would trade off readings, the winner receiving a magnum of champagne (Eileen Kaufman, interview, September 2000). Additionally, Kaufman received such prestigious honors as an invitation to read his poetry at Harvard University, the nomination for Great Britain's Guinness Poetry Award 1960–61, and a National Endowment for the Arts grant for creative writing. Nevertheless, he remained fairly anonymous, financially impoverished, and addicted to methedrine for most of his life.

Although Kaufman emphasized the connection between poetry and orality, it is interesting to note that he took a Buddhist vow of silence after the assassination of John F. Kennedy in 1963 and did not speak in public until 1973, after the Vietnam War ended. He concluded his ten-year silence by reciting Thomas Becket's opening speech in T. S. Eliot's *Murder in the Cathedral* and one of his own poems.

> All those ships that never sailed
> The ones with their seacocks open
> That were scuttled in their stalls . . .
> Today I bring them back
> Huge and intransitory
> And let them sail
> Forever. (*Cranial* 125)

In this poem, Kaufman focuses on the ship, which is a potent image in African diasporic literature.[2] In the beginning of the poem, these ships are powerless and incapable of movement and it is only through the will of the poet, "Today I bring them back," that they can be made functional as vessels of historical memory. Metaphorically, these ships sail back and forth between the Americas and Africa. Thus, the African ancestral connection is restored. Reciting this poem after his long silence was significant because Kaufman emphasizes that the poet must simultaneously carry the dual roles of witness and visionary in order to reclaim and harness the power of language. Maria Damon provides an explanation for Kaufman's self-imposed silence. She observers that his "preoccupation with anonymity and silence come, in his life story, to indicate strength and choice even as they continue to evoke their traditional negative association with the silencing of the dispossessed. The vow of silence carries with it the force of the powerful—the users of words—assuming the powerlessness of those whose voices are ignored" (42). Bob Kaufman died on January 12, 1986, in San Francisco of emphysema.[3]

Fortunately, Kaufman left behind a significant body of work. There are several instances in his earlier poetry where he shows the influence of a jazz aesthetic. In 1959 his broadside, *Abomunist Manifesto,* published by City Lights, achieved widespread popularity among the beat poets. The text includes a variety of sections written in styles that use prose, epistolary, and verse forms. There is even an "Abomunist Rational Anthem," which is written completely in scat phrases.[4] Overall, this extended poem was extremely significant because it functioned as a social and political critique of Western society at a time when most beats were apolitical. Here Kaufman playfully endows Jesus with a jazz hipster's vocabulary.

> TUESDAY-B.C.—minus 3–8 o'sun, p.m.
> Jeru. cool, Roman fuzz busy having a ball, never bother you unless someone complains. Had a ball this morning, eighty-sixed some square bankers from the Temple, read long poem on revolt. Noticed cats taking notes, maybe they are publishers' agents, hope so, it would be crazy to publish with one of those big Roman firms. (82)

By transforming the biblical Jesus, Kaufman creates a character that speaks in the vernacular.[5] He implies that the jazz poet stems from a long spiritual and historical legacy.

City Lights published *Second April,* another broadside, in 1959 as well. The text is composed of several prose sections, which Kaufman refers to as "sessions." Throughout the text, Kaufman interweaves his autobiography with historical and popular cultural events. For example, in this section Kaufman alludes to his Louisiana origins.

> Session golden horn before one . . . is Bayou St. John, Big Sur pornography dipped in, emptied . . . a thing, dipped, dipped in poems, the black child glistened in self-conceived madness . . . dipped in contemporary multiplied generations, played musical electric chairs, dipped in in-jazz the Kansas City maniac found world three, Zulu laughter, good old Fourth of July American heroin, Sumeria, Picasso modern limericks, madness, final mausoleums . . . ah . . . leu . . . cha . . . the time is now . . . is a thing, time is . . . they watch . . . (67)

The repetition of "dipped" accomplishes several things. Not only does it propel the movement of the passage, but it also implies birth, arguing that jazz was born in New Orleans, and it also alludes to Louis Armstrong, whose nickname was "Dipper mouth." Kaufman's use of language and imagery in this passage demonstrates a jazz aesthetic that he would continue to manipulate to various effects throughout his literary career.

Kaufman's first major collection, *Solitudes Crowded with Loneliness* (1965), contains several poems that make use of jazz in a variety of ways. There are lyrical poems, such as "African Dream," "Bagel Shop Jazz," "San Francisco Beat," and the startlingly beautiful "Walking

Parker Home," which Kaufman wrote after the birth of his son. The poem's closing strophe shows how Kaufman had become a master in capturing the lyrical qualities of the music and bringing them to bear in his poetry.

> In that Jazz corner of life
> Wrapped in a mist of sound
> His legacy, our Jazz-tinted dawn
> Wailing his triumphs of oddly begotten dreams
> Inviting the nerveless to feel once more
> That fierce dying of humans consumed
> In raging fires of love. (5)

There are several poems that celebrate jazz musicians such as Charlie Parker, Ray Charles, Lester Young, and Coleman Hawkins. For example, "Mingus" attempts to capture the musical essence of bassist and composer Charles Mingus.

> String-chewing bass players
> Plucking rolled balls of sound
> From the jazz-scented night.
>
> Feeding hungry beat seekers
> Finger-shaped heartbeats,
> Driving ivory nails
> Into their greedy eyes.
>
> Smoke crystals, from the nostrils
> Of released jazz demons,
> Crash from foggy yesterday
> To the light
> Of imaginary night. (27)

There are experimental poems like "Jazz Te Deum for Inhaling at Mexican Bonfires" and "Cincophrenicpoet" that abandon the conventional linear form. There are surreal poems like "Battle Report," with its opening strophe:

> One Thousand saxophones infiltrate the city,

> Each with a man inside,
> Hidden in ordinary cases,
> Labeled FRAGILE. (8)

Throughout the collection, Kaufman makes numerous references to jazz music, thus indicating its importance toward his political and social vision of African American culture.

Kaufman's last collection, *The Ancient Rain,* published by New Directions in 1981, shows that his continual involvement with jazz had become slightly abated. The majority of the poems in this collection reveal a poet more engaged with apocalyptic imagery than the celebratory qualities of music. For example, this prose passage from the title poem of the collection expresses the extent of Kaufman's vision.

> I see the death some cannot see, because I am a poet spread-eagled on this bone of the world. A war is coming, in many forms. It shall take place. The South must hear Lincoln at Gettysburg, the South shall be forced to admit that we have endured. The black son of the American Revolution is not the son of the South. Crispus Attucks' death does not make him the Black son of the South. So be it. Let the voice out of the whirlwind speak. (80)

Here, apparently, is the prophetic voice Kaufman would continue to use until his death.

In terms of Kaufman's use of a jazz aesthetic, *Golden Sardine* is perhaps his most mature work. The manner in which Kaufman uses jazz meter is quite similar to the meter of regular jazz music, where the improvised solo breaks away and expands the composition's melodic and harmonic structure. In Kaufman's aesthetic, the improvisatory gesture is a crucial element, thus often making his use of regular meter unpredictable. *Golden Sardine* is tour-de-force Kaufman, with the poet employing the various techniques he pioneered in his earlier books. City Lights Press, as part of their pocketbook series, published *Golden Sardine* in 1967. Uniquely designed, the book was sized to fit into the pocket of a coat or jacket, thus bringing poetry out of homes and libraries and into streets and cafes. Kaufman's collection consisted of poetry collected from scattered bits of manuscript found in a leather-bound valise by his friend and editor, Raymond Foye, after a fire in his apartment. The title of the manuscript was taken from a phrase written on a brown piece of wrapping paper. Overall, the poems show Kaufman's ability to successfully manipulate a wide variety of forms as he examines the political and social issues of his time. The collection opens with the poem "Carl Chessman Interviews the PTA (from his swank gas chamber)," a long piece that Maria Damon describes as a work that "joins social protest and physical fracturing through linguistic play" (41). The poem is a surrealistic prose narrative divided into several sections. Kaufman's subject is Caryl Chessman, a victim of the death penalty, who, despite evidence of his innocence and pleas for clemency from Denmark, Brazil, Uruguay, Great Britain, and the Vatican, was executed by the state of California.[6] Throughout the poem, Kaufman creates analogies to Jesus' crucifixion and other human tragedies as he describes the injustice of the American judicial system.

> Here, Chessman, is the message to all garcias everywhere,
> longitude people, beyond the margin,
> I am glad now, sad now, home, in TIME FOR THE
> MURDER, guilty California is quiet (33)

Although the book achieved literary notoriety, particularly in France, where Kaufman was celebrated as the "Black Rimbaud," it appeared that he had little interest in its success.

Golden Sardine is important in the study of jazz poetry because it marks the first time an African American poet of the generation following Langston Hughes would use bebop and scat improvisation to lend authenticity to his work. Additionally, the collection is significant because it is the work of an artist who is unafraid to take risks. The inclusion of poetic "failures" as well as "successes" certainly marks a heroic moment in literature. The result is a miraculous unevenness of work that belies the Western critical desire to constantly create masterworks that often end up being closed and inflexible. Surely Kaufman heard the surrealist Antonin Artaud's call from France advocating "no more masterpieces." And, in doing so, he frees up the page, allowing the possibility for improvisation and demonstrating that good art can become simultaneously possible and impossible.

There are several poems in *Golden Sardine* that are written in a jazz aesthetic. Poems like "Tidal Friction," "Why Write ABOUT," and "WAITING" do not necessarily use jazz as subject matter, but they certainly make use of jazz-inspired rhythms. One of the first poems in the book to deal directly with jazz is "Heather Bell *Chorus*." Kaufman indicates the musicality of the poem by defining it as a "Chorus." There is a duality of meaning that occurs in Kaufman's use of this descriptive word. It recalls not only the repeated set of musical phrases in a composition but also the idea of community. Generally, when examining Western notions of choral music, one envisions several human voices singing in a style where it is difficult to decipher individual voices. The sound is often collective. In African American culture, particularly in the tradition of the black church, the choral tradition exists as well. However, after listening to a choir perform, one observes that distinct individual voices can be heard among the collective, with various members singing in slightly differing cadences, timbers, or keys. Performing music in this fashion appears to imply that, although the communal voice is crucial in order to convey the general quality and spirit of the music, it is also informed by the collection of individual voices in which every member has a "story to tell or a song to sing." Separate as these individual narratives may be, combined they all serve the purpose of articulating the united testimony of the community. This practice also occurs in jazz music. Additionally, it appears that Kaufman is signifying on the Greek chorus—that is, the collective voice that would provide commentary to ancient texts like *Medea* or *Antigone*.

HEATHER BELL *Chorus*

You know Heather Bell, she lives around the corner from every-
body, Heather's problem is not staying around the corner . . . she's
an unusual girl, she has no desire to sleep with her father, partially
because her father is dead. It may also be said of her that she has
never willingly submitted to her stepfather . . . until she had
received everything she had been promised.

Heather is cool for a schoolgirl, she prefers the company of
   hipsters,
beats, homosexuals—impotent novelists . . . and a beat girl who
   looks
very much like a view of her as seen from the inside . . . Heather
loves jazz as much as she hates her mother who no longer
loves . . . Heather is an American matador. Heather's mother is an

> American bull. Heather needs a cape to tire her bull and prepare
> it
> for the kill . . . Heather fights rough, her cape is apt to be ripped,
> but how important is a cape when you know the important
> thing is
> to kill. Heather is cool & needs a cool cape. (48)

Kaufman chooses a very lyrical name that evokes two of the most important symbols in his work, nature (Heather) and music (Bell). He establishes the text's musical cadence by repeating the name several times. However, Heather Bell is not necessarily a distinct individual; she is a particular type who should be familiar to the reader: "You know. . . ." Kaufman places her as an outsider by saying that Heather "lives around the corner from everybody." Several times within the work, Kaufman indicates her differences within the various spheres of social life, family, school, art, sexuality. Heather prefers the company of "outsiders."

It would appear that Kaufman's mention of jazz in the second stanza is rather casual. However, it should be noted that he places Heather's love for jazz in direct opposition to what her mother "no longer loves. . . ." The absence of mother's love is crucial to our understanding of how Kaufman views jazz, and because mothers are often viewed as nurturing figures in literature, the contrast is all the more startling. The mother is often the first person to encode how we feel and function in the world. By veering away from that crucial connection, mother or lineage becomes fractured. Thus, jazz supplants the function of mother and becomes the nurturing source for Heather that further defines her outsider status. The importance of this phrase is additionally emphasized by its placement between ellipses. The ellipses serve a rhythmical function as well, indicating the "silence" between phrases.

In the fifth line of the second strophe, Kaufman describes Heather as an "American matador," a very important image that indicates her courage and her lack of passivity. Heather's mother is described as an "American bull." The bull is often characterized as combative and stubborn. When people are described as "bull-headed," it indicates their inflexibility. The bull image can also be extended to include mainstream American society. Kaufman implies that Heather will have to fight against mainstream America (Mother) in order to assert her vision of life. What Heather needs in order to combat the bull is a "cool cape," emphasizing the necessary merger between the interior and exterior that is crucial to practicing a holistic style of living. "Cool" is a very important concept in African American culture that describes a particular way of living. In *Juba to Jive: A Dictionary of African American Slang,* Clarence Major provides a definition of "cool," informing us that the word originally had Mandingo origins.

> **Cool** adj., v. (1650s-1990s) "gone out" (Mandingo); fast (Mandingo); . . . in the 1930s American tramps and criminals were using it to refer to the act of *killing someone;* to be under great self-control . . . generally it means anything favorably regarded . . . a cool person is one who is detached, aloof. In the forties "cool" music was fashionable, just as it was fashionable for the listener—and everybody else!—to be cool. "Cool" was the opposite of hot. (111; emphasis added)

The "cool" music that Major refers to was first made popular by Miles Davis and his nonet's 1949 recording called *The Birth of the Cool.* The music was particularly popular on the West Coast and was performed by several talented white musicians like Stan Getz, Gerry Mulligan, Pepper Adams, and Chet Baker. Additionally, it should be noted that, although notions of the term "cool," as it was used among Kaufman's fellow beats, later became vogue in American popular culture, the word had origins in the African American community. The adjective became a means of distinguishing those who distanced themselves from "square" America, either through music, walk, speech, or clothing that was imitative of African American musicians like Dizzy Gillespie, Thelonious Monk, Cab Calloway, or Babs Gonzalez. When Kaufman indicates that Heather is "cool," he is defining her in a context that is informed by bebop music and African American culture.

"Cocoa Morning" is another poem that places emphasis on the redemptive qualities of the music.

> Variations on a theme by morning,
> Two lady birds move in the distance.
> Gray jail looming, bathed in sunlight.
> Violin tongues whispering.
>
> Drummer, hummer on the floor,
> dreaming of wild beats, softer still,

Yet free of violent city noise,
Please, sweet morning,
Stay here forever. (54)

In a similar fashion to "Heather Bell," Kaufman immediately opens the text by establishing a musical connection. The opening phrase, "Variations on a theme," indicates the possibility of improvisation or the multiple ways in which the morning can be sung/heard or seen. Literally, the variations can apply to the "two lady birds" the poet notices. It is important to note that Kaufman introduces the possibility of sound "variations" before presenting the image, thus giving the ear primary importance over the eye. After describing the gray jail as looming, he returns to a musical description, "Violin tongues whispering." Because of the image's close proximity to the "Gray jail," the tongues take on sinister implications. This is additionally true because of the connection with jails and violence. Perhaps "violin tongues" is a pun on "violent tongues." The violin in this line can also be viewed negatively because it is often the dominant instrument in Western music and, although there are a few exceptions, it has seldom been used in jazz. Note how Kaufman uses the word "violent" alongside the word "city," an industrial image. This image captures the possibility of dissonance and can be seen similarly in the confrontation between the birds that are like two instruments in a band that achieve harmony only through counterpoint. Kaufman uses other contrasting images such as "gray" and "sunlight," "free" and "jail" to further emphasize the importance of dissonance. These variations Kaufman emphasizes are not unlike the changes that occur in the music. Thus, the jazz texture of the poem becomes obvious as the poet pursues these contrasts and counterpoints in various places in the text.

The continued use of variations creates an even more important distinction when one considers how Kaufman uses the drum in the next stanza. Prior to the invention of the drum kit and the global influence of rock 'n' roll, the drum has historically been viewed as a non-Western instrument. The phrase "Drummer hummer" establishes a change in the text's rhythmic structure. Again, Kaufman demonstrates another sort of variation. Rhythmically the phrase mirrors the poem's title with the stressed syllables of "cocoa" corresponding to "drummer." This percussive change that Kaufman introduces in the poem signals a musical change as well: from the bird songs of the first stanza to the human-controlled beats of the second. The drummer could be a person playing the drums or the percussive tap of a woodpecker or similar type of bird. In addition to its vernacular definition of referring to something exceptional, "Hummer" indicates a different manner (variation) of making music. The phrase could be connected to the tonal vibrations of the drum. The poem closes with the poet finding solace through the music of "sweet morning." Although jazz is not mentioned in any direct way, there is the inference that "natural" music is more significant than the artifice of urban structure. Since jazz solos are seldom notated prior to performance, the emphasis on improvisation and spontaneity is highly prized. Thus, the music becomes more integral to human emotion and less contrived. For Kaufman, music becomes a means of emotional security and entrance into the rhythms of the day.

There have been various interpretations of "Cocoa Morning." Bob Kaufman's close friend, jazz musician Steve Lacy, set the poem to music aware of the work's tonal lyricism. In an interview, Eileen Kaufman offered a literal reading of the text, commenting that Kaufman's favorite morning beverage was cocoa and that while he was composing the poem he was listening to "Variations" by Nicolo Paganini. "The girl described is myself and this girl from Europe who used to live with us . . . 'drummer-hummer' is in reference to an African boy who was visiting us and became sick and was sleeping on our floor that morning." Eileen Kaufman's observation provides a complex glimpse into Kaufman's composition method that certainly demonstrates a profound connection between literal and metaphorical readings of work that draws from a broad range of musical traditions.

"Round About Midnight" is one of Kaufman's most anthologized poems. The poem's title comes from the well-known 1940 ballad "Round Midnight" composed by bebop innovator Thelonious Monk. The piece has become a standard and has been performed or recorded by almost every major jazz figure. Although there are several instrumental versions of this jazz standard, singer Carmen McRae has recorded an interesting version in which she uses Bernie Hanighen's original words and weaves in the lyrics by Jon Hendricks in the second chorus. She closes out the song with a vocal reference to a Dizzy Gillespie tag.[7] In examining the collaborative process that often occurs between jazz musicians, Paul F. Berliner discusses Monk's well-known 1944 recording of the piece with trumpeter Cootie Williams, showing that composition in general was often a communal enterprise.

> According to some accounts, Williams added embellishments to the melody during the recording session. Consequently, his embellishments were incorporated as formal features of the melody when sheet music renditions were produced based on the recorded version. Subsequently, when Dizzy Gillespie recorded the piece in 1946, he added to its form an eight-measure introduction and coda that he had originally used as the coda of his version of "I Can't Get Started." By 1955, after the "imported introduction" had itself become a standard feature among renditions by various artists—including Monk himself—Miles Davis personalized the composition further by adding a three-measure interlude to the end of the first chorus, which other artists subsequently adopted as a formal part of the composition. (88)

Kaufman worked in a similar fashion, combining original phrases of poetry as well as other things that he heard. "He mixed it up. People never knew where his stuff began and ended" (Eileen Kaufman, interview, September 2000).

Monk's nickname was "The Mojo Man of Bop" and, like Kaufman, he experienced several years of public neglect while he pursued his artistic vision. Paul Bacon was one of the first jazz critics to recognize Monk's importance to jazz. In a 1948 review of Monk's recording of "Round About Midnight," Bacon describes his contribution:

> His beat is familiar but he does something strange there, too—he can make a rhythm seem almost separate, so that what he does is inside it, or outside it. He may play for a space in nothing but smooth phrases and then suddenly jump on a part and repeat it with an intensity beyond description. His left hand is not constant—it wanders shrewdly around sometimes playing a couple of notes, sometimes powerfully on the beat, usually increasing it in variety, and occasionally silent. (Williams 216–17)

I emphasize Bacon's description of Monk's technique in order to observe how Kaufman uses it in "Round About Midnight."

> Jazz radio on a midnight kick,
> Round about Midnight,

Sitting on the bed,
with a jazz type chick
Round about Midnight,

Piano laughter, in my ears,
Round about Midnight.

Stirring laughter, dying tears,
Round about midnight.

Soft blue voices, muted grins,
Exciting voices, Father's sins,
Round about Midnight.

Come on baby, take off your clothes,
Round about Midnight. (59)

When one considers how often Kaufman employs a jazz meter in his poetry, emphasizing offbeats and polyrhythms, the regularity of the meter in "Round About Midnight" is puzzling. This metric form is managed by using single syllable end rhymes in several of the stanzas. This technique would appear quite contradictory to Monk's predilection for disjunctive phrasing; however, it should be observed that Kaufman places end rhymes of startlingly different tonal value. For example, words like "kick" and "chick" are more heavily accented than words like "grins" and "sins." Also, end rhymes like "grins" and "sins" or "ears" and "tears" all contain the same lingering consonant sound. A similar effect occurs in the second and fourth strophes, where the poet uses "sitting," "stirring," and "exciting" as rhythmic elements at the beginning of the line. This technique not only evokes the musical quality of the poem but also the exciting pace of the evening. The repetition of the phrase "Round About Midnight" also contributes to the pace of the poem in a similar manner.

Kaufman's use of Monk's piece can be analyzed in a variety of ways. The slight variation of the title, which occurs in several recordings as well, establishes the connection to the original as well as the possibility of difference. The change in the title can also be read as a move toward describing the work in musical/literary fashion. For example, "round" is another word for "roundelay," which is a short simple song with a refrain. Kaufman's repetition of the phrase "Round about Midnight," points to the possibility that he is alluding to this early form. Additionally, "Round about" in African American vernacular indicates place, as in "I saw her round about here." In doing so, Kaufman emphasizes the variations that can occur in poetry as well as music.

Although the poem directly refers to jazz with phrases like "jazz radio" and "jazz type chick," there is no direct description of a musical performance or anecdote about a musician's life. Rather, the poem captures the sensuality of jazz by juxtaposing the music with phrases of objects that evoke eroticism. The final line, "Come on baby, take off your clothes," propels the poem toward the climactic event of the evening, repeating the closing phrase "round about midnight," as if someone was turning off the light in preparation for a sexual encounter. The power of this poem is that Kaufman demonstrates how music manages to transfigure our emotions and create a more sensual way of being.

In "Jazz Chick," Kaufman uses descriptive elements of jazz to portray the female form:

> Music from her breast vibrating
> Soundseared into burnished velvet.
> Silent hips deceiving fools.
> Rivulets of trickling ecstasy
> From the alabaster pools of Jazz
> Where music cools hot souls.
> Eyes more articulately silent
> Than Medusa's thousand tongues.
> A bridge of eyes, consenting smiles
> Reveal her presence singing
> Of cool remembrance, happy balls
> Wrapped in swinging
> Jazz
> Her music . . .
> Jazz. (60)

Kaufman pays particular attention to the music of the human body, which he encodes with sexual meaning. He achieves this by focusing on the sensual parts of the body (breasts, eyes, tongue, hips). He further emphasizes the eroticism of the body by using verbs like "vibrating" and "trickling." Additionally, Kaufman's use of sensual imagery encourages the reader to recall the original etymology of the word "jazz." It is interesting that, although the poem evokes sound to describe the woman's body, the use of silence is also emphasized. The hips are silent and the eyes are "articulately silent," an interesting phrase when one considers that the word "articulate" is often applied to speaking. Kaufman changes our common perceptions of silence, making it powerful rather than powerless. The woman's eyes are compared to Medusa's thousand tongues. Medusa, the monster from Greek myths whose hair was full of serpents, turned men into stone, literally silencing them. Kaufman's use of tongues and Medusa's serpents are also phallic images, thus emphasizing the sexual aspect of the text even more. However, it should be noted that Medusa and the violence of her implied sexual encounter are juxtaposed to the performer's sensual engagement with the music. The audience watching her is referred to as "fools" because they are caught up in the sexual reading of her body. It is jazz that becomes the balm to soothe their "hot souls." Thus, the music that is encoded on the body becomes just as potent as the snakes in Medusa's hair.

The final four lines of the poem further evoke how jazz can transform both the listener and performer. Kaufman underlines its importance by placing "Jazz" on separate lines. The appearance of the dancer/singer indicated by "Her music . . . ," is placed between two uses of the word, thus indicating her merger with the music. The poet's use of jazz in this manner demonstrates the ability of music to transcend place and transform people. By using jazz as an ornamental frame, he introduces an African American cultural expression to describe the body, thus revising the manner in which white poets have described the female form.

Jazz is used as a transformative agent in "Tequila Jazz." The poem captures the atmosphere of a party and the self-introspection that occurs over drinks and music. The reader is addressed as if he or she were in attendance.

> The party is on.
> People are on,
> Too.
> Are you on too?

Who crouches there in my
Heart?
Some wounded bird,
Hidden in the tall grass
That surrounds my heart.

Unseen wings of jazz,
Flapping, flapping.
Carry me off, carry me off.
Dirt of a world covers me,
My secret heart,
Beating with unheard jazz.

Thin melody ropes
Entwine my neck,
Hanging with
Tequila smiles,
Hanging, Man,
Hanging. (61)

The poem's title indicates the mood and atmosphere in which jazz is heard. Tequila, distilled from the *Agave tequilana* plant in Central America, is known for its hallucinatory properties and its association with Mexican culture. By using tequila to define jazz, Kaufman alludes to the connection between jazz and alcohol as vehicles of transformation. As he demonstrates through most of his jazz-influenced poems, when one hears music, one becomes more perceptive to the connections between the physical and rhythmic. The same thing occurs when one drinks; the physical images of the world become blurred, and the manner in which one walks or talks changes cadence as well.

In this poem, Kaufman uses the African American vernacular to emphasize the complex duality of a language "charged with meaning." To say that something is "on" means that it is informed or sophisticated. Thus the party where the music is being heard is the place to be. Being "on" could also indicate jazz is in the spotlight or the center of attention. Thus, the party becomes a locale of performance, not only in terms of music but also with regard to the interaction among people. The reader's sophistication or "hipness" is addressed when the poet asks, "Are you on too?" However, considering Kaufman's pervasive drug use, the question could have other implications, indicating that the speaker is trying to make a connection. The different meanings of "on" open the way for a poem that seeks to transcend the limitations of a single interpretation. In the second strophe, Kaufman jumps from the party's exterior to the body's interior by introducing the image of a wounded bird "hidden in the tall grass" of his heart. The bird is an image often associated with music, and the heart with emotion. By presenting these two images in conjunction, the poet implies that there is a hidden music within the body. Although the party and the people attending are supposed to be "on," the speaker also addresses the reader, asking, "Are you on too?" perhaps seeking complicity. However, what goes beyond the human-to-human communication that is insinuated in the text is the interior music of the body, the unheard "secret heart" that conceals emotion and legitimate human interaction.

In the third strophe, the bird, propelled by jazz wings, begins to move. It becomes a means of transport ("carry me off"), of moving outside the body, of reconfiguring the interior and the exterior. The heart—that is, the life line—is pumping a jazz rhythm. The fact that the rhythm is unheard indicates the speaker's inability to express outwardly what is in his soul. Kaufman insinuates that "silence" is a device to which only the enlightened individual in touch with his soul is privy. Thus, the personal aspect of the music of the body is as important as the personal language of the jazz soloist.

The final strophe provides a startling image. "Thin melody ropes / Entwine my neck" appears to indicate that music can also be a means of entrapment. Kaufman's use of the word "hanging" when viewed in close proximity to "neck" has the implications of a lynching, particularly when one recalls the brutal photographs of celebratory lynchers standing over charred bodies, smoking cigarettes and drinking whisky. At Kaufman's party, the loss of self-control creates a treacherous place in which one, absorbed by the combination of alcohol and music, loses equilibrium. Thus, the "Tequila smiles" imply a sinister guise in which overt emotion must be concealed. However, like the word "on," "hanging" has different meanings. If someone is "hanging," he or she is enduring or putting up with a slightly unpleasant situation, or the person could simply be "hanging out"—that is, just being there. Therefore, the use of the word makes the poem circular, with the end contradicting the beginning. At first everything is "on," but the party later becomes a prison from which the speaker cannot escape.

In "His Horn," Kaufman paints the portrait of an unnamed saxophone player. According to Eileen Kaufman, the poem refers to Charlie Parker.

> Swinging horn softly confirming
> Anguished cries of eternal losers
> Whose gifts outgrow their presence.
> We hear this lonesome Saxworld dweller
> Swing higher—
> Defiantly into a challenge key
> Screamed over a heartbeat
> Shouting at all beat seekers
> To vanish into the soft sounds of jazz
> And walk with him to smoky ends
> While his jazz walks forever
> Across our parched heartstrings. (63)

By employing religious imagery in the poem, Kaufman asserts that the jazz musician is not merely an entertainer. In the poem's first line, he brilliantly alludes to the African American spiritual "Swing Low Sweet Chariot."[8] The spiritual articulated the African American desire for peace and release from the secular world, and it was also sung as a liberation code to signal to slaves the moment and direction of escape. Although Kaufman does not use any of the exact wording of the spiritual, his allusions are obvious in the manner in which he uses sounds to recall the "feel" of the original piece.

The second and third lines of the text not only confirm Kaufman's use of religious allusion but also comment on the contributions of African American culture. The "anguished cries of the eternal losers" are articulated through the saxophone. Thus, music becomes a way to communicate a legacy of inequality for African Americans. However, what is crucial to our understanding of the text is that the "eternal losers" provide "gifts," or culture, that have long lasting effects. Here, one cannot help but think about the contributions that African American musicians have made to American popular music. Although the saxophone player articulates the voice of the community, he, like most artists, is an outsider. He is totally devoted to his art, living in a "Saxworld."

In the fifth line, the poem changes from its ethereal pace. With "Swing higher—" the poet commands and the music becomes a vehicle for defiance. By mentioning the "challenge key," Kaufman alludes to the cutting contests that were such an important part of a jazz musician's education. During a cutting contest, various instrumentalists would attempt to outperform or outimprovise whoever was on the bandstand. There are several stories about musical battles by musicians. Particularly prominent is the "Battle of the Saxes" between musicians like Lester Young and Herschel Evans, Coleman Hawkins and Eddie "Lockjaw" Davis, and John Coltrane and Sonny Rollins. The intensity and the drive to create innovative music made these contests prized moments in jazz lore. Lines seven and eight, with their strong verbs "Screamed" and "Shouting," demonstrate the change in tonal timber as well. The closing of the poem indicates that the musician has departed or gone to "smoky ends." However, his music continues; it becomes a way to nourish and sustain the black community. Thus, Kaufman establishes the importance of the jazz musician as a carrier of African American culture and a symbol of spirituality and liberation.

In "Crootey Songo," Kaufman uses the techniques of scat singing in order to create a poem that relies heavily on sound and less on meaning.

> DERRAT SLEGELATIONS, FLO GOOF BABER,
> SCRASH SHO DUBIES, WAGO WAILO WAILO.
> GEED BOP NAVA GLIED, NAVA GLIED NAVA,
> SPLEERIEDER, HUYEDIST, HEDACAZ, AX—, O, O.
>
> DEEREDITION, BOOMEDITION, SQUOM, SQUOM, SQUOM.
> DEE BEETSTRAWIST, WAPAGO, LOCOEST, LOCORO, LO.
> VOOMETEYEREEPETIOP, BOP, BOP, BOP, WHIPOLAT.
>
> DFEGET, SKLOKO, KURRITIF, PLOG, MANGI, PLOG MANGI,
> CLOPO JAGO BREE, BREE, ASLOOPERED, AKINGO LABY.
> ENGPOP, ENGPOP, BOP, PLOLO, PLOLO, BOP, BOP. (74)

Upon first encounter, "Crootey Songo" may have the appearance of being completely nonsensical. However, closer examination of the text reveals that Kaufman occasionally uses an approximation of phonetic spelling to indicate actual words or implies words by introducing certain sounds often found in bebop vocal language. Below, I have repeated the poem by attempting to supply some of the words or near-words Kaufman may have intended. My creative rendering of the text should by no means be taken as an authoritative explanation but rather as another way in which the poem can be "understood."

CRUELTY SONG

THE RIGHT LEGISLATIONS, FLOW GOOF ?
CRASH SHOO DOOBIE, WE GO WAIL WAIL.
GET IT BOP NEVER LIED, NEVER LIED NEVER,
?READER, WHO IS IT(HERE IT IS), HEAD A GAS, ASK(AXE), OH, OH.

DIRECTION, BOOM EDITION, SQUIRM, SQUIRM, SQUIRM.
THE BEATS STRESSED, UP I GO, LOCOEST, LOCO, LOW.
VOMIT(VOOM IT) TIL YOU REPEAT IT UP, BOP, BOP, BOP, WHIP A LOT.

FRICK(FUCK) IT, ?, CORRECTIVE, PLUG, MANGE, PLUG MANGE,
? ? BREATHE, BREATHE, AS ? , I CAN GO BABY.
ENGPOP, ENGPOP (ENGLISH-POPULAR?), BOP, BLOW LOW, BLOW LOW, BOP, BOP.

If my reading of the text does in fact approximate Kaufman's meaning, its emphasis is only secondary to the sound of scat that he hoped to create in this poem. He was never to write another one like it, and I suspect that, as an oral piece, the effect it has on a listener would be quite different. Regardless of what the poem may "mean," it marks an attempt by an African American poet to render the tonal quality of jazz by employing a different medium. Maria Damon has remarked that

> Kaufman's unmeaning jargon differs sharply from meaningless. His unmeaning—as in unnaming—aims to destroy actively the comfort of meaning, to burst its chains in service to the furious, spasmodic play of jazz energy. His jargon is both the special code of initiated hipsters (the underground cultural counterpart to an elite of educated expertise) and the original "jargon": etymologically, the babble of (yard)birds, gurgling—the bubbling up and over of untamable sound. (41)

In the poem, "O-JAZZ-O," Kaufman shows how jazz transcends human origins and becomes the primary element in the universe, the origin of all things.

> Where the string
> At
> Some point,
> Was some umbilical jazz,
> Or perhaps,
> In memory,
> A long lost bloody cross,
> Buried in some steel calvary.
> In what time
> For whom do we bleed,
> Lost notes, from some jazzman's
> Broken needle.
> Musical tears from lost
> Eyes.
> Broken drumsticks, why?
> Pitter patter, boom dropping
> Bombs in the middle
> Of my emotions
> My father's sound
> My mother's sound,
> Is love,
> Is life. (93)

The placement of jazz between the two zeros or the letter "O" creates an interesting title because it acts as a kind of Taoist equation, implying how integral jazz is to the functioning of the universe. The first three lines of the poem introduce the image of a string. The string is an important image because it is a symbol of connection. It represents the umbilical cord, a medium of sustenance for new life. Additionally, in musical terms, a string is used to define a melodic line or theme on which a composition is based. It is a musical undercurrent that is retained throughout the piece with the various harmonies and rhythmic changes orbiting around its periphery, serving as a connector of sorts. The line "At / some point" also has a dual meaning and can be read to refer to an unspecified moment in time or an unspecified position in the cosmos, a point of origin. Additionally, the line alludes to evolutionary development in that scientists cannot exactly pinpoint the origin of the species.

Beginning with line five, the poet offers another possible explanation for the origin of jazz by alluding to symbols of Christianity. Once again, Kaufman repeats his penchant for placing jazz in a sacred and religious context. However, the blood spilt on the Calvary cross in order to save humanity from sin is transformed and placed in a more collective and communal context. "For whom do we bleed" is obviously a reference to the suffering of the African American community similar to the poem "His Jazz." The music ("lost notes") scatters and becomes lost, perhaps alluding to the African diaspora, in which language and other cultural materials are dispersed. The image of a jazz musician's "broken needle" works simultaneously as a reference to drug use and a broken phonograph needle. This distinction is crucial to our understanding of the poem because symbolically it refers to the function of jazz in supplying the lifeblood of African and African American cultural identity. Because the needle is broken, the record is unplayable and the notes cannot be heard. Thus, the lifeblood is scattered and diffused into the diaspora, the result of which is a fracture of racial and cultural history.

The image of an object that no longer serves its function is used in the phrase "broken drumsticks." As mentioned earlier, the drum has particular significance in African and African American culture in terms of its ability to communicate between individuals and the community. Drumsticks that are broken disrupt the rhythmic continuum. In the line "Pitter patter, boom dropping," the image of the drum is reinstated. However, this rhythm can allude not only to the musician's tears but also to the sounds of nature. The use of rain as a symbol of nourishment and cleansing is certainly a well-established trope in several cultures. The "bombs" mentioned in the poem refer to a musical term used to describe the strong offbeat accents used by drummers that were particularly influential during the bebop period of jazz. Its importance to the text is that it evokes explosive changes. The final lines of the poem indicate the importance of jazz in connection to ancestry. The poet finds solace and self-definition through the music. It is something that is born of a father's and mother's love.

The connection between jazz and the human body is a recurring motif in Kaufman's poetry. His innovative use of scat phrasing, which he acquired by being particularly attuned to the music of Charlie Parker, Thelonious Monk, and Dizzy Gillespie brought an attention to the musical possibilities of poetry when language goes beyond "meaning." What is equally important is that he infuses his work with a heightened sense of spirituality that goes beyond the secular implications of music and poetry. Thus, he seeks to reestablish the bridge between African and African American culture by employing a more rhythmic vocabulary. For Kaufman, a poem that uses a jazz aesthetic should dictate the relationship between our physical and spiritual existence.

CHAPTER 4

Now's the Time: Stephen Jonas's Exercises for Ear

i have come to
chew up yr language

to make more palatable
the L's & collaterals

(at the service
entrance
—Stephan Jonas

A contemporary of West Coast poet Bob Kaufman, Stephen Jonas employed jazz materials in his poetry while living in Boston from the 1940s through the 1960s. Like Kaufman, in his adoptive home of North Beach, Jonas seldom ventured far from Boston's West End, which he jokingly referred to as the "ass side of Beacon Hill." Although there was the occasional foray to New York City to look at art, listen to music, and cavort with fellow poets, Jonas preferred the cultural offerings of Boston and remained there until his death in 1970. There is no record of Jonas and Kaufman having met, but the two shared similar interests. Both men found an aesthetic appeal in jazz, particularly bebop, and used it to inform their unique approaches to poetry. In addition, they had in common friendships with beat poets, run-ins with the law, prison terms, and mental breakdowns.

One similarity of particular interest was their desire to be perceived as "outsiders" to mainstream America. Both writers consciously cultivated an ambiguous racial identity that would constantly undergo revision. Kaufman chose to emphasize his outsider status by taking on the dual ethnic identity of Jewish and African American. Jonas made a conscious effort to be elusive about his past, thus constantly reinventing and repositioning himself in a racially myopic society. The notion of racial ambiguity in relation to one's self-definition has historically and often artistically been an albatross over African American writers. Most familiar is the racial ambiguity expressed by modernist Jean Toomer, author of *Cane,* who, toward the end of his life, refused racial categorization, partly in response to his immersion in Gurdjieff philosophy. As a child of racially mixed parentage, Toomer considered himself to be part of a new "American" race that encompassed elements of all humanity. With the publication of *Cane* in 1923, his reputation as a "negro writer" grew. This angered him because he preferred to be regarded simply as an "American writer." Eventually, he distanced himself from friends and colleagues like Langston Hughes, Zora Neal Hurston, Alain Locke, and Claude McKay, subsequently denying his black heritage.

By most accounts, Stephen Jonas was born somewhere in Georgia between 1920 and 1927 and was raised by his adoptive parents, who named him Rufus S. Jones. Although he never legally changed his name, Stephen Jonas was the name he often used as a writer. Racial lines, particular in the South, where Jonas may have grown up, were often difficult to decipher. In the essay "No Saints in Three Acts," Aldon Lynn Nielsen poses an interesting insight into Jonas's work in the context of his insistence on racial ambiguity.

> In America, where the "one drop" rule has, since the last century at least, classified anyone with African heritage as a black person, and in which during the period of slavery, a child's legal status followed that of the mother precisely so that white fathers could sire and sell legally black children, what do we read of Jonas now, we who read remains that are in his writings, make of this poet who may have been born black Rufus Jones and died as white Stephen Jonas. (4)

Nielsen adds that a thorough reading of Jonas's work reveals that he had such an "extensive and intimate knowledge of African American expressive culture" that it would be hard to imagine his racial origins being solely white. He goes on to say that Jonas's work is a "virtual casebook for the study of multiple directed racism" in which one can observe the interaction between race and culture that obfuscate issues of American identity (4).

Diane di Prima, poet and coeditor with Amiri Baraka of the 1960s influential journal *Floating Bear,* described Jonas as a "very fine Puerto Rican poet from Boston." In his autobiography, Baraka describes his first encounter with Jonas, whom he had met through poet John Wieners.

> [Wieners] had a crazy half-black (maybe Cape Verdian) friend poet Steve Jonas, who plagued him. Jonas rambled nonstop about Pound. Black and Jews and Poundians all, scrambled by talk of Art. We'd look at all the "kikes" and "niggers" in his work, gloss it, look over it, justify it, and right on, Pound, right on!" (162)

In a letter to Baraka, Jonas arrogantly addresses racial identity and the political responsibility of the writer.

> I have no time for Revolutionist & "guerrilla writing" indeed . . . Who're you publishing to? Nobody reads anymore—Its a lost art. i don't like "kikes," "niggers" & "pore" "white trash" a sample of each I encountered at yr. pad. None of which has to do with racial prejudice—its cognitions. You are a Poet & a gentleman. (Nielsen 17)

The photograph of Jonas that appears on the jacket cover of his *Selected Poems* shows his light complexion, high cheekbones, and wavy black hair and could easily lead readers to assume a racially mixed heritage. That he appeared "other than African American" was a distinction he would constantly manipulate to suit his needs. Jonas's appearance enabled him to traverse several racial demarcations. To some he appeared to be Native American, biracial, or Latino; to others, Cape Verdian or African American. By most accounts, he took advantage of this ambiguity, allowing himself to "enter" and interrogate various minority cultures as an insider, a privilege unavailable to the white poets with whom he associated. In the introduction to Jonas's *Selected Poems,* editor Joseph Torra discusses this complexity.

> Jonas often passed as Hispanic or Portuguese and didn't feel comfortable when someone referred to him as black. But in some ways, he liked his "blackness" and the fact that he could travel in circles not immediately open to whites. His associations

> and friendships were nearly always with whites, but in black and white worlds, he was an outsider—a rootless, social renegade, which at times created in him an insecurity and self-doubt that he struggled with throughout his life. It seems unlikely that he ever came to terms with his racial identity. (2)

There are several other factors besides Jonas's desire for racial ambiguity that may have contributed toward his outsider status. He was openly gay in a period when gay pride was in its infancy. Several of the poets in Jonas's orbit were gay as well; however, the issue of homosexuality is seldom used as poetic material. Often falling in love with straight white men, addicts, or runaways, his advances were seldom reciprocated, leaving him without a much-desired long-term relationship. His sexuality obviously ostracized him from participating fully in both the conservative African American and white communities of Boston.

Although Jonas occasionally used pharmaceutical drugs to push his creative drive, he was not an addict. However, his Anderson Avenue apartment became a favored hangout for his addict friends, who would use it as a place to stash stolen merchandise used to buy drugs. In addition, prostitutes, runaways, and various "street people" found Jonas's home to be a welcome haven. He was an unselfish host, leaving the window of his apartment open for late night visitors to crash in on his floor and feast on surplus food he found while foraging through restaurant dumpsters. On various occasions he would have "magical evenings" in his apartment, in which people would gather to talk about issues ranging from politics to alchemy. The evening colloquia in Jonas's apartment certainly served as a place that challenged the often-stifling "traditional" academic atmosphere of Boston area universities and made learning a more collaborative, explorative, and intimate journey.

In the late fifties, Jonas became involved in a book and record club scam in which he joined clubs and ordered merchandise using fake names. Once the records and books arrived in his apartment, they were read, listened to, and later sold by his friends for drug money. In 1958 he was sentenced to six months at the federal penitentiary in Danbury, Connecticut, for mail fraud, reportedly telling the judge that in a country of grand larceny, petty larceny was no crime. Upon his release, he returned to Boston to continue his writing.

Jonas experienced a series of mental breakdowns that often left him incapacitated and unable to function. It was perhaps these bouts of mental illness and incarceration that would enable Jonas to further identify with the controversial American poet Ezra Pound. Jonas's collection, *Orgasms/Dominations,* uses several of the methods Pound used in constructing *The Cantos.* In the collection are references to American politics, tarot cards, the vernacular, historical figures, and other bursts from Jonas's encyclopedic mind and his extensive collection of books and music, most of which were stolen from the Boston Public Library. Unfortunately, Jonas adopted Pound's anti-Semitic rhetoric, believing that the assassinations of his heroes Abraham Lincoln and John F. Kennedy were the result of a foreign-influenced usury that was Jewish in origin.

However, the poet Jonas felt most attuned to was Charles Olson. Charles Olson, Melville scholar and author of the epic *The Maximus Poems,* was an influential poet among Boston's avant-garde who were opposed to the elitism of the Ivy League–trained poets who felt affinity with the poetry of T. S. Eliot and W. H. Auden. Living in the nearby seaport town of Gloucester, Massachusetts, Olson was in close proximity to the poets on "the other side of Beacon Hill from Robert Lowell," who admired his ability to work with varying materials that transcended the traditional boundaries of poetry. In his seminal essay, "Projective Verse," which first appeared in 1951, Olson wrote that "a poem is energy transferred" and that it is "a high energy-construct and, at all points, an energy-discharge" (16). This idea certainly appealed to poets who viewed jazz as the foundation of their aesthetic. Further, he advocated that the poet's use of breath be the means of determining the poem's use of measure and line breaks. The use of voice to determine line breaks became an important practice for several "New American Poets." It became a crucial statement that freed up the restraints that Jonas and others observed in the confessional work of poets like John Berryman, Robert Lowell, Sylvia Plath, Anne Sexton, and those influenced by the New Criticism of Allen Tate and John Crowe Ransom. Jonas would take Olson's ideas a step further by using meter to reflect not only breath but also the rhythmic and tonal qualities of jazz music.

In his introduction to the 1968 Ferry Press edition of Jonas's *Exercises for Ear,* Gerrit Lansing wrote, "The School of Boston, in poetry, middle this century, is an occult school, unknown" (ii). A 1956 poster elaborates the "School of Boston's" debt to jazz. The poster reads "EZRA POUND EATS WORMS . . . You are invited TO A POETRY READING where five Boston cats are blowing their poetry REAL HARD: J. Dunn, J. Spicer, J. Wieners, R. Blaser and S. Jonas . . .

Nothing has been so good since Bird died." It is obvious that this reading espoused a poetry that was firmly connected to the music by its prevalent use of the jazz musician's vocabulary.

In the company of poets John Wieners, Joe Dunn, Robin Blaser, and Jack Spicer, Jonas found a comfortable environment where his work could be heard and his explorations taken seriously. These five poets all lived within blocks of each other and met several times a week to share the fellowship of their work. In an interview with Joseph Torra, Robin Blaser discussed Jonas's relationship to the poet Jack Spicer, noting that the two poets were writing in "one night stands" and that Jonas often crafted large thirty-page poems in one weekend. Jonas's prodigious work made use of not only the vernacular and jazz music but also polemically complex treatises. His adept use in blending several sources caused Spicer to question his own writing and eventually led Spicer to write his breakthrough jazz-influenced poem, "Song for Bird and Myself" (Torra, "The School of Boston 1950" 7). It was through correspondence and late night conversations that Jonas introduced and taught Spice the intricate dynamics of the music. Thus, practically everything Spicer knew concerning jazz came through Jonas.

Jonas found in Spicer a brother and kindred spirit not only because of their homosexuality but also because of their cultural interests.[1] The two also shared skepticism concerning much of the New Criticism poetry that was being widely published at the time. It is interesting to note that for someone who had such a profound influence on Spicer and the other Boston poets, Jonas is not included in Donald Allen's significant anthologies, *The New American Poetry, 1945–1960,* and *The Poetics of the New American Poetry* (1973), in which the work of both Jack Spicer and Robin Blaser prominently appear. These two books have since become canonical documents of 1960s "alternative poetries."[2]

The Ferry Press first published Jonas's masterwork, *Exercises for Ear,* the title possibly alluding to Lester Young's tune "Exercise in Swing," in 1968 in England. The collection consists of 174 Roman-numbered untitled poems of varying lengths linked by subject and/or rhythm patterns. The complete title, *Exercises for Ear: Being a Primer for the Beginner in the American Idiom,* points to a practice among jazz musicians of hearing by ear—that is, not reading the musical notes from the printed score but concentrating on the sound, the tone, the timber, and the musical attack of their instrument. A musician who plays by ear has mastered the art of tonal memory. After hearing a tune repeatedly, one is able to play it back line for line, nuances and all. Yet Jonas's book is a score, a "school text," in which one learns to negotiate their way through the tonal values of individual words and move toward hearing the sound and rhythmic qualities of the various "exercises" as single or unified musical compositions. To read Jonas is to become more attuned to the importance of sound as a means of imparting musicality into the text.

Despite the profound influence jazz music played in the work of Steven Jonas, it should be mentioned that his musical tastes were fairly eclectic. In a letter to his friend Raffael De Grutolla, Jonas wrote a list of the music he would listen to on a typical day. The list included recordings by European classical composers like Bach, Vivaldi, Rameau, Scarlatti, Corelli, Mozart, and Pergolesi, as well as jazz fare from Carmen McRae, Frank Sinatra, and the Modern Jazz Quartet.[3] This is a trait Jonas shares with most jazz musicians known to have a wide range of listening interests.

In his preface to Jonas's *Selected Poems*, Gerrit Lansing points to the book's connection with musical apprenticeship.

> First it is to say these Exercises are that, real ubungen not romantic etudes designed to tickle a faceless concert hall crowd. They are practice on the poet's keyboard, or for study by those who aim to listen like poets top the twang of the specific. It is no accident that they are all short, pithy as the best of the Anthology, because each focuses one particular sonic or rhetorical means (ear is brain, Jonas never lets us forget). (19)

This is the "practice" on the poet's keyboard, the sounding out and percussive drive on the blank page. Jonas often referred to his poems as songs or "poem-chunes," confirmation that he placed his work within a musical framework.

Sound was also an important element in the manner in which Jonas spelled. In a letter to Cid Corman, he wrote:

> "the correct way" just don't make it. When I write, I write listening to the sound of the word and I come as close to the spelling of it as spelling will permit me. Usually that is not close enuf. What I'm trying here to get over to you Cid is that I am a Poet (I hope so) drunk with a music of langwidge. (Jonas, "Stephen Jonas" 1)

Where language is wedge, Jonas plies the vast and open sea of music, a "langwitch" where the text is a bubbling cauldron. Thus "language" becomes "langwidge," not only more accurately capturing the sound of the word, but also implying the "wedge" that occurs between the spoken and the written. This impulse is found in writers like Ezra Pound, Melvin Tolson, Gertrude Stein, Bob Kaufman, and several others in which emphasis is placed on the linkage between spelling and sound, indicating that a poem must be seen as well as heard. This aesthetic vision certainly has its predecessors in the African American oral tradition where this practice was used in secular and religious songs, as well as speeches. It also has its roots in the African practice of word-spirit, the *veve* in Haitian voudoun, where the drawn word becomes the spoken and signifier—that is, the word made flesh. Thus, in Jonas's poetics, language solely constructed in terms of meaning can become an impediment to sound. Jonas felt that poets had become too philosophical and were stepping further away from the original musical and tonal impulses in poetry. It was his belief that sound took precedence over the meaning of words in context because for Jonas meaning appears and occurs in the manner in which the text is orchestrated.

Timing is an important element in music, particularly jazz. How and where an instrumentalist chooses to place a note is crucial and so significant that it has the power to change the direction of the piece. The same importance given to tempo can be seen in the visual appearance of Jonas's work. Significantly, *Exercises for Ear* is also a visual text where the shape of the work on the page propels its energy and movement. He ignores the straight linear verse, the Tin Pan Alley poetry made so popular by legions of other poets and instead chooses to construct poems that reflect the complex cadences of everyday speech. All of the poems included in *Exercises,* whether or not they "use jazz" as a subject matter, are composed with a jazz-based aesthetic. Aldon Lynn Nielsen writes that Jonas's poetry uses "typography to apportion aural and visual space in much the same way that Miles Davis used silence to shape and underscore the causeways of his music" (35). It is the practice of improvising on a phrase, changing directions, sewing the fragments then unraveling the stitches. This method employs a variety of sources that have particular resonance in African American culture. Jonas often combined allusions to African American musical forms like gospel, jazz, and R & B to set the cadence of his texts and often composed while listening to recordings by artists like Billie Holiday, Lester Young, Charlie Parker, Miles Davis, John Coltrane, and Ornette Coleman.

In a letter to Amiri Baraka, Jonas provided his fullest statement regarding the use of music in his work.

> Music rots when it gets too far from dance. poetry
> atrophies when it gets too far from the music.
>
> . . .
>
> More to home, the gospel music cum handicapping and
> spontaneous footwork is remembered in the music of the
> MJQ [Modern Jazz Quartet].
> Jazz is to be listened to by an American Poet.
> Interesting to note how they refresh the medium—
> returning to "roots" of foot, hand and body movement.
>
> . . .
>
> Melody is the most artificial thing in music. Song
> (lyric) is the most artificial equivocal language (Poetry).
>
> . . .
>
> American speech is mostly articulation—most of the
> Prose we read is so much dialogue.
>
> . . .
>
> Music can still be made in poetry without doing
> violence to the natural habits of speech. (Nielsen, "Saint in Three Acts" 14)

Jonas's manifesto echoes Charles Olson's essay "Projective Verse," with its emphasis on the physical body and breath as being vital elements in the making of poems. Olson wrote that a poet must "go down through the workings of his throat to that place where breath comes from" (26). Jonas's remark about the "natural habits of speech" intersects with Olson's poetics. Both poets express a desire to eliminate any contrived or artificial delivery of poetry. Olson's emphasis on "natural breath" comes from his desire to return poetry to its ancient Greek origins, while Jonas's desire to return poetry to its musical and physical roots comes from an African American musical tradition where the physicality of the performer/dancer is as significant as the music. Additionally, Jonas's emphasis on the importance of the "natural habits of speech" mirrors William Carlos Williams's insistence on using everyday language as the brick of poetry. Williams was an inspirational figure, especially for

Jonas and other poets of his generation, because he rebelled against the heavy influence of the more formal European-influenced metric line and sought to show the variables present in American speech patterns.

Although in music the melody is often a necessary component, it is what occurs outside of it that is particularly vital in jazz. The practice of "playing off of the melody" happens when the musician mentally hears the tune and uses it as a reference point to improvise around it. Simply put, it is Jonas's unique use of spelling and punctuation that offsets the more formal perimeters of grammar and language.

Jonas's statement also mirrors the scholar Stephen Henderson's criteria, discussed earlier, for defining a "black poem," particularly "using the poem as a score or chart" (47). Although Jonas's political views can be connected to the political ideas of Ezra Pound, rather than Black Nationalism, he did make use of several of the movement's aesthetic arguments. For example, Jonas's insistence that the poem be viewed as a musical entity and that it use language from the "jazz life" demonstrates the connection he shared with black arts poets like Amiri Baraka, Sonia Sanchez, and Etheridge Knight.

Jonas's attention toward jazz innovators actively engaged in redefining musical standards certainly fed into the manner in which he wrote poetry. His poem about Lester "Pres" Young articulates the crucial positioning jazz had in his work.

CXVIII

& there was "Pres"
  horn horizontal aslant
    blowing nothin' but
    free verse
& all them jitterbugs
  outta' their skulls
        on B's flyin'
from the second balcony
the while cool hippies looked on
    in *gran dispetto* (Jonas, *Selected* 76)

This poem celebrates not only the musical mastery of Lester Young during a performance with Count Bassie's band, but the physicality of his performance as well. Musically, Young's tone is sensual, delicate, and precise, and he was admired not only for the manner in which he played his horn but also for the way he held it, slantwise, on the bandstand. For many, Lester Young, with his porkpie hat, soft-spoken speech, and elegant slant, became the signature that was admired and copied by many "cool" aficionados.

Young's break with traditional jazz playing established by tenor saxophonist Coleman Hawkins became the impetus for Jonas's poem. The opening line alludes to the biblical chapter Genesis, "And there was light." Thus, Jonas emphasizes the spirituality, as did Kaufman, of Lester Young's playing. Similar to his use of the phrase "poem-chunes," Jonas connects poetry and music in the line, "Blowing nothin' / but free verse," combining the two separate identities of poet and musician. Jazz becomes an organic and implicit connection in the creation of poetry. Perhaps what Jonas takes from Lester Young is his attention to the subtle qualities of tone. In this poem, the placement of a word/tone establishes meaning, cadence, and mood. The lines "horn horizontal aslant / blowing nothin' but" make use of assonance to reflect the tone of Young's performance. It is in this fashion that Jonas guides/orchestrates the reader to regard the importance of ear/hearing as an integral aspect of form. In the Jonas pantheon, the musician was the high priest of art, speaking through a medium that appealed directly to both soul and mind.

In the next poem, Jonas addresses the work of another, perhaps more controversial, artist.

XXXVI

it's to dave brubeck
i initially
          owe
three short bars
      sans musical no-
                        nation
that the horn player,
shinin' thru,
              deciphers (36)

Jonas's choice of Dave Brubeck as a figure in this poem offers insight. Brubeck is a white musician who achieved notoriety with his quartet during the 1950s. He was classically trained and often played musical quotations from Chopin and Wagner during his performances. This practice perhaps had more in common with European Romanticism than the improvisational techniques of African American–rooted jazz. Even though Brubeck swept *Downbeat* and *Metronome* magazines in 1956 in a readers' poll of top jazz musicians, he was constantly overlooked by influential jazz critics like Leonard Feather, who failed to include him in his list of the top forty musicians of that same year. Most African American jazz musicians familiar with the racial myopia that often judges the worth of American artists found his mass-market appeal fairly predictable. Brubeck and saxophonist Paul Desmond's "West Coast Jazz" were thought to be basically "safe," doing little to challenge the ears of an astute listener.

Jonas's poem is in three stanzas, or "three short bars." In the text, the poem acknowledges that its musical configuration comes from Brubeck. However, the following line, "sans musical no- / nation," is the key to understanding what Jonas gets from Brubeck. Jonas uses the French preposition *sans* (without) to perhaps allude to Brubeck's classical musical training under the French composer Darius Milhaud, as well as to indicate how jazz appropriates from a variety of musical traditions. Since the word "musical" is sandwiched between the French "sans" and the English "no," emphasizing the negation of music, Jonas could be saying that there is no musicality in Brubeck's playing. But the hyphen used after "no" carries over to the next line. Here Jonas's innovative line breaks demonstrate how poetry can exhibit the note-bending qualities of jazz. Thus, "notation" becomes the implied reading rather than the actual "no- / nation" in the text. In doing so, Jonas points toward a political understanding of the creation of art, implying that a national identity is predicated upon how art (music, poetry, etc.) is used. The final section (bar) indicates that a written text, or any other artistic form, can only be "deciphered" by using the technique of improvisation ("slippin' thru"). Thus, improvisation can become a political as well as a musical tool. Jonas's continual forays into U.S. history, particularly his reading of Jeffersonian Democracy and economic theory, indicate that he viewed himself in a similar fashion: a poet/musician capable of deciphering the complexity of a sociopolitical culture.

In "XCIV," Jonas pays homage to saxophonist Stan Getz.

ah would that
        life were the long-
  est side Getz
        ever cut & Death
an ex-
        tended play (65)

A former member of Woody Herman's Thundering Herd and an admirer of Lester Young, Stan Getz was a pioneer in what became known in the 1950s as West Coast Cool, a "laid back" version of jazz pioneered by Miles Davis but mainly played by white musicians. Critics accused it of lacking the intensive, gritty, and percussive drive of bebop. Getz had a distinctively soft and mellow sound. By beginning the poem with the exclamatory breath "ah," Jonas replicates what he hears in Getz's playing. Additionally, the poem's spatial disposition seeks to mirror Getz's playing. For the most part, Getz's, like Young's, improvisational vocabulary was so subtle that often what was left out, the silent pauses, were an equally significant part of the music. The spacing of the poem and the extension of words like "longest" and "extended" result in a poem that expresses one of the most enduring qualities of the music, the subtlety of silence—that is, Kaufman's "silent beat."

Poet/critic Aldon Lynn Nielsen makes a comparison between Jonas and Charlie Parker, saying that his "sonic and visual experiments test the limits of speech and writing as surely as Parker tested the limits of harmony and rhythm" ("No Saints in Three Acts" 32). Bird not only transformed the direction of jazz; he was an influential figure for many writers, particularly poets who viewed his heroic improvisations as a model to uproot standard forms. When writing about the aesthetic influences on students at Black Mountain College, Olson commented in *Muthulogos* that "there was no poetic. It was Charlie Parker. Literally, it was Charlie Parker. He was the Bob Dylan of the fifties." "CXVII" recalls a Charlie Parker performance in Boston and demonstrates how Jonas handles the almost sacred musician.

once i saw bird so high
    that he came wingin'
over from the apple
w/ a busted foot & a gig
    to make at roll-a-way

he came in on the chorus
    from a wheelchair &
    just made the bridge
on one wheel
                oh, man the hippies
at mass. & columbus
                were moderately
shook! (76)

The poem begins with Jonas's unique ability to use words with double meaning. He uses "high" to indicate height/flight or intoxication. "Wingin" works in a similar way. The word is typically associated with birds and flight, but Jonas could also be referring to its meaning in the African American vernacular: to improvise, to pretend to understand —that is, to "wing it." By employing words with double meanings, Jonas is able to put one over on the reader in a similar fashion to Bird. What becomes interesting in the poem is Bird's ability to rise to the occasion and survive what could have been a disastrous performance. The final phrase, describing the audience's response, is also ambiguous. Were the hippies "moderately shook" because of Parker's inability to play fully, or were they "shook" because of his ability to find an opening in the music even though he was "high"?

Jonas's highly tuned ear was not only engaged with sounds emanating from the phonograph and jazz club, it was also pointed toward the cadence of the street. In "XVI" he emphasizes the importance of sound as a causeway toward creation.

how
muthafucker
            am i
'spose to hear
    a fuckin'
            muse
if you keep
            on
        talkin'/ (27)

Jonas calls attention to tone in the poem by placing the word "how" on a single line. The word as tone takes on additional significance because of its resonance, echoed in the words "muthafucker," "'spose," "fuckin'," "on," "talkin'." Jonas also uses the apostrophe to tighten the tonal connections. The "n" consonant sound in "fuckin'" and "talkin'" has a longer, deeper resonance than an "ing" ending. In order to hear these tones, it is crucial that Jonas's poetry be read aloud. Thus, Jonas's emphasis on the importance of hearing is further established. It is also interesting to note that the speaker of the poem, who is engaged in the process of creation, chooses to emphasize hearing as well. It is only through the ear that the muse can first be encountered. There is an irony that, although the speaker desires the other person present to keep silent, the real creation of music, and subsequently poetry, comes in his reprimand. By stressing silence in an art form that celebrates sound, Jonas implies that we need to reassess our way of hearing music to include the spaces between audible sounds.

Jonas's use of the black vernacular as demonstrated in the above poem and his other rhythmically constructed texts that derived influence from the African American community are similar to the work of the black aesthetics/black arts movements of the 1960s. Poet Haki Madhubuti (Don L. Lee), one of the major theorists during this period, wrote about the importance of using the "word and sounds of the street" as opposed to words found in Western-influenced dictionaries. In *Dynamite Voices: Black Poets of the 1960s,* Lee provides a gloss on the word "muthafucka" to illustrate the disparity between the languages of black and white America. Noting that "muthafucka" is not "synonymous with the western 'motherfucker,'" he provides four examples of its usage in black speech:

(1) "I fired on the muthafucka!"
(2) "Ain't the muthafucka layen there?"
(3) "You jive muthafucka!"
(4) "You stupid muthafucka!" (34)

Lee demonstrates that in the above cases of its usage, the word is descriptive and can be used in a variety of contexts. By providing and critiquing a word that some critics would consider inappropriate, Lee, like Jonas, makes use of the ability to transform/rewrite notions of criticism by using the vernacular to demonstrate the differences in textual assumptions. Appropriating the vernacular allowed for the "freeing up" of language restraints for several writers and performers. The manner in which Lee and Jonas choose to spell "muthafucka" makes it apparent that the way the word "sounded" among African Americans was a prime concern. The role that "sound" plays in the composition of jazz poetry is certainly significant because its use implies the desire to release the text from the constraints of the page and return poetry to its musical origins.[4]

"LXI" brilliantly demonstrates Jonas's sensitivity to the musical tones found in the African American vernacular.

> like my jazz
>   low-down
> & my blues mutha-
>   huckin'
>   dir-
>   ty
> now don't chu' go
>   'N blow no whistle
>   on me 'cause
> i'll tell the man
>   all ya biz'ness
> this i got from
>   miz mess
> hoodsie-cap's
>   in her horn
> where she-it she keeps
>   her stash (50)

Structurally, the poem takes the form of a twelve-bar blues, with "like my jazz / low-down / & my blues mutha- / huckin' / dir- /ty" and "now don't chu' go / 'N blow no whistle / on me 'cause" keeping the traditional blues cadence. Reading the poem aloud, one notices that Jonas adheres so closely to the blues form that the lyrics could successfully be put to music. His use of hyphens, apostrophes, and creative spelling maintain the text's rhythmic integrity. The language of the poem comes directly from the vernacular. His use of "she-it" acts as a rhythmical extension of "shit," thus further emphasizing the musicality of the text. Additionally, "she-it" (shit) is not only a word that can indicate surprise or anger; it is also a word that was popularly used in the 1940s and 1950s to describe low-grade heroin. The use of the word "stash" (a place where drugs are hidden) and "the man" (the police) illustrate how well Jonas captures and records "low down jazz," the music of the streets.

Jonas's engagement with the vernacular may have been fueled by his interest in the nineteenth-century poet Paul Lawrence Dunbar. Although Dunbar wrote poems that used "formal" language, his most popular were his "dialect" poems, which reflected his view of black life in the antebellum South.[5] Poems like "In the Morning" and "When Malindy Sings" were memorized and recited by black children in elementary school or church talent shows. In a 1965 letter to poet and friend Gerrit Lansing, Jonas wrote:

> I also got a copy of Paul Lawrence Dunbars (Negro dialect verse & song from back at the turn of the century) I have a first edition—have there been others? I recall William C. Williams Autobiography, mentioning him as one of his early childhood memories of his, I think, his father, reading Dunbar to him. His music (tho' like most of the Blues, is iambic pentameter. But it has its moments and the rhythms are eyeopeners to vistas,—new). (Jonas, "Stephen Jonas" 6)

Jonas's comment is significant because it indicates his awareness of an African American predecessor who made use of the vernacular as a means of establishing a distinctly African American cadence in the work. Certainly Jonas noticed how Dunbar used the rhythmic qualities of the black vernacular in a poem like "A Negro Love Song."

> Seen my lady home las' night,
>   Jump back, honey, jump back.
> Hel' huh han' an' sque'z it tight,
>   Jump back, honey, jump back.
> Hyeahd huh sigh a little sigh,
> Seen a light gleam from huh eye,
> An' a smile go flittin' by—
>   Jump back, honey, jump back . . . (Hill and Bell 608)

Dunbar's poem makes use of the percussive qualities of the black vernacular that appear in Jonas's work as well. This is particularly evident in the repetition of line "Jump back" and in his consistent use of assonance found in the phrases "Hel' huh han'" and "Hyeahd huh sigh."

In "LXV," Jonas merges song lyrics and common speech, applying a similar tactic used in jazz composition.

> . . . blues aint nuthin
>   but which gender you
> makin' it w'th
>   split
>
> & you want
>   *some*-body to
> please come hear
>   & gimme sum'um
>
> this mornin'
>   -don't call no
> doktor 'cause he
>   cant do'me no good
>
>   lord-lord
>   lord
> jus'
>   gimme sum'um
>   'cause i doan' kere (52)

In the opening line, Jonas establishes linkage to a well-known trope often used in African American music. "Blues aint nuthin' but a pain in my heart," sang Billie Holiday. "Blues aint nuthin but heartache" is a refrain to a song made popular by Bessie Smith. Jonas's awareness of diverse mystical/spiritual traditions contributes to his ability to manipulate and expand the meaning of form and language. By using ellipses and the reader's familiarity with the poem's opening line, Jonas places the reader in the middle of a song that has already started. Thus, he signifies and continues a dialogue that responds to his blues predecessors. The opening line manages to evoke the pathos often found in the blues lyric.

Jonas implies that the manner in which the blues is used is based upon gender. This is particularly interesting when one considers Jonas's homosexuality. It appears that the poem evokes a bisexual lifestyle, one that is based on desire and physical availability. The second stanza emphasizes this: "& you want / *some*-body." The use of italics underlines the importance of the physical body as a means to satisfy sexual appetite. For the speaker, sex is an addictive drug. The third stanza confirms this connection. It is the function of doctors ("doktor") to heal the sick and to prescribe drugs that relieve suffering, but the speaker knows that relief is only temporary.

In the form of the poem, Jonas uses line breaks to reflect the poet's breath. Additionally, when the poem is read aloud, one becomes aware that the poem can be sung. Jonas accomplishes this by incorporating bits and pieces of blues lyrics like "blues aint nuthin'," "gimme sum'um / this *mornin'*," "don't call no / doktor 'cause he / cant do'me no good," and "lord-lord / lord," whose cadences are well established in popular culture and familiar to most listeners. The use of these fragmented lyrics further demonstrates that Jonas not only had an ear for music, but also knew how to manipulate it to serve his poetic needs.

In "XXVI," Jonas uses African American dance as a metaphor for writing poetry while at the same time cleverly alluding to Western concepts of poetic measurement—that is, feet. What becomes paramount via this double entendre is the crucial role African American culture plays in establishing a poetics grounded in the "American idiom." The reader of Jonas's collection should remain cognizant that, like a school primer, the work is meant to function on an instructional level as well.

when the old
measure's gone

      & the new
stresses feet

tho' the heart
   stagger & the head

be still
      let the feet go

          black & bare
          let 'em go

                black & bare
                let 'em go

                        & etc. (32)

The poem may allude to William Carlos Williams's "variable foot," in which he advocated the importance of listening to the variations of meter found in American speech and disrupting the formal constraint found in conventional poetry. Jonas also demonstrates varied cadence by line displacement. Although the poem is not given a linear treatment in order to indicate a disjunctive meter, the repetition of "black & bare" creates a pattern of regularity or continuity that the poet finds in African American dance. Additionally, the repetition of "go" establishes an almost predictable cadence that propels the poem's movement forward.

In "XXXV" Jonas demonstrates how music can be subversive.

> a musick
> a spreck
>   a formal rack-
>   et in time
> a yak-yak
>   a means
>   of talkin' back (36)

Here Jonas highlights the pronunciation of words like music ("musick") to underscore the significance of sound in the construction of a poem. The act of "misspelling" is subversive enough when one considers the pervasive conformist elements of 1950s and 1960s American academic poetry. However, Jonas's tonal spelling becomes a pun as well, and perhaps a comment on popular music. No doubt, Jonas was aware of the popular song "Yakety Yak," by The Coasters, with its repeated refrain, "don't talk back," or perhaps, "don't talk *black*."

> Take out the papers and the trash
> Or you don't get no spendin' cash
> Tell your hoodlum friend outdoors
> You ain't goin' to rock & roll no more
> Yakety Yak
> Don't talk back

By the 1960s, rock and roll had become America's popular music. Jonas was aware that the music's roots were African American and that its increase in popularity subsequently meant more influence by the large record companies that ultimately sought to make a profit and maintain the status quo. In his poem, the line "a formal rack- / et in time" alludes to the racketeering practices of the industry as well as to a loud and indecipherable sound. Music is measured by time signatures (tempo). If a musician is playing "in time" to the music, it means that a consistent rhythmical pattern has been established with little or no deviation. Often the measured or "formal" constraints of most music yields little opening for the improvisatory gestures of the jazz soloist. In Jonas's aesthetic, music and poetry function as vehicles of argument—that is, "talkin' back." Jonas's change in the lyrics from "Yakety Yak" to the more percussive "Yak Yak" is a way of responding to the staid influences of musical commercialism.

There are several "chunes" in *Exercises for Ear* that further affirms the connection between jazz and poetry. "CLV" is one of the more interesting poems that demonstrates how Jonas is able to combine the aesthetic issues of both art forms.

when the man
        blows his saxophone
we listen
          as to a poet
speaking of his a-
                bandon'd or
          slower, in a lower
octave, speaks of the
                everlasting
                      enigma (92)

Although the poem does not directly name a particular jazz musician, Jonas uses the article "the" to imply specificity. This creates an assumption that the reader of the poem is privy to recognizing the musician alluded to. The inclusion of the pronoun "we" further indicates that the performance is a shared experience. The lack of punctuation throughout the poem creates a fluid situation where lines become interconnected. It is particularly key that "we listen" can refer to both the saxophone player and the poet, making a shared connection between the two art forms. In the next few lines, "speaking of his a- / bandon'd or/slower," Jonas uses our expectations of what the line should read ("speaking of his abandoned lover") in order to demonstrate the importance of sound as it applies to music poetry. By manipulating our expectations, he "bends the note," a standard musical practice in jazz, particularly in the ballad performances of Lester Young, to which the collection's title alludes. The use of the musical term "octave" is interesting because its juxtaposition to "speaks" reaffirms the connection between jazz and poetry. Not only does the poet speak via the medium of the poem; the musician speaks through music. This connection further reinstates Jonas's view that the original impulse behind poetry must be musical. The "closing" lines of the poem, particularly the word "enigma," is quite interesting in terms of its connection to the earlier imagery in the poem. "Enigma" comes from the Greek *ainissomai,* meaning to speak allusively. Jonas, although self-educated, had a good ear for the etymologies of English words. Therefore, his use of "enigma" manages to simultaneously refer to the often-elusive qualities of music and poetry.

The brilliance of Stephen Jonas and the jazz-inspired poems in *Exercises for Ear* demonstrates the work of a poet who found meaning by returning poetry to its musical roots. Since sound is such an important element in Jonas's work, the poems appear more closely akin to musical scores than to traditional conceptions of poetry. His attention to and use of the materials of African American culture extend the early jazz innovations of poets like Langston Hughes and Sterling Brown. However, what comes across most strongly in Jonas's work is his desire to portray things as he heard and saw them, not to sculpt an art that is unblemished and beautiful, but to "blow real hard" and give us the grittiness of life.

CHAPTER 5

Hot House: Jayne Cortez and the Music of Illumination

> *I cut my hair into a permanent tan*
> *made my feet rebellious metronomes*
> *Embedded record needles in paint on paper*
> *Talked bopology talk*
>
> —*Jayne Cortez*

Jayne Cortez is one of the most astute performers and creators of jazz poetry. Her engagement with the music is unmistakable, and she reads/sounds her work with a musician's sensibility. Barry Wallenstein has written that Cortez's voice is "the perfect instrument for jazz: flexible, warm, hard-edged and swinging" (614). Her poetry displays a sophisticated, sometimes surreal, vocabulary that skillfully conveys the varied nuances of poetic and musical forms. Quincy Troupe describes Cortez's poetry as carrying "us beyond ourselves and into her personal world filled with all kinds of fascinating images that seem to spring out of nowhere" (91). Her adept skill at calling forth an unusually visceral vocabulary makes her a significant improviser. In the 1960s, music and cultural critic Stanley Crouch described her as "the real thing."

> She is from the streets and free of their platform-shoed slavery; she is a country girl sophisticated by the ravages of urban complexes; she does know black music and had a crush on Duke Ellington in the sixties when the myopic nationalist front was too busy sneering at his glittering and radiant process. (99)

By combining various aspects of African diasporic culture, Cortez has remained a poet of extraordinary depth and musicality. The infusion of diverse musical and spiritual traditions has led to a body of work that demonstrates how a jazz aesthetic can successfully be applied to the craft of poetry. Critics like Jon Woodson have tended to classify her work as "surrealist" because they often perceive the exoticism of her language as being unconnected to real-life situations. This is perhaps a misreading of surrealism, which is principally engaged in expanding and heightening perceptions of realism. Although her work has appeared in surrealist journals like *Arsenal* and Penelope Rosemont's historically significant anthology, *Surrealist Women,* Cortez has chosen to refer to her work as "superealism," which the critic D. H. Melhem defines as "the intense vision of reality" that moves "beyond the intellectual and unconscious aspects of Surrealism . . . into a divine and infernal realism" (181). The manner in which Cortez uses language may appear exotic to readers grounded in the tradition of European surrealism, but she has more in common with Caribbean poets like Aimé Césaire and Léon Dumas than their European counterparts. What Cortez shares with Césaire and Dumas is a poetics that originates from a distinctly African and African American realism in which the power and creation of nature plays an integral part in everyday existence. It is Cortez's excellent ear for music from the black tradition (blues, jazz) and her impeccable sense of timing that propels the linguistic energy of her work and blurs the distinction between musician and poet.

Jayne Cortez was born on May 10, 1936, in Arizona on the Fort Hauachuca army base, where her father was stationed. She attended a segregated school of mostly black and Native American children until she was seven, when the family moved to San Diego and later to West Los Angeles. In a 1982 interview with D. H. Melhem, Cortez talks about her fondness for Arizona.

> I remember I hated to leave Arizona, because I had a cat and there were these insects, the ants and the bees. I used to get bees in the summertime—catch them in the middle of a flower, hold the petals together so they couldn't get out, and they would buzz, buzz, buzz! Anyhow, I used to play games with all of the little insects. And of course there was my favorite tree. (Melhem, *Heroism* 197)

Cortez's apparent intimacy with nature has been a recurrent descriptive element in her poetry. Even when she is writing about urban landscapes, as in her poem, "I am New York City," her gaze is that of an urban naturalist, meticulously taking inventory of her surroundings, "i am new york city / here is my brain of hot sauce / my tobacco teeth my / mattress of bedbug tongue."

The aesthetic elements of performance, orality, music, and language that Cortez would later use in her poetry to great effect came to her as a child while playing African American word games like the dozens.

> We played the Dozens, signified, told jokes, and performed for each other. . . . We did it constantly. It was an everyday ritual. Oral poetry in an oral atmosphere. When I used to go to jam sessions and other musical events, I would sometimes write down my reactions to the music and the scene. (Melhem, *Heroism* 200)

Playing the dozens has made a significant impact on the aesthetic development of several African American writers. Writers such as James Baldwin, Sonia Sanchez, and Amiri Baraka have all remarked that this game allowed them to develop an attention toward some of the most inventive and innovative qualities of rhythm and language. The game, which is often played by boys, consists of two players and is verbally elaborate. The two participants must insult each other's relatives as a test of their emotional strength while a group of friends cheer each stinging retort. The first person to become angry loses. It is apparent, by the very nature of the verbal joust, that the players need to be able to improvise on the spot or be subject to the ridicule of the crowd. In his introduction to *Yo' Mama's Disfunktional,* a critique of urban America, Robin D. G. Kelley provides an accurate description of the game.

> I grew up in a world in which talking about somebody's mama was a way of life, an everyday occurrence. For all of us, boys and girls, it was a kind of game or performance. Whether we called it "capping," "snapping," "ranking," "busting," or simply "the dozens," most of it was ridiculous, surreal humor bearing very little resemblance to reality: "Your mom's so fat she broke the food chain"; "Your mama's skin's so ashy she was a stand-in for Casper the Friendly Ghost"; "Your mama's so dumb she thought ring-around-the-collar was a children's game." More than anything, it was an effort to master the absurd metaphor, an art form intended to entertain rather than damage. (1)

The orality that the game inspires certainly helped Cortez develop her skills of improvisation. There is a correlation between the skills that African American games (such as signifying, the dozens, and skipping rope) provide and the improvisatory gestures of jazz music. Jazz musicians often take fairly common songs and restructure the melody and harmony, creating an entirely different mood and rhythmic structure. For example, John Coltrane's version of the old English folksong "Greensleeves" demonstrates how a musician can take an established piece, rework it, and signify on it so as to relieve the complacency of the original. This technique infuses not only more energy and rhythmic complexity into the piece, but cultural complexity as well.

Music played an important role in Cortez's early development as an artist. She studied piano and bass, played cello, and took courses in music theory and harmony while attending the Manual Arts High School in Los Angeles, California. Her family had an extensive collection of recordings, and she was exposed to the music of Duke Ellington, Count Basie, Jimmy Lunceford, Billie Holiday, Ella Fitzgerald, and to the bebop rhythms of Charlie Parker and Thelonious Monk (Melhem, *Heroism* 198). Access to these recordings enabled Cortez to develop a strategy of writing poems that made significant use of jazz. Thus, she served an apprenticeship not unlike the self-taught jazz musician who repeatedly listens to albums in order to capture the technique and nuance of the performer. Subsequently, her early musical training and her renowned public performances and recordings would show an affinity to the music. In her delivery, one can hear the phrasing of Billie Holiday, the staccato plunk of Thelonious Monk, the sophisticated orchestral colors of Duke Ellington, or the hard-driving swing of Count Basie.

Cortez expressed early interest in other art forms as well. She took courses in drawing, painting, and design. Courses in drama, and her position as artistic director of the Watts Repertory Theatre Company from 1964 to 1970, enabled her to further develop her outstanding oral delivery. D. H. Melhem described a 1981 performance by Cortez, observing that her voice ranged from "shimmering silk to steel [and] the stunning imagery of the poems; the democratic ambiance and group sense allowed each performer alternately to star" (181).[1] It is obvious from Melhem's description that poetry becomes an integral component of the ensemble and not simply a solo act. In his biographical article on Jayne Cortez, Jon Woodson remarks that her interest in drama influenced her poetry by enabling her to "amplify her feelings for the performance styles of a number of black musicians and singers" and that her "ability to chant her poetry using evocative, jazz-influenced vocalizations has marked her as a creative artist uniquely able to reach audiences for whom books of poetry had little appeal" (70).

Although Cortez had been writing since she was fourteen, it was not until she came in contact with the ideas expressed by the black arts movement that her work began to closely scrutinize the issues of race and American domestic and foreign policy. Her first collection, *Pisstained Stairs and the Monkey Man's Wares,* was published in 1969. The collection was dedicated to the Watts Repertory Theatre Company and was written as part of a performance event focusing on African American music and poetry. In the book, Cortez combines black speech and various African American musical traditions. However, the main focus of the book is on black musicians, with several poems responding to the work of Bessie Smith, Leadbelly, Charlie Parker, Ornette Coleman, Clifford Brown, Sun Ra, Billie Holiday, John Coltrane, and Fats Navarro. In the 1969 review that appeared in *Negro Digest,* poet Nikki Giovanni wrote the following:

> We haven't had many jazz poets who got inside the music and the people who created it. We poet about them, but not of them. And this is Cortez's strength. She can wail from Theodore Navarro and Leadbelly to Ornette and never lose a beat and never make a mistake. She's a genius and all lovers of jazz will need this book—lovers of poetry will want it. (35)

According to Woodson, Cortez writes about blues and jazz artists because "for her they constitute a pantheon of revolutionary heroes and heroines who have prepared the way for the new order that they sing about" (70). Woodson is not specific as to what this new order is, but it is obvious he is underlining the importance of nationalism in the black arts movement. When asked in a 1980 interview to comment on her work and its relationship to Black Nationalism, Cortez remarked that she is "a Black person in a Black family in the Black Nation, so nationalism is a natural fact. I think that Black Nationalism has its place in the growth of the United States of America. I think the Black nation—the oppressed African American nation—has a future (Melhem, *Heroism* 203). Cortez's early poetry appears to be influenced by some of the categories in Larry Neal's outline "Some Reflection on the Black Aesthetic." Under the heading, "History as Unitary Myth," Neal gives equal importance to black artists and political figures, as they are considered to be the foundation of a new black nation (Neal 12–15). Cortez's early work shows an engagement with the views expressed by many black arts aestheticians who believed that in order for art to have any relevancy, it must address the sociopolitical and spiritual needs of black people. Thus, Cortez's references to African American musicians are a means of acknowledging the critical role African American music has played in the spiritual and historical development of the black community.[2]

It was Cortez's involvement in the black arts movement that brought her in contact with several influential writers and artists. The highly charged atmosphere of creativity and cooperation between artists of various disciplines and her 1954 marriage to jazz innovator Ornette Coleman and later marriage to sculptor Melvin Edwards have all made an impact on how Cortez has chosen to craft and produce her poetry. In the "Lonely Woman," Cortez directly responds to an Ornette Coleman composition that appeared on the recording *The Shape of Jazz to Come* (1959), featuring Coleman on alto sax, Don Cherry on pocket trumpet, Charlie Hayden on bass, and Billy Higgins on drums. Interestingly, Coleman's music was a response to a painting he had seen of a wealthy-looking white woman with a "lonely expression" and tears running down her face (Litweiler 51). In *Ornette Coleman: A Harmolodic Life,* John Litweiler describes the musical performance:

> "Lonely Woman" turns the conventional bop ensemble structure inside out, with its fast tempo set by the drummer, the bass playing accents rather than meter or velocity, and the two horns playing the slow, rubato theme over it all. Pity, sorrow, sympathy, and resignation emerge in succession from the theme, qualities amplified in Ornette's solo, which is in Higgins's fast tempo and in identifiable strains, however freely the lengths to which he improvises in the song's two keys. (68)

Cortez's poem, which appeared in *Pisstained Stairs and the Monkey Man's Wares* and the anthology *New Black Voices* (1972), provides a linear narrative to the musical composition that certainly veers away from the painting's original subject.

Lonely Woman

A wasted flow of water hiding
  sliding
down the face
of a lone-ly one

This black woman's
oblong tears
render
softly felt wetness
warm like sperm
to melt
the calling—calling
flesh
  Is there any reason
  for this not so
  dry—Dry season

Cutting tongue of fear
please
won't you hear
the stretch marks
of Loneliness
bent—in this
cold woman's tear
Night Raining
in
The Woman's Quarters
Listening to
Crickets
small—weak
dark like me
—sit—
Stripped——nude
from the trembling cadence of fire
Lit——
in Ornette's horn

Crickets that cry

Come—weep—with—us
come—weep—with us
come weep with us
Lone-ly wo-man

Lonely Woman
come weep with us (*New Black Voices* 233)

What is strikingly apparent is the musicality of the poem. Cortez uses several devices to establish the rhythmic structure of the text. The poem opens up with two rhyming verbs, "hiding" and "sliding," to establish a somewhat regular cadence. Rhyming words, like "Reason" and "Season" and "fear," "hear" and "tear," create a conventional, lyrically based, rhythmic undercurrent. However, rhyme is not the sole vehicle of rhythm in the poem. Cortez's short one-word line breaks and dashes create a staccato and a dissonance that is mirrored in the Coleman performance. The dashes and the single- and double-syllable words enable the reader of the poem to value not only the intricate rhythms of the text but also the tonal qualities that the changing cadences evoke. For example, in the lines "Crickets / small—weak / dark like me" and "Crickets that cry / Come—weep—with—us / come—weep—with us," Cortez makes use of the long vowel "e" to conjure the shrill sound of crickets. Thus, the music of nature is reflected in the music of jazz and poetry. The "lonely woman's" suffering is echoed in that line as well. Cortez obviously politicizes the poem by writing about the sexual exploitation of black women during slavery through the use of words like "sperm," "Woman's Quarters," and "stripped—-nude." However, the exploitation Cortez writes about is not limited to one particular historical period. Cortez creates linkage to the present by saying "dark like me."[3] By insisting on the connection between the poet and the lonely woman, she undercuts the original intent of Coleman's piece. It is obvious that the poem's lyricism evokes a more concrete reading than perhaps Ornette's tangential music can. However, it should also be remembered that Ornette Coleman's music was certainly visionary in terms of how its often-brutal energy and use of musical keys that were slightly askew disturbed several listeners, reflecting the tenor of the times. In reading Cortez's poem, one also continues to hear the haunting refrain that opens and closes the Coleman piece.

In 1971, Cortez published her second book, *Festivals and Funerals,* which was praised by Eugene B. Redmond in his extensive study, *Drumvoices: The Mission of Afro-American Poetry: A Critical History,* for being "musical, daring, ambivalent, complex and technically dexterous" (296). The collection is dedicated to her son, jazz percussionist Denardo Coleman. Coleman began playing the drums at age six and four years later made his recording debut on Ornette Coleman's *The Empty Foxhole,* recorded in 1966. Denardo has since been a very instrumental participant in several of his mother's performances and recordings.

In *Festivals and Funerals,* Cortez still uses musical phrasing inspired by jazz, but the poems also make use of what Cortez refers to as "fusions" in which traditional African art and music merge with African American art and music. In her interview with D. H. Melhem, Cortez says that "Africa represents a link with the past. Africans and African Americans have many things in common. Our tastes, gestures, beliefs, ancestors. We share the same blood. We are connected in pigmentation and in our struggle against oppression. We are lovers of life" ("A Melus Profile" 73). It is Cortez's Pan-Africanist vision that manifests the linkage between art and politics, thus making her less of a regional poet and instead one of a larger geopolitical constituency. Additionally, her aesthetic sense comes from influences beyond Western modernism. In describing her creative process for composing the 1971 collection, Cortez remarked: "I use dreams, the subconscious, and the real objects, and I open up the body and use organs, and I sink them into words, and I ritualize them and fuse them into events. I guess the poetry is like a festival. Everything can be transformed" (Melhem, *Heroism* 205).

Cortez's comment concerning the transformative qualities of poetry finds affinity in the manner in which art functions in many non-Western societies. Her role in creating an art form that validates the transformative process places her squarely in African culture, where dance and music are integral to spiritual fulfillment. Woodson writes that *Festivals and Funerals* presents poems that show Cortez moving toward more "theoretical concerns: colonialism, African nationhood, revolution, mythology, and the role of the artist in revolutionary politics" (71). Although Woodson's observation is generally correct, Cortez's earlier poetry has always expressed these concerns. What does occur in this collection is a language that is rawer and precariously placed between what Woodson defines as the "extremes of creation and destruction," which evoke the political climate of the times. In *Heroism in the New Black Poetry,* D. H. Melhem writes that the book marks a crucial moment in Cortez's development as a poet because of her fusing of African and American language and culture and her employment of the "self/body as metaphor, surrealistic imagery, jazz influenced rhythmic repetition both simple and incremental, parallel structures, lack of punctuation, improvisational features, and worker-oriented perspectives" (184). Several of the poems written in the collection are monologues in which Cortez uses her experience as a factory worker.

> I worked in a shirt factory; then I worked in a belt factory; and I worked in other factories. I also worked as a waitress, a telephone operator, and an office worker, typing and operating business machines. I learned a lot from women in the factories. We talked about many, many things. I got advice and tips on how to confront reality. How to be an independent woman. How to get your heels clicking when you're being abused. How to cook. What to do about health problems. It was a real sisterhood. (*Heroism* 201)

This experience had a profound impact on Cortez because it attuned her to the improvisational qualities of feminism and confirmed her desire to work as an independent artist.

Some of the political and cultural subject matter taken up in *Festivals and Funerals* are also treated in Cortez's third book, *Scarifications,* with drawings by her second husband, Melvin Edwards. The book was published in 1973 with her own Bola Press. Although Cortez self-published her two early collections, Bola Press became a larger financial venture and continued to be an avenue where Cortez could have control over her own works. As Aldon Lynn Nielsen points out in *Black Chant,* Cortez followed the example of artists like Betty Carter, Charles Mingus, and Amiri Baraka, realizing early in her career that "black artists would require full control over the production of their works if they were to escape the censorious mediations of white editing and of capitalist recording industry demands for certain modes of product" (221). One of the most significant poems in the book is "I am New York City," in which Cortez uses several long Whitmanesque lines to evoke the surreal brutality of the urban landscape. The poem begins:

> i am new york city of blood
> police and fried pies
> i rub my docks red with grenadine
> and jelly madness in a flow of tokay
> my huge skull of pigeons
> my séance of peeping toms
> my plaited ovaries excuse me
> this is my grime my thigh of
> steelspoons and toothpicks
>   i imitate no one (Cortez, *Coagulations* 9)

In 1973 Cortez recorded a version of the poem with bassist Richard Davis on a Strata-East release titled *Celebrations and Solitudes*. Describing Cortez's vocal technique, Aldon Lynn Nielsen writes that "Cortez tends usually to read these lines in descending pitch sequences. She reads a first line, organized around one tone and then reads the next descending from a lower starting pitch. Her lines are, in this sense, chantlike, allowing for melodic effects within the chosen tonal range of the individual line"(222). Cortez's tonal reading over Davis's walking bass line replicates a stroll through the city. The recording displays Cortez's ability to successfully integrate her writings with Davis's music, something that has often been tried unsuccessfully by Kenneth Rexroth, Jack Kerouac, Kenneth Patchen, Lawrence Ferlinghetti, and several others. Cortez writes and delivers her lines as if they were a cappella breath units, the measures of which are derived from African American music. When asked about the difficulty of working poetry into music and music into poetry, Cortez responded:

> That part is not hard. The part that is hard is stretching the human voice. Everybody else in the group has another kind of voice, a musical instrument that's much louder than yours. That's the problem. How not to let the different pitch levels control your work. Most of the musicians who've played with me have all been musicians who play jazz. They are used to inventing off of different rhythm patterns and different sounds. So they relate to what I'm doing in the same way. They interject their own sound and attitudes. And I do the same thing. I listen to them and respond to their ideas and attitudes. I like working with music. It's a collective experiment. A collective composition. (*Heroism* 204)

It is important to emphasize that Cortez views herself as a collaborator. This places her as a member of a community of musicians, relaying ideas through sound as well as word. The several recordings that Cortez has made all demonstrate that she is a performer who places herself in a role similar to that of Billie Holiday, who viewed herself not as a lone singer with a backup band, but as part of a collective ensemble of "instrumentalists."

Mouth on Paper, published in 1977, continues with themes similar to those expressed in earlier works and shows Cortez's further development into a poet of incredible breadth and music. There are several poems about jazz in the collection. "Rose Solitude," written for Duke Ellington and also recorded as "Essence of Rose Solitude" on the *Celebrations and Solitudes* album, is an example of a poem that incorporates several facets of what attracts listeners to jazz. According to Cortez, "Rose Solitude" was not inspired by a particular piece of music by Ellington, but by the "creativity of Ellington." Cortez, who attended Ellington's funeral on May 27, 1974, at the Cathedral Church of Saint John the Divine in New York City, was also inspired by the emotions expressed by some of the mourners.

> I happened to be sitting next to an older West Indian woman who said these lines to me, "Like Nat (King) Cole, like Satchmo," and I thought about that; I thought about the qualities of the people she mentioned. I thought about their music, and I was sitting there, and I was thinking about Duke Ellington and watching all of the images in this church, the different moods, the different faces, the agitation of the wind outside, and I thought about the music. The poem is an accumulation of those thoughts, images, and other memories. (Melhem, *Heroism* 208)

The poem opens with images of elegance and sophistication that for many are synonymous with Ellington's personality and music.

> I am essence of Rose Solitude
> my cheeks are laced with cognac
> my hips sealed with five satin nails
> i carry dreams and romance of new fools and old
> flames
> between the musk of fat
> and the side pocket of my mink tongue

> Listen to champagne bubble from this solo (Cortez,
> *Coagulations* 36)

It is interesting that the sensual images—"cognac," "satin," "musk," "mink," and "champagne"—that Cortez attributes to Ellington have little to do directly with his music. They are images that evoke glamour and refinement and place Ellington in the public eye. Although Ellington's masterful use of African American and European music demonstrates his astute understanding of various musical forms, it must be recognized that Ellington's portrayal as a sophisticate was also manipulated by the recording industry in order to transform Ellington's early image as blues artist to someone who composed "fine art."[4] In the first strophe, Cortez takes advantage of our familiarity with Ellington's cultured image and humorously evokes his "facile" style in lines like "listen to champagne bubble from this solo." Perhaps Cortez had Ellington's 1934 version of "Solitude" in mind, which Gunther Schuller describes as being "excessively sentimental" with a "saxophone-quartet chorus absolutely dripping with a heavy saccharine vibrato"(65). Later, as the poem progresses, Cortez's poem subverts Ellington's surface image to reveal the complexity of his music. In *Stomping the Blues,* Albert Murray remarks:

> The preeminent embodiment of the blues musician as artist was Duke Ellington, who in the course of fulfilling the role of entertainer, not only came to address himself to the basic imperatives of music as a fine art but also achieved the most comprehensive synthesis, extension, and refinement to date of all the elements of blues musicianship. Indeed so all-inclusive was Ellington's synthesis that it amounts to a special vocabulary and syntax of orchestration. (214)

In this strophe, Cortez makes use of alliteration in words using the "s" and "m" consonants. By expressing the tonal qualities of these two consonants, she establishes a rhythmic pattern in each line that remains consistent throughout the text. Additionally, the inclusion of the "I" pronoun in both capital and lowercase, creates an additional rhythmic pattern with an incantatory effect that is continued throughout the text.

In the next strophe, Cortez links Ellington to jazz legends Nat King Cole and Louis Armstrong.

> Essence of Rose Solitude
> veteran from texas tiger from chicago that's me
> i cover the shrine of Duke
> who like satchmo like Nat (King) Cole
> will never die because love they say
> never dies (Cortez, *Coagulations* 36)

The strophe's opening is very similar to the opening of the first, except that "I am" is dropped. However, because of the repetition of "I" that is established earlier, the continual link is implied. Additionally, by omitting "I am," Cortez pares the line down to the essence of the image. The second line, with its stress and repetition of "t" in "texas," "tiger" and "that's" creates a percussive drive. Even the first word of the line, "veteran," has a strongly accented "t" consonant. The next line, "i cover the shrine of Duke," places Ellington beyond the level of mere artist/performer and establishes the spiritual essence of his music, a quality that is also found in the work of Kaufman and Jonas. Also quite possibly alluded to is the jazz standard "I cover the Waterfront," made popular by Billie Holiday. This allusion may mark a moment of improvisation in the poem where Cortez veers away from the expected. It is a well-documented practice among some musicians that during moments of improvisation a performer may quote and slightly twist a phrase from a popular song. However, "solitude" also implies the loneliness of the artist engaged in the creative process, what Welsh poet Dylan Thomas referred to as his "lonely craft or sullen art / exorcised in the still of night / when only the moon rises." It is important to recognize that although Ellington's compositions and performances achieved a wide range of respect from musicians and critics, he was never awarded a major prize for his work. Thus, "solitude" can also be attributed to public neglect and lack of acknowledgment for his contributions to American music. Aldon Lynn Nielsen makes an interesting observation about the collaboration between Davis and Cortez on the 1973 recording *Celebrations and Solitudes*.

> Davis slides in and out of citations. At one point he alludes briefly to the melody of Ellington's "Sophisticated Lady," surely one of the Ellington orchestra's most popular of collaborative works, thus doubling the signifying directions of the jazz text. For if Cortez's poem "Rose Solitude" is an overironized praise song for Ellington, then Davis's quotation from "Sophisticated

> Lady" must be taken not only as a further tribute to Ellington but also as an ironic praise for the praise song's author, Cortez. (226)

Additionally, there is a lyrical moment within the last two lines of this strophe that may also allude to a song because the phrasing sounds so familiar, as implied by "they say." The use of, or allusion to, popular phrasings also enables the reader to recall the public appeal and popularity of this musical trinity: Ellington, Armstrong, and Cole. Although all three musicians began their careers as devotees to the musical impulses found in blues and jazz music, it was toward the end of their lives that their renditions of popular songs increased their public appeal. This is particularly true for Nat King Cole songs such as "Mona Lisa" and "Dinner for One, Please James" and Louis Armstrong's "What a Wonderful World" and "Hello Dolly." Although Ellington never really fell into this predicament, he was more often expected to play his popular standards like "Take the A Train," "Sophisticated Lady," or "Prelude to a Kiss" as opposed to any of his "sacred works."

In the next two strophes, Cortez veers away from the concrete imagery that occurs earlier and employs a new and highly charged vocabulary that she would define as "superealism." What becomes paramount in the development of this praise song to Ellington is the connection to the African diaspora, evoking the gods Shango and Erzulie. Here, Cortez brings the ancestors home.

> I tell you from stair steps of these navy blue nights
> these metallic snakes
> these flashing fish skins
> and the melodious cry of Shango
> surrounded by sorrow
> by purple velvet tears
> by cockhounds limping from crosses
> from turtle skinned shoes
> from diamond shaped skulls and canes
> made from dead gazelles
> wearing a face of wilting potato plants
> of grey and black scissors
> of bee bee shots and fifty red boils
> yes the whole world loved him

> I tell you from suspenders of two-timing dog odors
> from inca frosted lips
> nonchalant legs
> i tell you from howling chant of sister Erzulie
> and the exaggerated hearts of a hundred pretty
> women
> they loved him
> this world sliding from a single flower
> into a caravan of heads made into ten thousand
> flowers (Cortez, *Coagulations* 36–37)

Here she testifies: "I tell you" becomes the continuous refrain that drags us through her imagery of animals and plants. The practice of "testifying" originated in the African American church but later found use in music and other forms of art. In *Juba to Jive,* Clarence Major defines "testifying" as a verb used to "ritually comment upon any cultural experience understood by all black people; a secular or religious confession" (469). The images that Cortez brings to this strophe are strikingly different from the "saccharine" imagery that occurred in the first strophe. She no longer alludes to the romantic and glamorous world of mink, satin, and champagne, but to the natural world with its snakes, fish, and gazelles. Not all of the animals appear in their natural forms. There are snakes that are made from metal, turtles that have been made into shoes, and "canes made from dead gazelles," thus Cortez blends together the manufactured with the natural. Perhaps Cortez's intention is to imply a comparison between the media created image of Ellington versus his real persona. In this strophe, Cortez introduces imagery that not only reflects the complexity of Ellington's personality and style but also serves as a counterpoint between African and Western cultures. She describes powerful African gods expressing emotions that evoke tragedy, thus Shango, the Yoruba god of fire and rain, is "surrounded by sorrow," and Erzulie, the voudoun goddess of water, hearth, and home, is "howling." Perhaps this connection applies to jazz music's African origins and expresses how this musical form was created out of oppression. This technique of combining references to Western and African culture plays a prominent role in the composition and performance of jazz. Cortez's use of animal imagery emphasizes Ellington's link to the African continent, thereby implying that what occurs in the ballrooms is more complex and goes beyond secular merriment. Thus,

Ellington's performance acts as a kind of musical exorcism, reinstating the profound influence of the diaspora. By subverting several of the images in this strophe, the irony in the line, "they loved him," is further heightened. It is significant to note the density of repetition contained in several of the beginning words in each line; this technique drives the energy of the poem forward. In addition, several nouns are made plural, using alliteration to emphasize the importance of sound in the text. The poem concludes:

> Ask me
> Essence of Rose Solitude
> chickadee from arkansas that's me
> i sleep on cotton bones
> cotton tails
> and mellow myself in empty ballrooms
> i'm no fly by night
> look at my resume
> i walk through the eyes of staring lizards
> i throw my neck back to floorshow on bumping goat
> skins
> in front of my stage fright
> i cover the hands of Duke who like Satchmo
> like Nat (King) Cole will never die
> because love they say
> never dies (Cortez, *Coagulations* 37)

In this final strophe, Cortez's use of rhyme in "me" and "chickadee" creates a tight pattern that signals a change in the text's rhythm. Thus, the repetition of the "i" pronoun that follows becomes more pronounced and intensifies the cadence. Additionally, Cortez appropriates the "I" and blurs the distinction between the speaker and the subject (Ellington). This technique alludes to the practice of "mounting the gods" in voudoun, where the initiate takes on the spiritual and physical attributes of the Loa. Although lines like "i throw my neck back to floorshow on bumping goat / skins" may sound surreal and exotic to some readers, they probably refer to Ellington's first appearance in segregated nightclubs like the Cotton Club, where he and his band members were expected to perform their "jungle music" in costumes made to look like animal skins. This recalls Cortez's animal imagery in the opening and also reflects the perversion of Africa in a Western setting. References are made to Ellington standards, such as "cotton tail."[5] Cortez returns to the lyrical phrase, "i cover the hands of Duke," which implies the silencing of the piano and provides closure. Her ending is similar to that of a musical piece where the melody is repeated to create a sense of closure. However, her omission of a period at the end of the final line and the lack of punctuation throughout the poem indicates that the closing is open ended, thus fortifying the concluding message, "because love they say / never dies."

On November 13, 1981, Cortez performed, with a jazz ensemble, several poems from her forthcoming collection, *Firespitter,* at Joseph Papp's New York Shakespeare Festival Public Theater. The performance was a rousing success. D. H. Melhem writes that Cortez "functioned as the poetic instrument in a jazz ensemble where each performer, in turn or as inspired, led the group into improvisation" (*Heroism* 191). For several listeners, Cortez became the quintessential "jazz poet," one who manages to bridge the gulf between literature and music. Although other art forms have been equally important, it was the 1981 concert and the 1982 publication of *Firespitter* that began to define her in the public eye. The label "jazz poet" does not seem to bother Cortez or limit the direction of her work. For her, jazz becomes an aesthetic device in which her poems can be sculpted, no matter what the subject.

With the publication of *Firespitter,* Cortez also became defined as a surrealist. Woodson writes that the poems in *Firespitter* move away from the "chaotic style of free verse and the emphasis on black speech" that was commonly used by many African American poets in the 1960s to the "controlled evocation of otherness employed by the American surrealist poets" (73). Woodson's remarks about Cortez's earlier work are a bit puzzling, for Cortez was certainly working under the formal constraint of a jazz aesthetic, where the sequence of musical events is often predictable. This is particularly true with improvisation in which a designated moment in a performance opens up to the flow of creative and free flowing thought, then closes or is passed on to another performer. As mentioned earlier, Cortez did publish in the surrealist journal *Arsenal* and appeared in the City Lights publication *Surrealism and Its Popular Accomplishes,* and she has often been labeled as a surrealist. She also continued to publish in journals like *Essence, Black World, Callaloo,* and *Black Scholar.* Jon Woodson notes that "by being linked to this [surrealist] school, Cortez has not given up anything or moved away from her past creations. She has been discovered for what she is—an artist committed to the same revolutionary program as the surrealists and one who has employed many of the same materials and methods as Andre Breton, Ted Joans, and other poets of the surrealist school" (74). This may be true, but it must be noted that it is the American surrealists who have made use of the earlier established forms of African American music such as jazz and blues because of the perceived chaos and disjunction of the music. This view of African American music is problematic because it appears to focus solely on the emotional makeup of the music as opposed to the longstanding rhythmic traditions of other non-Western cultures.[6]

Several poems in *Firespitter* are devoted to jazz musicians like Charles Mingus ("Into this Time"), Count Basie ("Solo Finger Solo"), Chano Pozo ("I see Chano Pozo"), and Duke Ellington ("If the Drum Is a Woman").[7] In "Solo Finger Solo," Cortez recounts the history and music of one of the "swingingest" bands of all time. In *The Swing Era,* Gunther Schuller writes:

> That the Basie band has been from its inception a master of swing could hardly be disputed. It is and always has been a magnificent "swing machine." For over forty years the Basie band has upheld a particular concept and style of jazz deeply rooted in the Southwest and Kansas City in particular. It draws its aesthetic sustenance from the blues, uses the riff as its major rhetorical and structural device, all set in the language and grammar of swing. (225)

In the poem, Cortez begins with Count Basie's widely recognized musical signature: the quick musical tags that would accompany his soloists. Not seeing these tags in a favorable light, Schuller remarks that by 1938 Basie's piano mannerisms were becoming a cliché and predictable, turning into "empty mechanical ciphers" in which "the fingers twiddle out mindlessly" (245). Making the connection between Basie and literature, Albert Murray wrote that the bandleader picked up the same "principles of composition that Ernest Hemingway learned from the style sheet for prose writers at the *Kansas City Star*" (175). The newspaper asked its contributors to use short sentences, short first paragraphs, and "vigorous English" and said that the language should "be positive, not negative. Never use old slang . . . slang to be enjoyable must be fresh"

(175). Murray comments that "Basie stripped his own Harlem Stride-derived piano style down to the point that he could make one note swing"(175). Cortez's poem begins:

> When evening goes down into its jelly jelly jelly
> into drain pipe cuts and stitches and vaccinations
> protruding from arms
>
> And spirit of the five-by-five man pushes
> his sweet potatoes in the air
> feather daddy leaps into a falcon of tropical bird squats
> rubber legs swing into off-beat onijos onijos
> then into your solo finger solo
> the blues chantress jumps up and
> repeats her nasal volcanic chant calling
>
> Count Basie   Count Basie   Count Basie
> (Cortez, *Jazz Fan* 23)

Cortez begins the poem by alluding to the song "Jelly, Jelly." The song was originally recorded in 1940 by vocalist Billy Eckstine for the Earl Hines orchestra, not Count Basie. Although the word "Jelly" was African American slang for sexual intercourse during the 1930s and 1940s, Cortez's use of it is slightly ambiguous because the images that follow are linked to illness, "Cuts," "stitches," and "vaccinations." In the next strophe, another singer is introduced, "the five-by-five man," Jimmy Rushing, the popular Basie vocalist who joined the band in 1935 and was with them for fifteen years (Fernett 51). Rushing had the nickname "Mr. Five-five" because of his physical stature: stout, short, and squat. "Feather daddy leaps" may possibly refer to saxophonist Lester Young, who had the hit "Lester Leaps In" in 1938 with the Basie band. The "blues chantress" that Cortez refers to may be Helen Humes, who joined Basie in 1937 after Billie Holiday's brief stint and was with them for four years (Basie 211). In the poem, Cortez uses active verbs like "pushes," "leaps," "squats," "swing," and "jumps" to indicate the high level of excitement that marked the band's performances. The repetition of "onijos" mirrors "solo" in the next line, giving the two lines that particular rhythmic bounce that was one of the most salient musical characteristics of the band. The line "Count Basie Count Basie Count

Basie" that is repeated in several variations throughout the poem is another musical signifier as well; the heavy accented "Count" and the tonal extension of "Basie" establishes a musical pattern that demonstrates how Cortez successfully merges music and poetry. The poem continues:

> And Count Basie
> you burn through this timbale of goose flesh rhythms
> a drop of iodine on your starfish lips
> the intonation of your kiss of melodica trilling
> into a labyrinth of one o'clock jumps
> into corpuscle flashes of the blues torpedo
> the erupting volcano of the blues shouters chanting your name
> Count Basie   Count Basie   take em to Chicago Count Basie
> (23)

Several of the stylistic devices Cortez used in the poem's second stanza are repeated here: the reference to a song made popular by the band, "One O'clock Jump," and the reference to "Count Basie" as a device to continue the rhythmic drive of the text. The "volcanic chant" of the "blues chantress" transforms to a "blues shouter chanting"; the change is significant because it marks a variation on a previously established image. Additionally, the adjectives and verbs intensify: "gooseflesh rhythms," "melodica trilling," "corpuscle flashes." These devices heighten our excitement as we push through the text.

> And Count Basie
> you punctuate this strong bourbon mist of gamma globulin breath
> a mixture of chords like serpentariums coiling
> from the deep everglades of your body
> and when the luscious screams of three-headed root doctors split
> Kansas City reeds in unison with this triple tapping
> double stopping   slow grinding   loosey butt night swinging
> with the blues chantress
> erupting volcano of the blues torpedoes chanting your name (23)

The lines become more extended in this strophe, showing how in poetry, as with music, rhythmic drive and intensity can open the way to improvisation. The line, "you punctuate this strong" is particularly noteworthy for its flow of alliteration. Throughout the stanza, the rhythmic value of the verbs lingers. Cortez accomplishes this by placing the "ing" suffix on verbs that occur either at the beginning or end of the line, like "coiling," "tapping," "erupting," and "swinging," or by placing extra spacing between them in words like "stopping" and "grinding." Again, stylistic devices are being repeated with slight variations as in the final strophe where the images from the "blues chantress" that appeared earlier are further merged. Cortez's use of words like "serpentariums," "everglades," and "three headed root doctors" recall the voudoun rituals that are practiced in Louisiana, often referred to as the birthplace of jazz. In doing so, Cortez acknowledges Basie and his connection to the geographical and spiritual origins of jazz.

> Count Basie
> you reach through the bottom of the music
> way down between cross rhythm vamps
> below air stream of the lowest octave
> into depths of a sacred drum
> and Count Basie   Count Basie   Count Basie
> how powerful and dignified and exquisite and direct and
> sharp
> your solo finger solo is (23)

In the final strophe, the intensity of the language and rhythm begins to dissipate with the imagery becoming more descriptive of Basie's musical technique. Cortez's vocabulary veers towards terms that refer directly to music: "rhythm," "vamps," "octave," "drum," and "sharp." Also changed is the "volcanic chant," for the band is winding down and Cortez brings the performance back to Basie as the singular focus. The line "how powerful" and its repetition of the conjunction "and" slows the cadence. It also replicates the sound of a train slowing into the station. The refrain "Count Basie Count Basie Count Basie" has a similar effect. The rhythms of the railroad are one of the recognizable sounds used by musicians from the Kansas City and Southwest bands of which Basie was such an integral part.[8] The repetition used in the final line, "your solo finger solo is," effectively brings the poem to a Basie-like tag.

In 1984 Cortez published *Coagulations: New and Selected Poems* with Thunder's Mouth Press, marking the first time she used an outside publisher. Illustrated with drawings by Melvin Edwards, the book contains poems from her earlier collections: *Scarifications, Mouth on Paper,* and *Firespitter,* as well as a section of new poems called *On all Fronts.* In the new poems, Cortez continues her commitment to political change and dedication to the jazz aesthetic. Aldon Lynn Nielsen writes that "Cortez's work, both on the page and on the stage, simply refuses to countenance reductive distinctions between lyric poetry and vernacular song" (231).

Somewhere in Advance of Nowhere, Cortez's next book, was published by Serpents Tail/High Risk Books in 1996. Many of the poems that appear in the collection were performed by Jayne Cortez and the Firespitters on two outstanding CDs, *Cheerful and Optimistic* (1994) and *Taking the Blues Back Home* (1996), both produced by her son, Denardo. In the book, there are several poems with jazz references: "About Flyin' Home," "The Guitars I Used to Know," "Why Not," "A Miles Davis Trumpet," "So What," and a beautiful poem eulogizing several artists, "States of Motion." Among these poems, "Why Not," dedicated to the vocalist Babs Gonzalez (Lee Brown), is a good example of how Cortez can adapt language to a particular musical style. Gonzalez's vocalese renditions on the 1954 recording *Tales of Manhattan* were particularly noteworthy because they, according to Wallenstein, "enlarged our understanding of how poetry/talk joins with jazz performance" (601). On the recording, Gonzalez makes use of scat singing, street poetry, and the jailhouse toast tradition. "Why Not" employs similar techniques. I will only quote the first and final stanzas in order to demonstrate their effectiveness and debt to the music.

> Why not
> let Babs
> dominate
> this night
> with his
> thirty year
> rite of
>   oo bop sha bam
> Horns imitating him
> as he imitated them
> in up tempo grooveness
>   of Expubidence

a riffology collaboration
    a sha ba dah ba doot doot
    in front of
sheel-lee-ah doo bee dah
    rejection into
    an injection of
oo daba doo bay doo yey doo yey doo
    Itself
    a home
    demonstration
    of those
    flat sharp
    natural sensations
    swinging
    at the end of the wind
    of a big ole nasty
    tenor saxophone ya ya ya yawl lapowl
    and why not (68–69)

The poem begins a few spaces away from the left margin. Using a technique similar to the rhythmic changes found in bebop, Cortez begins the poem on the offbeat. The short one- or two-word lines create a percussive and disjunctive effect. This is particularly true in the first seven lines where the alliteration created by the "t" consonant occurs. After the tightly rhythmic seven lines come the often-quoted vocalese phrase "oo bop sha bam," made famous by Dizzy Gillespie.[9] Clarence Major defines the phrase as being "existential" and "perhaps a mystic effort to comment on the inscrutable in the black man's social, moral, and spiritual condition in the United States, or simply another way of talking to that 'sense' of mystery often referred to as God" (333). Throughout the poem, Cortez makes continual use of bebop phrasing, thus emphasizing sound, in a manner similarly used by Bob Kaufman, as an important tonal and rhythmic component of the text. Cortez also plays with language by extending words: for example the noun or adjective "riff" becomes "riffology," giving the word a scientific aura. Cortez provides a glossary in the back of the book for words like "Expubidence," which evokes the bebop linguistics of Gonzalez. Also the noun or verb "groove," which indicates one's style or manner of playing, becomes the abstract noun "grooveness." Like Gonzalez and other vocalese artists, Cortez bends and extends the sound and meaning of words.

In the closing stanza, Cortez repeats some of the same rhythmic cadences used in the opening.

> Why not
> let Babs
> leave
> his hot
> orikisms
> in bandstand blood of the blues
> in amber lights of city tubes
> oo ya cooing and oop pop a dahing
> on his way to
> ee ee ee doo blah blee
> blee blah doo ee ee ee ee ee
> and why not (69–70)

Cortez economizes her language. By using several single-syllable words, she creates a punctuated rhythmic stress in the text, giving the poem the characteristic bounce that can be heard in Gonzalez's recording. Additionally, more use is made of alliteration. The repetition of the "b" sound in words like "Babs," "bandstand," "blood," "blues," and the scat phrase "blah blee / blee blah," obviously inspired by the bebop vocabulary, create the musical influx. Here, Cortez introduces words like "orikisms" to evoke the connection to Africa, "blood" to emphasize the violence of sociopolitical struggle, and "amber lights" to evoke the performative aspect of African American culture and the locale (nightclubs) where some of the music's most innovative experimentation took place.[10] Cortez's use of these images cryptically suggest that the production of African American art is linked to political and social struggle. By infusing the political in her work, Cortez encourages us to look beyond the mere artifice of poetry (or any other art form) and consider its relevancy in effecting change. In her refusal to gloss over any of the hardships one encounters when presenting their art to an inhospitable society, Cortez reveals the complexity of being African American. These politically charged images create a tension within the poem that suddenly gives way to the brief riff of jazz's "existential language." Her use of bebop phrasing appears at a crucial time within the poem and enables us to view the bebop riff as a kind of language of liberation. This cleverly refutes the often-used description of the language being "nonsensical." Cortez ends the poem, "and why not," using the hard sounding "t" as the closing note. However, the phrase is also rhetorical, making "why not" an open-ended question and therefore an open-ended closing.

For many years Jayne Cortez has gone beyond the often stiff and staid public readings that most poets are guilty of; rather, she infuses her readings with an unmistakable political and musical energy. The same can be said for her work on the page. Cortez's most recent collection, *Jazz Fan Looks Back,* was published in 2002 and brought together all of the poetry she has written that specifically uses music as its subject. The work includes poems written from 1968 to 2000 that Cortez has defined as her "poetic response to African and African American music, Blues, Jazz, Black Music, the Music and its environment" (7). This collection further displays the poet's knowledge of the music, use of line breaks, spacing, and a heightened visual and aural sense make her a poet who successfully combines and reintegrates the art of music and poetry. In an interview with D. H. Melhem she remarked:

> My role as a poet? I want to be creative, inventive, imaginative, free, secure, and make poetry. I'm interested in using the latest technology to reach a wider audience. I believe in diversity and in exchanging ideas. Travel means I have access to information from other sources. I think that poets have a responsibility to be aware of the meaning of human rights, to be familiar with history, to point out distortions, and to bring their thinking and their writing to higher levels of illumination. (*Heroism* 210)

As evidenced in the above quote, Cortez feels that poetry has a responsibility to advocate social and political change. Her desire to disseminate her work among a wider, more multicultural audience shows that she seeks to reconnect poetry and music to its early folk origins. It is obvious that Cortez will continue to push beyond the conventional parameters of art and use jazz as a vehicle to express her political ideas.

CHAPTER 6

Interstellar Space: Nathaniel Mackey's Musical Weave

words, words' amanuensis . . . Packed up,
departed, booked . . . "Cold water
and dirt," a voice we heard sang,
wasted.
Whatever we spun it was a drink we
took. Goatskin, ecumenical kiss,
runaway tongue, whatever we drank
it
—Nathaniel Mackey

Nathaniel Mackey is one of the most complex and innovative African American writers to employ a jazz aesthetic. His extensive use of jazz goes beyond that found in other contemporary poets, who mainly rely on jazz for anecdotal subject matter and poetic rhythm. Rather, he encompasses a wider and more erudite use of the absorptive qualities of the music, making his poetry and prose an improvisational weave through the complexities of African diasporic culture. It is this approach to poetry that creates a body of work that is as beautifully lyrical as it is evocative and complex. By employing an aesthetic that uses elements of African and African American culture, as well as other ethnic traditions, he fashions a literature that is truly multicultural. His spontaneous drive toward a language informed by tonal improvisation is as easily recognizable in the Canto Moro music of Spain as it is in the jazz tradition. Mackey's engagement with the "alternative poetics" that rose out of the 1960s and the musical traditions of the African American avant-garde enables him to create work that slips outside the conventional and sometimes rigid boundaries of genre. His unique approach to poetry is marked by the disjunctive use of rhythm, the jagged cadences, the pauses, and the linear and nonlinear riffs of some of the most interesting musical experimentation of black artists like Sun Ra, John Coltrane, Pharoah Sanders, and Anthony Braxton, linking his work inextricably to the ancient and postmodern connections between poetry and music. Having studied the saxophone as an amateur for several years, Mackey benefits by having a musician's knowledge of jazz, which is a crucial element in the fashioning of his poetry.

Equally important are Mackey's intensive explorations of esoteric traditions that are mainly derived from books. In an interview with Charles Rowell, Mackey discussed his connection to books and music: "I'm something of a bookish poet and I try to leaven that bookishness with musicality. I mean, music is very important in my work in a lot of different ways, including rhythm and explorations of a variety of rhetorical tonalities" (Rowell 706). The result of this passionate use of both text and music is the creation of a body of work that is intellectually challenging because it speaks to the possibility of multiple modernisms, becoming a response to those who view the designations "modern" and "postmodern" as Eurocentric. Commenting on the complexity of Mackey's work, Peter O'Leary has observed that his work "bears importantly on the vitality of the ambivalence—between cosmic world-poem and particularized cross-cultural poem; between white avant garde poetics and African American poetic lore" (521). Mackey's notoriety as poet, novelist, and scholar reflect the way he chooses to live his life, and it is that same holistic approach to writing that allows all his work to escape categorization.

Mark Scroggins writes that Mackey aims to "recapture in poetry the contemporary individual's search for origins and identity among the multifarious cultural traces making up a world of simultaneity and to recapture the moments of spiritual breakthrough" (180). This search for "origins" has profound resonance in the African American community and particularly among the avant-garde in jazz. It strikes an interesting chord with musicians like Sun Ra, who engaged in a highly speculative Egyptcentric form of symbolism from Africa's historical past while saying he was extraterrestrial, or the Art Ensemble of Chicago, who use African symbolism in performances to simultaneously evoke the historical and contemporary legacies of Africa and the Americas while the trumpeter, Lester Bowie, appears in a lab coat as the scientist/mixer. That search for origins and reverence for ancient cultures has also found its way into the white avant-garde. Writers like Charles Olson and Robert Duncan, who were equally fascinated by the Mayans and the Greeks, have made a profound impact on Mackey's poetic sensibility.

Nathaniel Mackey was born in Miami, Florida, on October 25, 1947, to Sadie Jane Wilcox and Obadiah Mackey. When Mackey was four, his parents separated and the mother took the four children to live in California. It was there that he developed an early interest in music, particularly the music he was exposed to in the Baptist church. He was in a setting where he could observe the dynamic manner in which people respond to music. The "possession" and the trancelike state experienced by the parishioners were certainly different from the staid musical performances of the concert halls. For Mackey, the church was a place where music had the ability to profoundly affect not only the spirituality of the parishioners but also their physicality. Anyone who has seen a congregation in a Baptist or Evangelical church must have witnessed the electrified, highly musical atmosphere, with its shaking pews and the convulsions of the sanctified. Mark Scroggins notes that Mackey's observations in the church would enable him to realize the close relationship to other religious practices like Voudoun and Santeria and create an "abiding sense of kinship between the musical and the spiritual" (181). This connection between music and the spirit can also be found in the work of Kaufman, Jonas, and Cortez.

According to Mackey, this interest in music was not manifested in his creative work until much later. In high school, he was interested in mathematics and saw himself developing a career in that area. Additionally, he showed no interest in becoming a writer, although he was an avid reader and went well beyond the typical school fare of Longfellow and Tennyson, reading works by American poets William Carlos Williams, Amiri Baraka, and other writers who called for an attentive ear toward the "American voice." It was also during high school that he began to read work by Robert Duncan, Charles Olson, Robert Creeley, Denise Levertov, and the writers who appeared in Donald Allen's influential anthology, *The New American Poetry.* It introduced him to the work of several writers who were outsiders to the often-conservative writing that came out of the academy. These writers were significant because they stressed the importance of using everyday speech as poetic material and advocated that the poet should take great care to listen to the rhythmic cadences found in the American idiomatic speech as opposed to cadences inherited from the British tradition. What Mackey admired in these poets was their use of contemporary language, their attention toward non-Western cultures, and an inclination toward experimenting with form and subject matter. Even more important was the manner in which some of these poets used jazz to inform the subject and structure of their work. This direction led Mackey to further explore the music of Miles Davis, John Coltrane, and Dizzy Gillespie. Listening to bebop and hard bop called for a new way of approaching music that was not based solely on recognizing the melodic line, and Mackey feasted on these early musics before he expanded his explorations into jazz's avant-garde. In an interview with Ed Foster, Mackey commented that he had been listening to rock and rhythm and blues and first found the new music difficult, but after repeated listening he became more attentive to the music's unique vocabulary (50). Although, at this point Mackey's interests were primarily rooted in American music, there may have been an awareness that what he was listening to drew from a wider range of sources that went beyond American borders.

As a student at Princeton University, Mackey became interested in post-bop, often termed as the "New Jazz" and performed by innovators like John Coltrane, Albert Ayler, Ornette Coleman, Cecil Taylor, and several others who were pushing the perimeters of American music. Mackey was attracted to the heroic efforts of these musicians who went against the popular musical tastes of the day and placed themselves on an aesthetic limb. Their references to other musical cultures and new vocabularies not only brought in voices from Africa's past but considered the future as well. This continual interest in the experimental end of the musical spectrum would lead toward his developing aesthetic. Writing about the importance of the avant-gardists in terms of the liberating qualities found in musical experimentation, Mackey explains:

> This tendency involved a departure from—even outright abandonment of—bebop's reliance on the recurring chords referred to as "the changes" of a particular piece . . . To listeners accustomed to recurrent reminders of a tune's head in the form of the soloist's confinement to the changes, the new music seemed structureless and incoherent. (Scroggins 181)

Mackey's comment on the seemingly structureless and incoherent qualities of the "new music" is noteworthy because a similar observation can be made when one reads experimental literature, where seemingly abstract qualities appear fragmentary and not necessarily linked. However, Mackey's comment that the music "seemed" to function this way implies that it may be an illusion, and after one "lives with the work," structure and coherence are eventually revealed.

After graduating from Princeton in 1969, Mackey enrolled in Stanford University's Ph.D. program in English and American literature and continued to explore his earlier interest in avant-garde literature. It is often problematic to define African American artists like Mackey as being avant-garde because the label is based upon a particular view of Euro-American modernism. Several black artists have rejected labeling their work as experimental because they see the work as part of a long-established African tradition. For example, Ishmael Reed, a writer often labeled as experimental, remarked:

> I consider myself a classical Afro-American writer. I work out of the Afro-American cultural tradition, out of the folklore, and my work probably has more in common with black folk art, the visual . . . which emphasizes fantasy, humor, and satire . . . The distortion of my characters also originates from African tradition, if you look at the sculpture . . . I wouldn't call myself an avant-garde writer . . . [*Mumbo Jumbo* is] not experimental writing . . . It looks different but that's because people don't know our tradition . . . Even in Scott Joplin you get a mixture of European parlor music and ragtime. (Nielsen 50)

The term "avant-garde," when read under the illumination of Reed's comment, reveals the political ramifications such a designation implies for the African American artist, in whom the influence of non-Western aesthetics are often unacknowledged by white critics.[1]

While at Stanford, Mackey co-founded the journal *Hambone,* which he continues to edit from his home in Santa Cruz. Although the magazine was originally designed to showcase the work of African and African American writers, after the first issue *Hambone* became a journal that published "cross-cultural work emphasizing the centrifugal" (Scroggins 182). Editing the journal put him in touch with such innovative artists/writers as Sun Ra, Kamau Brathwaite, Cecil Taylor, Clarence Major, and others. After receiving his doctorate from Stanford, he taught at University of Wisconsin–Madison and University of Southern California before becoming a full professor at University of

California–Santa Cruz. In addition to being an influential figure in West Coast cultural life through his work as a writer and scholar, he runs a weekly radio show, "Tanganyika Strut," on KUSP-FM that showcases jazz and various ethnomusics. It is through his position as editor and professor that his strong advocacy of innovative writing has made him an invaluable voice in the academy.

Mackey was also attracted to the work of William Carlos Williams because Williams viewed himself as an outsider of mainstream America, and it was this estrangement that allowed him to connect to black culture. In the essay "Sound and Sentiment, Sound and Symbol," from Mackey's critical book *Discrepant Engagement: Dissonance, Cross-Culturality, and Experimental Writing,* he discusses what may have attracted Williams to black music.

> William's engagement with black music was greatly influenced by his sense of himself as cut off from the literary mainstream . . . Seeing himself as a victimized poet, Williams celebrated the music of a victimized people. In a gesture that has since been overdone ("the white negro," "the student as nigger," analogies between "women and blacks"), he saw the parallels between their lot and his own. (241)

In the essay, Mackey examines Williams's poem "Ol' Bunk Johnson," showing how the poet went against the expected rules of grammar and how he appropriated the black trope. It is in this spirit of rebellion and camaraderie found in the American avant-garde that often crosses racial barriers that Mackey places his lineage. In discussing the rhythmic qualities of poetry, Williams remarked:

> Each piece of work, rhythmic in whole, is then in essence an assembly of tides, waves, ripples—in short, of greater and lesser rhythmic particles regularly repeated or destroyed. [Therefore] the rhythm unit is simply any repeated sequence of lengths and heights. Upon this ether the sounds are strung in their variety—slipping, clinging, overreaching, triumphing but always going forward even through moments of total disorder in advance. (66)

Williams's comment describes the way rhythm has been used in free jazz. The use of varying cadence and dissonance can be found in the work of musicians like John Coltrane, Anthony Braxton, Marion Brown, Cecil Taylor, and in poets like Norman Pritchard, Harryette Mullen, Steve Jonas, and several others discussed here. Like the jazz artist who weaves elements from various musical traditions, the linkage has a particular lyrical appeal through which the music can be easily disseminated. One factor that made Mackey interested in Williams was his use of an open form that employed "noise" as a key aesthetic element. Here, Mackey comments on the importance of "noise" on innovative writing.

> Open form (itself a discrepant, oxymoronic formulation, not unlike Williams's "variable foot,") is a gesture in the direction of noise. Baraka's valorization of "honking" by rhythm and blues (R&B) saxophonists, [Clarence] Major's "remarkable verb of things," Duncan's invocation of "disturbance," Creeley's bebop influenced deviation from expected narrative accents, Olson's insistence that things "keep their proper confusions," his advocacy of "shout" as a corrective to discourse, [Edward Kamau] Braithwaite's "calibanisms," and [Wilson] Harris's "language as omen" all in their distinctive ways validate noise. (20)

It was Williams's innovative use of form, sound, and material that Mackey found provocative and useful in his own work.

Amiri Baraka has perhaps been one of Mackey's most significant influences for several reasons. Mackey first encountered Baraka's work in the Langston Hughes anthology *New Negro Poets: USA* and in his liner notes to *Coltrane Live at Birdland*. Baraka's engagement with both the white modernism of the beats and African American modernism certainly gave Mackey a lot to consider and led him to examine the issue of race as a cultural component in the development of an aesthetic vision. What Mackey admired was the way Baraka's poems "appeared to obey an aesthetic analogous to that of the music—mercurial, oblique, elliptical —and what particularly caught [his] attention in that was the ratio of statement to imaged evocation, the way it kept changing" (Naylor 659). In Baraka, Mackey found a Renaissance man who wrote not only poetry but also plays, novels, and music criticism and often made these genres interchangeable. Baraka was constantly reinventing himself, and by the late 1960s he had changed his name from LeRoi Jones to Amiri Baraka and had repudiated his avant-garde Greenwich village beat leanings to become a Black Nationalist. In "The Conversion of LeRoi Jones," his senior thesis at Princeton University, Mackey explored the aesthetic choices Baraka made during this transition and how it affected his reading of American art and culture. Baraka's "conversion" certainly made an impact on Mackey and most young African American writers who followed his work closely and were well versed in the debate as to whether art was to be Western influenced and ornamental or rooted in African American culture and designed to effect socio/political change. When Baraka left the Village and became an advocate for the black aesthetic movement, Mackey was "fascinated and somewhat disturbed by [Baraka's] aesthetic about-face, his insistence that modernist and postmodernist poetic innovations were somehow 'white' and ought to be disavowed" by black artists (Scroggins 169). Baraka himself commented that his earlier work was "a cloud of abstraction and disjointedness that was just whiteness" (*Black Magic* n.p.). His comment articulated the desire to create a work that was more immediately communicable to the African American community by placing particular emphasis on using the black vernacular and concrete imagery as a means of communicating cultural ideas. In *Target Study* (1965) and *Black Art* (1966), not only does Baraka's use of language change, but the work becomes less insular and self-absorbed.

In an interview with Ed Foster, Mackey addressed Baraka's importance to him as a writer.

> Amiri Baraka was important to me at a time when he was very much involved with a literary scene that was predominantly white that was in many instances otherwise white were it not for him . . . The separateness of the black literary tradition has to do with the segregation of black people, the subtle and not so subtle apartheid which is the history of this country and continues to be part of the social fabric and the assumptions that govern a great deal of social life, most of the social life in this country. I don't feel an obligation to assert a sense of a separate black literary tradition. (50)

It is apparent from this statement that Mackey sees his work rooted in a larger and more eclectic tradition. However, it should be emphasized that innovative black literary and jazz traditions are ones of absorption in which a variety of cultural tropes are re-configured. In "The Changing Same: Black Music in the Poetry of Amiri Baraka," Mackey examines how Baraka's earlier poetry mirrors the development of the "new thing" jazz and how it is subsequently related to the innovative developments of white avant-gardists as well. Most important, the essay shows how Baraka has used jazz music as an aesthetic guide not only in his literary productions but also in his way of critiquing American society.

Charles Olson, who also appeared in the Allen anthology, made a significant impact on Mackey's development as a writer, too. Olson's essay "Projective Verse" influenced the aesthetic vision of many of the experimental writers of Mackey's generation. Using breath to dictate line placement has musical resonance reflecting the manner in which a musician can modulate a particular tone by controlling his or her breath. This idea returns poetry back to its original, ancient impulse. Olson writes that projective verse should "register both the acquisitions of [the] ear and the pressures of the breath" (17). Various aspects of the poetics Olson outlined in his essay can be observed in the work of Mackey. What Olson brings to poetry is its original impulse as an oral performance in which sound is not ancillary to meaning. Olson's use of blank space becomes an important element in Mackey's work in which music and the visual aspect of word placement plays a prominent role. In "That Words Can Be on the Page," from *Discrepant Engagement,* Mackey discusses Olson's uses of space and emphasis on the individual word.

> The idea of words as objects lends itself . . . to the idea of poems as objects as well. One of the meanings of Williams's "no ideas but in things" is that a poem is first of all a thing, a constructed natural object, and only secondarily a platform for ideas, that objectification rather than ideation makes it a poem. Creeley, as a footnote to Williams's oft-quoted dictum, comments that "things are made out of words." The sense of words as physical things, building blocks or bricks, can be seen on Olson's often masonlike way of addressing them. (132)

In reading this passage, one should bear in mind that there is a correlation in jazz where the note, the manner in which it is played, the pitch, where it is in a composition, all take on similar significance in terms of creating the tone, mood, and effect of the text. Equally important is the architecture of the poem, how the work is structured in terms of the integral relationship between sound and symbol. Mackey handles word placement in a similar fashion to Olson. The use of blank space becomes a crucial element in his poetry because it is within those opaque confines that the individual word works as correspondent. For example, the third section of Mackey's collection *Eroding Witness* (1985) includes the following poem:

> and when the Moon struck
>
> soon, all sun put back
> inside the ground, the
> Way gone,
> would all go down
> to on all fours,
> wear shells and
>
> furs and chase
> our tracks (57)

By not placing the poem in a linear form, the poet emphasizes the importance of structure and sound. This slows down the reader's pace; that is, the poem cannot be quickly glossed over, forcing the reader to constantly return to the intricacy of the line breaks and the words chosen. In reading the poem and considering the blank space, the individual word takes on importance. As with Olson, the individual word becomes the brick. For the most part, the words are monosyllabic. This allows one to focus not only more directly on the meaning but also on the sound and visual quality. Close reading reveals use of alliteration in consonant sounds (way, would, soon, sun, shell, etc.). The poem reveals a particularly lyrical musicality that becomes more pronounced via the use of blank space. The scant use of punctuation and its appearance in key places within the poem contributes toward its musical tension. The majority of Mackey's poetry certainly makes use of this practice. What occurs is a slow unfolding in which the linear event is revealed. In reading the poem, one also becomes aware of its lyricism, the words extending like a jazz riff, through the ear, down the page. For Mackey, how the poem sounds is a key factor of its success. Charles Rowell said in an interview:

> I want to write poems that, when heard, appeal to the ear's desire for rhythm, for music, for the quickness of movement

> and the shifting of reference and register that is meaningful to a listening audience—that is not only meaningful in the thematic sense but meaningful in the sense that that's one of the things that exercises the ear. (Rowell 713)

Mackey's comment on "exercising the ear" echoes the title of Stephen Jonas's collection *Exercises for Ear.* It is apparent that these two poets share an interest in expanding the aural possibilities of poetry and seek to engage the listener/reader in the sonic qualities of language.

Olson's explorations into cultures outside of the Western tradition are important to Mackey. In the essay "Human Universe," Olson writes:

> The difficulty of discovery (in the close world which the human is because it is ourselves and nothing outside us, like the other) is, that definition is as much a part of the act as is sensation itself, in this sense, that life is preoccupation with itself, that conjecture about it is as much of its coming at us, its going on. In other words, we are ourselves both the instrument of discovery and the instrument of definition. (53)

The idea of being the instrument of discovery and definition finds deep resonance in Mackey's approach to poetry, where one of its most salient qualities is its erudition and knowledge of other cultures. The poems become vessels in which Mackey posits his reading of various texts and anthropological studies, creating work that is open ended in the sense where everything becomes material for the poem. Olson's exploration in ancient history, particularly the Mezzo American cultures of Mexico, and his use of that material for poetry further influenced Mackey's own explorations into cultures outside the West. It is the exploration and subsequent appropriation of diasporic traditions that allow Mackey's poems to be historical/cultural messages in a bottle—that is, a way to reclaim the past. What Mackey shares with Olson is that broad reach over different histories and cultures that is infused with the self, a kind of spiritual searching that is grounded in the intellect as well as the heart. Mackey has remarked that poetry has "become . . . an instrument to articulate not simply [his] personal experiences and emotional reactions to those experience but also [his] engagement with intellectual matters, with philosophic, aesthetic matters, with world traditions of various sorts and local traditions of various sorts" (Rowell 704). As Olson's immense serial work *The Maximus Poems* made use of local

Gloucester, Massachusetts, history, as well as Greek and maritime history, Mackey has continued to maintain similar focus on his serial length poem, *Song of the Andoumboulou.*

Another poet who influenced Mackey perhaps even more significantly than Charles Olson was Robert Duncan. Duncan, a poet of visionary proportions, was also a contributor to Allen's anthology. He was extremely well versed in ancient religious traditions and mysticism. His extensive readings in areas such as alchemy, Gnosticism, phenomenology, anthropology, and psychoanalysis form the basis of most of his work. When one encounters the poetry of Robert Duncan, one becomes aware of his desire to transform poetry from mere literary artifact into a work of potent spiritual impact. Duncan believed in the ancient link of words to power, and his poetry demonstrates the connection. His highly structured forms and their reliance on ancient mysticism indicate that literature is meant to do something more, that it is a mutual explorative event between the reader and the poet, initiate and priest. In the essay "The Truth and Life of Myth," from his book *Fictive Certainties,* Duncan is explicit about the importance of the creation of poetry by metaphorically linking it to the biblical story of the creation of humankind.

> The poem that moves me when I write is an active presence in which I work. I am not concerned with whether it is a good or a bad likeness to some convention men hold; for the word is for me living flesh, and the body of my own thought and feeling, my own presence, becomes the vehicle for the process of genetic information. (15)

Duncan's lifelong immersion and serious study in the occult and non-Western traditions is pronounced throughout his work. In his interview with Edward Foster, Mackey specifically describes Duncan's contribution to his poetics.

> Duncan is someone whose work is very important to me. One aspect of that importance is the fact that Robert was so insistent upon the heterodox tradition in the West, that marginalized tradition within the West which was in significant ways victimized by the very will to order . . . being imposed on other parts of the world. You know, the suppression of witchcraft, the suppression of the occult, the suppression of the irrational, so

> on and so forth. The way in which the heterodox lyric tradition in the West has tried to avail itself of those things that go counter to and are contrary to that very rationalist Cartesian order is one of the things that make the question of the lyric and of subjectivity not as cut and dried as some of the dismissals of the lyric and of subjectivity have tended to suggest. (49)

It is obvious that Mackey's fascination and engagement with religious and cultural practices within and outside of Western tradition makes him part of a heterodox tradition. It is often ironic that avant-garde artists draw from the past as they push the work forward to the future. Additionally, this commitment to a heterodox tradition can appear not only in the content of the poetry but in the form as well. Duncan, Olson, and several others of Mackey's innovative forefathers all changed the standard notions of what poetry is and what it should do by manipulating the appearance of the poem on the page. Certainly the heterodox tradition extends to Mackey's jazz influences as well—Albert Ayler, Sun Ra, Anthony Braxton, and Cecil Taylor—who all embraced not only musical traditions outside of mainstream America but spiritual traditions as well.

Mackey's eight poem series, *Septet for the End of Time* (1983), relies heavily on the importance of numerology in non-Western cultures, as well as on the work of French composer Olivier Messiasen's *Quartet for the End of Time* (1941). The series opens up with epigraphs from three different longstanding non-Western traditions. As in most literary works, the epigraph serves a crucial role in that it provides an overall guideline/direction to how the text should be encountered. Mackey's epigraphs also work as musical codas in the sense that the language (tone, theme) is often repeated, though fragmented, throughout the poem. The first of these epigraphs comes from Marcel Griaule's *Conversation with Ogotemmeli,* which recounts the practices of the Dogon people of West Africa.

> "Seven," said Ogotemmeli, "is the rank of the master of Speech; 1 + 7 = 8. The eighth rank is that of Speech itself. Speech is separate from the one who teaches it, that is, the seventh ancestor; it is the eighth ancestor. The eighth ancestor is the foundation of the speech which all the other ancestors used and which the seventh taught." (Mackey, *Eroding Witness* 80)

The Dogon are known particularly for their scientific knowledge and astronomical observations that were much later "discovered" by the West. The Dogon has influenced artists as diverse as Guy Davenport, Mel Edwards, Jay Wright, Cecil Taylor, and Jackie McLean. Not only does the Dogon tradition provide a lens for reading the text, but it also provides us with a "living link" to our ancestors. It is Mackey's contention that, through them, we inherit/learn speech/language.

> Language is passed on to us by people who are now in their graves and brings with it access to history, tradition, times and places that are not at all immediate to our own immediate and particular occasion whether we look at it individually and personally or whether we look at in a more collective way and talk about a specific community. (Foster 54)

John Cage and Anthony Braxton have effectively used the integration of numerology and modern music. With Cage, particularly, numbers are used to create "random compositions," in the sense that the ego of the artist is not involved in the creation of the text and the music comes from elsewhere. For Mackey, the poem is a sacred text, a living organism that is simultaneously controlled and not controlled by the artist and thus capable of imparting the wisdom of both the profound and the profane.

The second epigraph in the text is a quotation from the Koran in which numerology and sleep (dreaming) play prominent roles.

> Some will say: "The sleepers were three: Their dog was the fourth." Others, guessing at the unknown, will say: "They were five: Their dog was the sixth." And yet others: "Seven" Their dog was the eighth." (Mackey, *Eroding Witness* 80)

Mackey's use of the Koran also brings in literate traditions that have been marginalized by Western culture. The Koran is also important because, although it is a written text, it was said to have been first communicated orally by the angel Gabriel to the Prophet Muhammad. In most Islamic countries, the Koran is still transmitted orally. The transmission is particularly striking because of its musicality. Mackey's use of the epigraph also implies that the act of accurately witnessing an event is crucial in terms of numerology, in which symbolic significance is placed on particular numbers. Devin Johnston has observed that

Mackey's "invocations of music in his writing often function as markers of loss" (Johnston 563). The fragmentary and spatial quality of his work appears to indicate those missing spaces. By referencing mysticism, various religious traditions such as Islam and Christianity, and the cosmology of the Dogon, Mackey, like an alchemist, mixes myriad readings and simultaneously embraces the "outsider." Mackey's interest in the esoteric is not superficial, but rather a personal Weltanschauung that engages close examination. His desire to connect deeply with spiritual traditions is shared with Kaufman, Jonas, and Cortez.

The third epigraph, "Thy soul is provided like the star Septet," comes from the Pyramid Texts of Unas. By introducing numerological readings from three different traditions, all mainly rooted on the African continent, Mackey provides his readers with a numerically designed and multifaceted compass to uncover the poem's "meaning." Thus, as we read the text, we read it under the gaze of different numerical traditions. This practice is similar to Duncan's poetry in which the reader becomes part of the heterodox reading of the text.

The use of "noise" as an integral component of Mackey's poetry should not be underestimated. Mackey has remarked that most listeners of African American music usually recognize that instruments have a speechlike quality. "But built into that," Mackey adds, "is some kind of dissatisfaction with . . . the limits of conventionally articulate speech, verbal speech" and that one of the reasons music moves into nonspeech (moaning, humming, shouting, etc.) is that the "realm of conventionally articulate speech is not sufficient for saying what needs to be said" ("Cante Moro" 86). There are also the screams and honks, the unexplained language of the gut, found in the work of John Coltrane and Pharoah Sanders. Mackey tries to bring the "inarticulable" into his poetry, creating a work that transcends typical expectations. For example, "Song of the Andoumboulou: 29" begins

> He spoke in tongues, for a
>   time at least. Spoke in
> tongues until tongues' lipped
>   itch exhausted us.
>   C'rib
> whispered into one ear,
>   Crash commandeered the
>   other . . . (*Whatsaid Serif* 69)

Rather than use the bebop phrasing found in the work of Bob Kaufman and Jayne Cortez, Mackey's vocabulary is very specific, giving the reader the opportunity to follow the narrative. However, the references that he uses regarding language and the "spoken," point to the "inarticulable." Thus, "speaking in tongues" evokes the incomprehensible language of the spiritual. Even the barely audible whisper cannot be completely discerned.

Mackey's first collection of poetry, *Eroding Witness,* was selected for the National Poetry Series in 1985 by Michael S. Harper. The collection, which included Mackey's earlier works *Four for Trane* and *Septet for the End of Time,* demonstrates Mackey's debt not only to jazz and the Olson/Duncan/Baraka nexus, but also to the traditions of Voudoun, Dogon cosmology, and Santeria. The book explores cultural and mythical realities that demonstrate Mackey's engagement with the sacred. Scroggins writes that the work "evolves from narrow-lined, left-justified stanzas to a more open, exploratory form, [with] pages spreading across the age like seeds thrown by a sower" (186). Mackey's use of space allows the poem to reflect the disjunctive rhythms often found in modern jazz and places further emphasis on the tonal variants of single words. Consider here his variant use of the word "what," in "Song of the Andoumboulou: 20."

> I was the what-sayer.
> Whatever he said I would
> say so what.
> Boated whether
> we came by train or by
> bus . . . (22)

The repetition of the "w" consonant is strategically placed in order to emphasize its tonal quality. Thus, the sharp accented consonant propels the rhythmic drive of the passage.

Overall Mackey's work here demonstrates a particular allegiance to jazz. This connection is especially made to musicians like John Coltrane, Pharoah Sanders, Archie Shepp, Marion Brown, Ornette Coleman, Cecil Taylor, and several other exponents of the music labeled by Baraka as the "New Thing." Mackey has often defined his poetry in a jazz context, saying that he is "post-bop," in the sense of coming out of the black improvisational music and intellectual tradition that many African American artists were engaged with during the sixties, when he first began to take up writing on a more serious level. During this period, musicians like John Coltrane were developing compositions that blended African American music with music from India, Africa, and the Middle East. Musical collectives, like the Association for the Advancement of Creative Musicians (AACM), founded in Chicago by Muhal Richard Abrams, were making recordings that revitalized "the African-American musical sensibility through the oppositional language of modernism" and creating "the basis for a grand signifying riff on mainstream variations" (Radano, "Jazzin' the Classics" 80). Additionally, the AACM was a part of the black aesthetic movement (black arts) that sought to return black artistic production to its African cultural origins. According to Radano, African inspired cultural nationalism was the official platform of the collective.

> Creative Music was a dialect of the mother tongue, a creation with African origins that had been spiritually preserved in the slave culture of the United States. Evoking images of the musician-seer of tribal Africa, many AACM musicians spoke in priestly terms of black music's spiritualism, which, they believed, revealed a kinship with the ancient mythmakers, the original cultural guardians of black people. (87)

In section II of *Eroding Witness,* Mackey includes a series of poems titled "Song of the Andoumboulou." This series is of particular interest because Mackey infuses references to jazz alongside narratives of Africa and the Atlantic crossing. Mackey makes extensive use of Dogon cosmology, and the poems are narrated in a fashion that evokes the griot troubadour/historians of West Africa. This connection is very apparent when these poems are accompanied to music, as demonstrated on the recording *Strick: Song of the Andoumboulou 16–25.* The musicians, Royal Hartigan and Hafez Modirzadeh, use musical instruments from various cultures, giving Mackey's narrative an air of historical authenticity. In his performance, there is no sudden change in vocal inflection and Mackey speaks/sings the poems in a cadence that is consistent with the music's rhythmical pulse.[2] He begins this serial poem with an epigraph from Francois Di Dio's liner notes from *Les Dogon (Disques Ocora).*

> The song of the Andoumboulou is addressed to the spirits. For this reason the initiates, crouching in a circle, sing it in a whisper

> in the deserted village, and only the howling dogs and the wind disturb the silence of the night. (31)

The inclusion of epigraphs in Mackey's work provides directions as to how the work should be read. Generally, the works are spiritual in nature and are important in terms of understanding the religious nature of Mackey's work. He imbues his work with a sense of spirituality that implies that it is meant to be more than a mere "literary text" and is designed to reconnect the reader to African culture.

Writing "Song of the Andoumboulou: 6" was to have a particularly profound effect on Mackey's continual reading of the diaspora and issues concerning the creation of art. The poem is written in epistolary form and is addressed to the "Angel of Dust" by an author simply named "N."

> Tonight my mind struggles, for example, to reject all reminder of thought. It doubles up in some extravagant way as if to ask you back the question always implied by that scowl of yours. But the truth is that I don't even believe any such question exists. I see the things of your world as solid in a way the world of my "myriad words" uncoil can't even hope to be. Not "ethereal," mind you. Not insubstantial, unreal or whatever else. Only an other (possibly Other) sort of solidarity, as if its very underseams—or, to be more exact, those of its advent—sprouted hoofs. (50)

Mackey continued to explore the interplay between reality and language expressed in this poem by writing *Bedouin Hornbook* (1986), *Baghostus's Run* (1993), and *Atet A.D.* (2002). The three books are a continual series of letters written by N., a jazz musician and member of a band called the Mystic Horn Society.[3] In both works, Mackey displays an astute awareness regarding the role language and music play in the creation of one's aesthetic and cultural values. Improvisation as a means of achieving a deeper connection to music is expressed throughout the letters. Its importance is particularly evident in this opening letter from Bedouin Hornbook.

> __________14.VI.78
>
> Dear Angel of Dust,
>
> You should've heard me in the dream last night. I found myself walking down a sidewalk and came upon an open manhole off

> to the right out of which came (or strewn around which lay) the disassembled parts of a bass clarinet. Only the funny thing was that, except for the bell of the horn, all the parts looked more like plumbing fixtures than like parts of a bass clarinet. Anyway, I picked up a particularly long piece of "pipe" and proceeded to play. I don't recall seeing anyone around but somehow I knew the "crowd" wanted to hear "Naima." I decided I'd give it a try. In any event, I blew into heaven knows what but instead of "Naima" what came out was Shepp's solo on his version of "Cousin Mary" on the Four for Trane album—only infinitely more gruffly resonant and varied and warm. (I even threw a few licks of my own.) The last thing I remember is coming to the realization that what I was playing already existed on a record. I could hear scratches coming from somewhere in back and to the left of me. This realization turned out, of course, to be what woke me up. (1)

I have quoted this passage at length to show how Mackey imaginatively uses improvisation not only to apply to the manipulation of sound but to demonstrate how physical objects (pipes) can be manipulated as well. In this letter, N. relates a dream to the Angel of Dust. What is interesting about N.'s narrative is his insistence on the auditory events ("You should've heard me in the dream"). The instrument he fashions comes from underground (manhole). This is an apt metaphor for the subversive nature of the music in that it comes from the "underground," often away from the public eye. The dream continues until N. realizes that his performance already exists on record, that it is unoriginal. Once the act of improvisation is lost, the moment of awakening occurs. Perhaps Mackey means to indicate that there is an integral link between our dreamscapes and our artistic creations. Concerning Mackey's use of music in these two books, Mark Scroggins has written that the "melody and rhythms the instruments play, as interpreted by N., become inseparable from the ideas and emotions with which the poem deals" and that there is an "astonishing marriage of narrative, critical theory, and high-spirited wordplay" (187).

For Mackey, "new jazz" was an important touchstone because it made "a significant break . . . with the tradition of the black musician as an embodiment of instantaneity, instinct, pure feeling, in some unmediated way uncomplicated by reflection and intellect" (Foster 56). Mackey's comment is very revealing. The musicians who came out of the "new thing" certainly went beyond the role of mere nightclub entertainers. Artists like Archie Shepp, Cecil Taylor, and Sun Ra were accomplished poets as well. By demonstrating the complexity of African American intellectual thought, the new jazz was trying to combat the facile public image of jazz artists as mere entertainers. In Mackey's work it is difficult to pinpoint a singular narrative or coherent story. Often the "voices" that appear in his work do not proceed in a singular fashion. Scroggins writes

> They are complex and initially bewildering works, for they proceed on a basis of complex contemporaneity and heterogeneous, perhaps indeterminate origins. There is a dense web of intertextual reference running throughout Mackey's poems: references to other texts, to musical compositions (especially jazz), and to his own previous writings. (183)

It is precisely these qualities that Scroggins describes in Mackey's work that can also be found in free jazz. Ekkehard Jost defines the music in a similar fashion.

> With the advent of free jazz, a large number of divergent personal styles developed. Their only agreement lay in a negation of traditional norms . . . The initiators of the free jazz drew widely different consequences from the renunciation of harmonic-metrical patterns, of the regulative force of the beat, and of the structural principles of the "jazz piece." As a result, the conventions that arose in free jazz with regard to instrumental technique, ensemble playing, formal organization, etc. were never universally binding as those in traditional areas of jazz. (10)

Mackey's unique aesthetic makes it difficult to generalize his use of jazz materials. The next two poems that I will examine indicate a direct debt to jazz by their dedication.

Next to Charlie Parker, John Coltrane has been the most popular subject of jazz poetry.[4] Most such poems were written between 1967 and 1969, after Coltrane's death, and are often poetic responses to particular musical pieces, his personality, or his artistic legacy. The poem "'John Coltrane Arrived with an Egyptian Lady'" from *Eroding Witness* (1985) shows how Mackey goes beyond mere jazz personality portraiture to develop a complex historical narrative.

no sheet of sound enshroud
the Fount of the fevered
Brook becoming one
with God's Eye, not
a one of these notes

come near to the brunt
of the inaudible
note I've been reach-
ing towards

To whatever
dust-eyed giver
of tone to whatever
talk, to whatever slack
jaws drawn against bone

To whatever
hearts abulge with
unsourced light, to whatever
sun, to whatever moist
inward meats

of love

Tonight I'll bask
beneath an arch of
lost
voices, echo
some Other place
Nut's nether suns,
These
notes' long fingers gathered
come to grips of gathered
cloud, connected lip
to unheard of
tongue (66–67)

The title of the poem immediately establishes a connection between Coltrane and Africa. The significance of Egypt as an important center of spirituality and mysticism is integral to understanding not only the poem but also the music of John Coltrane, who expanded his musical repertoire by exploring music from India, Africa, and the Middle East and also became interested in their religious and spiritual aspects. For example, albums such as *Ascension, A Love Supreme,* and *Interstellar Space* were extended musical prayers. By introducing an Egyptian woman into the poem's title, Mackey simultaneously alludes to the connection between African Americans and the continent, and especially to Egyptian mythology. Therefore, Coltrane's connection to Africa is inextricably linked, and his music is viewed as part of the African continuum that Ishmael Reed talks about in his earlier quoted comment concerning the black avant-garde.

The poem begins with a musical line, "no sheet of sound enshroud." Music critics like Ira Gitler described Coltrane's music as being "sheets of sound." Grover Sales likened Coltrane's later work to a "torrential downpour." Although these descriptions were not intended to be negative, some Trane enthusiasts saw them as labels that implied there was no forethought that went into the composition, that the notes were simply laid out and fell out of the sky like rain, thus undermining the intellectual complexity that underlies the structure of Coltrane's work. By alluding to Gitler's description in the opening line of the poem, Mackey presents a familiar image of Coltrane's musical prowess. This image is meant to recall the cleansing effect of rain and, by extension, the music. This connection places Coltrane's performance in a spiritual rather than a secular context. By alluding to the spiritual nature of Coltrane's music, Mackey is able to manipulate our reading of the text. In addition, Mackey establishes a musical line that makes use of assonance in words like "sheet," "sound," and "enshroud." This creates an even flowing rhythmic quality to the text that allows the reader to enter its imagery/ideas more easily. Had Mackey created a disjunctive opening, our entrance into the text would have been more difficult. This practice is mirrored in John Coltrane's music. He would often open a piece with a brief lyrical passage before entering the "free jazz" space of his performances. The alliteration continues in the next two lines, "the Fount of the fevered," with Mackey employing different consonant sounds. Although our entrance into the poem is made easy by the use of alliteration, the images Mackey conjures are those from Egyptian mythology. Our familiarity with Egyptian religion comes mainly from the hieroglyphic texts found on the burial chambers. This connection is established in the first line by the use of "sheets" and "enshroud," recalling the mummification process. Additionally there is reference to the underground river, "fevered Brook," which was used to transport the soul of the dead. Although Mackey establishes the connection to the Egyptian underworld, he is saying what the music is not, using a phrase from African American vernacular, "not a one." Thus, the opening line becomes a command. This is apparent when one considers the text to be a "belated prayer," as indicated above.

The closing line of the first strophe, "not / a one of these notes," opens up the possibility of a dual reading. Due to the absence of punctuation, it could be read as the closing line of the first stanza, making "come near" a new declarative sentence. This interpretation works if we are to read the first line as a command. On the other hand, the two lines could be seen as part of the same sentence. If so, this linkage creates musical continuity within the poem that does not necessarily disrupt the text's narrative movement. How we choose to read these two lines is significant because they come at a crucial moment within the text, where the "I" (speaker) is introduced. It is in this strophe that we learn that the speaker is reaching toward a particular note as well. The fact that the note is "inaudible" addresses Coltrane's musical exploration. There have been several comments made by musicians like Rashid Ali and Pharoah Sanders to the effect that Coltrane played so many notes because he was trying to exhaust the instrument and find the "right one." In terms of spiritual exploration, finding the "right one" is often an ongoing process. When one tries to reach the "inaudible note," the process of selecting that note is infinite. There is irony and contradiction in the line "come near to the brunt / of the inaudible / note I've been reach- / ing towards," for how can a musical note exist and be inaudible?

The cadence established by the repetition of "whatever" in the next two stanzas enables the text to maintain its rhythmic regularity. By beginning the opening line of the stanza a bit away from the linear perimeters of the left margin, the preceding space initiates a breath or pulse before the riff-like line begins. The use of consonant endings (er) in words like "whatever" and "giver" throughout the stanza and their strategic placement at the end of each line make the two passages musically compatible. Additionally, the repetition of the prepositional "to" maintains the prayerlike tenor of the text. However, what is paramount to understanding the poem is that "whatever" allows for the incorporation of various spiritual sources. Mackey thus veers away from what has often become a standard Afrocentric reading of Coltrane, demonstrating that the music is drawn from many cultural traditions.

Following the two stanzas, the speaker locates him- or herself: "Tonight I'll bask / beneath an arch of / lost / voices." The reader is presented with an unnamed historical legacy (lost voices) that can range from the "voices" of individual musicians to those of the ancestors. What is crucial here is not necessarily the type of voice but the awareness that they are there, located somewhere ("some Other place") in the cosmos, as a canopy to the living. The lost voices could be the spaces or silences between Nut's star-filled body, the Egyptian sky goddess who draped herself over the Earth. The poem's closing is ambiguous and open ended with the conclusion that the music comes from somewhere else, thus affirming Mackey's reading of jazz as a mystical and spiritual endeavor. The closing "connected lip / to unheard of / tongue" projects the music back onto parts of the body. "Tongue" can also refer to language, connecting music with the "unheard" language of the gods. Mackey's use of space within the contrapuntal movement of the poem is significant in that it endeavors to capture the often disjointed and pulsating rhythms of Coltrane's later work.[5]

Another poem that responds to the spiritual/mystical qualities of the new jazz is this one, dedicated to jazz great Pharoah Sanders:

Capricorn Rising
for Pharoah Sanders

I wake up mumbling, "I'm
not at the music's
mercy," think damned
if I'm not, but
keep the thought
to myself.

Sweet mystic beast on the
outskirts of earth,
unruly airs, an awkward
birth
bruises the bell of its
horn . . .

Life after life each like it
was endlessly yet
to arrive yet
already there, a
thin bread of duress,
a
sea-weary drift of boatlifted
Haitians . . .
The hiss of
the sea
whispering words of
power,
pinkish kef-pesh tools
part the lips of the
dead.
Lacking teeth but licking
the air for some
taste of Heaven,
hungered by
its name, what of
it I refuse
forks an angel's tongue,
what of it I refuse awakes
the wide-eyed
stone (83–84)

The title of the poem comes from a recording by tenor saxophonist Pharoah Sanders. Sanders is known primarily for playing with John Coltrane on several recording dates and public performances. Sanders was an important contributor to such "new thing" compositions as *Ascension, Om, Meditations,* and *Live at the Village Vanguard Again,* most of which were recorded in 1965. With a sound similar to Albert Ayler, Sanders was recognized for the often-harsh screams and speech-like quality of his music. Coltrane had often remarked that what Sanders brought to his performances were his spirituality and desire to get to the "human foundations of the music." After Coltrane's death in 1967, Sanders went on to make several recordings (*Tauhid, Journey to the One, Rejoice,* and others) that continued and expanded Coltrane's exploration of Asian, Middle Eastern, and African musical sources. Sanders's music was also particularly popular among the black artists who were part of the black aesthetic movement, mainly because of his interest in and placement of ancient African history as a primary propellant for the spiritual direction of the music.

According to astrology, Capricorn, the tenth sign, is often depicted as a half goat, half fish being that represents the dual nature of land and sea. The goat is also a symbol of lust and creativity. Mackey makes use of the various symbols associated with Capricorn throughout the poem in such a way that an awareness of the implications of mystical traditions outside of contemporary western culture becomes important to our understanding. The poem opens with the speaker having just awoken from either a deep sleep or a trance. Immediately upon awakening, he denies having been influenced by the "music's mercy" but knows that it is not the case. Mackey employs alliteration by using the "m" consonant ("mumbling," "music," "mercy," "myself," "I'm") in order to propel the text's rhythmic drive. There are several indications in this first stanza that the music is a conduit to spiritual power; however, it appears prudent that the speaker conceal his musical possession.

The next stanza begins as an evocation to a "mythic beast on the / outskirts of earth," obviously alluding to the constellation Capricornus, which can be seen in the equatorial region of the Southern Hemisphere. Thus, the reader is provided a locale based on celestial navigation/sightings. Mackey simultaneously alludes to Pharoah Sanders's instrument, "bruises the bell of its / horn" and the "mythic beast," suggesting that life evolves from the sea and music evolves from the horn. The repetition of "b" ("beast," "birth," "bruises," "bell") performs a similar function as "m" in the first stanza. This creates a kind of opening refrain, or theme, before the poem begins to undergo a change in rhythmic patterns. In the third stanza, the words "life," "yet," and "a" are repeated twice, condensing the rhythmic pattern and perhaps leading toward a more improvisatory moment within the poem. This change certainly becomes apparent when one notices how Mackey has created more blank space within the rest of the poem. The use of similar sounding words becomes tighter: "drift" and "lifted," "Haitian" and "hiss," "whispering" and "words," "power," "pinkish," "kef-pesh," and "parts." The use of alliteration and assonance becomes integral to the musical quality of the text. By placing such studied emphasis on rhythm and sound, Mackey additionally places further emphasis on place and culture. The specifics of the locale are addressed. A group of Haitians are performing a sacrifice to Agwe, sovereign of the seas. In *Divine*

Horsemen: The Living Gods of Haiti, Maya Deren describes part of the ritual that may give us more insight into the poem. The initiates have placed a sacrificial ram and other foods on a barque and have located Agwe's home beneath the sea.

> In that split second, when the water lay almost level with the rail, the men slid the barque on to the surface of the sea. Our boat lurched and righted itself and there, below us, and already behind, the barque was drifting swiftly away in our backwash. It looked incredibly lovely, the high-piled offerings, crowned with the sparkling white cake, drifting in the deep blue of the sea. As we watched it silently, it seemed to hesitate to a stop, and then, as if a great hand had reached up from below and grasped it, it disappeared abruptly into the quiet water. (130)

The poem closes with the repetition of the phrase "what of it," which not only maintains the rhythmic flow of the text but also underscores the urgency of the speaker's seeking to come to terms with the spiritual mystery of the event. Thus, the poem responds on three levels: to the spiritual interests and performance of Pharoah Sanders, to the mystical indeterminacy of music, and to the numinous power of the sacred ritual conducted by the initiates. Mackey's poem successfully integrates all three levels to create a text that captures the spirituality found in jazz music.[6]

Nathaniel Mackey's use of free jazz in poetry seems to mirror all of the aesthetic variants found in the music. Mackey's ability to reference cross-cultural sources in his poetry instills within the reader moments of dislocation. Like the complicated styling of innovative musicians such as Anthony Braxton, Cecil Taylor, Albert Ayler, Archie Shepp, and John Coltrane, Mackey refuses to compromise his poetic vision. He does not present work that uses jazz in a simplistic, solely musical fashion. The strength of his work comes from his ability to infuse within it the spiritual qualities that drive the music and enable it to step out of the secular. Mackey's use of short lines and disjointed spacing creates texts that are complex in their narrative structures. The manner in which Mackey manipulates the structural forms of poetry, by infusing within them the "chaotic" lines and timing often associated with the "new thing," enable him to fashion texts that have a variety of ethnomusic references. However, most important is the reclamation of

African culture that occurs in his work. This practice certainly speaks to the work of Coltrane and others who sought and studied musical traditions outside Western culture. Thus, when encountering Mackey's poetry, one must continue to take into account its close proximity to jazz's experimental impulse that not only advocates the new but also reaches back to the past.

CODA

The Mixtery of Jazz Poetry

Notes is good enough for you people, but us likes a mixtery.
—An ex-slave from the Georgia Sea Islands

For me, jazz works primarily as a kind of discovery, as a way for me to discover the emotional mystery behind things. It helps me to get to a place I thought I had forgotten.
—Yusef Komunyakaa

The jazz poem has infused in American literature a more heightened awareness of the inherent connection between music and poetry. Most important, it has reaffirmed the key role African American culture has played in the development of a literature that emphasizes the importance not only of the literal meaning of words but also of the musicality of language. This book has focused on examining innovations in jazz poetry through the work of Bob Kaufman, Stephen Jonas, Jayne Cortez, and Nathaniel Mackey. True, there are several aesthetic elements that these writers share: rhythm, improvisation, dissonance, etc. However, what also links them is their spiritual connection to the music. In the introduction to a festschrift celebrating the artistry of musician and composer Anthony Braxton, Graham Lock discusses the word "mixtery."

> What fascinated me about "mixtery" was its connotations, simultaneous and inextricable, of "mixture" and "mystery." Here, it seemed, was a word that neatly encapsulated several major characteristics of African-American creative music. "Mystery" covered both the spiritual aspects and the ritual functions of the music; "mixture" suggested the complex network of gradations the music could spin between such apparent

> polarities as improvised/composed, what's new/what's in the tradition, external influences/native lineages. (9)

Lock's reading of "mixtery" can be applied to the jazz-influenced poetry of these writers. The creative work of these four poets expands the aesthetic possibilities not only of poetry but of music as well and contributes to the continual and broadening role African American culture plays in defining postmodern literature. These writers have expanded the innovative and improvisational impulses of jazz by adapting them to literature in a manner that facilitates a critique of Western culture. Their work celebrates the salient qualities of an art form that has become inclusive by drawing on other ethnomusical traditions. Kaufman, Jonas, Cortez, and Mackey are all part of a tradition that uses several of the standard musical tools of jazz to craft a work that is distinctly individual while also voicing the collective consciousness of the African diaspora.

African American poetry contains a long historical legacy of early poets, such as Jupiter Hammon, Phillis Wheatley, and Lucy Terry, who all had in common the desire to critique and comment upon the black condition in the United States. Although these poets used the European literary forms of their time, it was their choice of subject matter that made their work vastly different from their European counterparts. For several African American writers and artists, there has always been a continual gaze toward Africa as well as the "re-membered" experience of the diaspora. It has been this perpetual connection to history, particularly how it has been expressed through the musical forms of black America that has kept the collective memory alive. During slavery, the various ethnic groups that were separated in order to suppress any linguistic communication had to improvise and be inventive in order to preserve the community. Music played an integral role in forming and maintaining a cohesive community among African Americans. As outlined in the first chapter, banning the drum subsequently led to communication through handclaps or feet stomping in order to preserve the cultural connections. It was the dancing in New Orleans's Congo Square, with its gestures of arms and legs evoking the forbidden gods and thus bringing them to the Americas, that would later appear in the work of modern dance innovators like Katherine Dunham, the Nicholas Brothers, Alvin Ailey, and Bill T. Jones. It was the ancient Mandean hymns, like "Naima," remembered and sung, that would later find their way into the saxophone of John Coltrane. It was English, the new language, and the imposition of antiliteracy laws that denied Africans access to Western ideas that opened the way for an inventive vernacular that retained the improvisational and rhythmic drive of Africa and later enabled African American poets like Sonia Sanchez, Amiri Baraka, and Ted Joans to continue to critique American society and communicate the historical legacies of African and African American culture to their listeners/readers.

In a symposium on jazz and poetry, Yusef Komunyakaa remarked on the importance of the continual infusion of music in African American culture.

> We refused to become only an antithesis—lost and incomplete. So music was the main thread that linked us to the future, was a process of reclaiming ourselves. Being in motion—improvisation, becoming—this was the root of our creativity, our accentuation of the positive even when the negative pervaded. Our music became an argument with the odds, a nonverbal articulation of our pathos. In this sense, even the blues dirge is an affirmation—the theft of possibility, words made flesh. Music has always been the bridge to what Houston Baker calls "the journey back," this needful voyage back to the source, the spawning bed of our cultural existence. (Kelly 646)

The role that music played, what Komunyakaa refers to as "nonverbal articulation of our pathos," was later to be verbally articulated through poetry. Thus, poetry manages to combine the aural qualities of music and the textual qualities of literature. The manner in which jazz poetry functions has been expressed differently among white writers of the "lost" and "beat" generations who used jazz as a way to describe their rootlessness. Perhaps what they saw in the music was a lack of form or an alternate aesthetic choice compared to the conservative verse of the academy. The outsider status that they placed on jazz may have been in part due to their own sense of isolation. For the people who are "in" the music and the culture that it springs from, the labels of "alternative" and "outsider" are problematic. Whatever the reasons poets of various ethnicities have for employing jazz as an aesthetic medium, certain commonalties prevail in their work. Among the various ways in which jazz poetry is defined, the commonly shared elements are the refrain, the emphasis on tonal quality and the spontaneity of improvisation. There are several other poetics that make use of musical form. For example, the Andalusian Cante Jondo (referred to as "Deep Song") and the traditional gypsy chants from Spain with their North African origins and deep emotions are remarkably similar to the blues and have been explored in the poetry of Frederico Garcia Lorca, Stephen Jonas, Nathaniel Mackey, and many others. Diane Wakoski and Louis Zukofsky have used Western musical forms, such as the polyphonic fugue, with its variations on themes and tonal colors. Non-Western musical traditions, such as the Indian Raga, have figured prominently in the work of Allen Ginsberg.

In the essay, "Fabulating Jazz," Frederick Garber discusses the effect of jazz on modernist art forms. In particular, he examines films like *Young Man with a Horn* (1950), *Round Midnight* (1986), *Bird* (1988), and *Mo' Better Blues* (1990), showing how these works characterize jazz and its performers. Garber argues convincingly that jazz music is "both auratic and textual" and that when soloists perform they draw upon the music's history (73). His examination of how the aural and textual qualities of the music have been applied to film is particularly insightful and can be similarly applied to the work of jazz poets. Thus, the same terminology used to describe the music can effectively describe the poetry as well. As the critical discourse on jazz poetry continues to develop, perhaps it would be appropriate to use a new vocabulary that comes directly out of the music, as opposed to the traditional terminology applied to literature. Throughout this work I have often analyzed the poetry in jazz musical terms such as "scat," "riff," and "beat" in order to underline the profound impact the music has made in the construction of these texts. For a jazz poem to be successful, it is essential that the poet's ear be tuned to the musicality of particular words and phrases and that there be an additional awareness of their instrument counterparts. "How you sound," Baraka once remarked to indicate that the aural nature of a work of literature is of prime importance. Is the language formal and stilted or does it evoke the often illusive and abstract "jazz feel?" When poets like Jayne Cortez or Nathaniel Mackey directly refer to musicians or compositions in their poetry, they are calling on our aural memories. These memories become adjunct to the poetry so that when we read, we subconsciously recall the music. Thus, a jazz poem that successfully emphasizes the aural qualities of a text blurs the distinction between poetry and music.

The textuality of the work is especially important because it echoes the early applications of the form. For example, it is almost inconceivable that poets like Stephen Jonas or Bob Kaufman would have used the musicality inherent in the black vernacular so skillfully had it not been for the pioneering work of poets like Paul Laurence Dunbar, Langston Hughes, or Sterling A. Brown. The innovative contributions of these literary ancestors, in terms of subject matter, language, and form, weave through the work of each subsequent generation, enabling each writer to extend and push the form further. The same correlation can be made for the contributions of early musicians such as Buddy Bolden and Louis Armstrong. Where, for example, would Lester Bowie or Wynton Marsalis be without their groundwork?

The poets examined in this book are similar in terms of how the music informs their work and particularly in their desire to push further away from the boundaries of a predictable narrative or linear form. Their poetry provides fascinating examples as to how the two art forms of poetry and music can work in tandem. It is important to emphasize that all of these poets were well acquainted or worked directly with jazz musicians, thus providing them with a more intimate knowledge of the music. Generally speaking, Bob Kaufman and Stephen Jonas primarily employ bebop cadences and tonal shifts to structure their work, while Jayne Cortez and Nathaniel Mackey make more use of the highly stylized vocabulary of hard bop and free jazz. While Kaufman and Cortez's poetic line appears to be spontaneous, making use of a more surreal vocabulary, Jonas and Mackey's lines are more studied and emphasize the concrete, though through different means. Mackey emphasizes the mystical and esoteric, while Jonas emphasizes the vernacular. However, these poets are not bound by a particular jazz style, and the range of their work shows an intimacy with the historical developments of jazz.

It is unfortunate that there is a lack of general popular and critical awareness of the innovative work of these poets. As the jazz poetry canon gets formed and the works of "mainstream" poets such as Jack Kerouac, Hayden Carruth, Michael Harper, and William Matthews take their places in the newly constructed pantheon, avant-garde writers such as Clark Coolidge, Will Alexander, Kofi Natambu, Ed Roberson, and several others are pushed to the periphery. This book aims to provide a sensitive reading of four poets who have written some of the most innovative and formally complex poetry in response to jazz. The trend to create an "unthreatening" canon is blatantly obvious in the recent resurgence of interest in the beat poets and the prominence of white writers such as Jack Kerouac and Allen Ginsberg over the innovations of African American writers such as Bob Kaufman, Amiri

Baraka, and Ted Joans. In *The Beat Generation,* a recent compilation by Rhino records, recordings of poetry performances by Bob Kaufman, Amiri Baraka, and Ted Joans are inextricably left out, while the often less engaging work of Kenneth Rexroth, Kenneth Patchen, and Rod McKuen are included. As Yusef Komunyakaa has pointed out:

> Jazz shaped the Beat aesthetic, but that movement seemed a privilege only whites could afford. Blacks, fighting for inclusion, didn't have to ostracize themselves voluntarily. Of course, this was a cultural paradox. To many the Beat Movement was nothing more than the latest minstrel show in town with the new Jim Crows and Zip Coons, another social club that admitted hardly any women or blacks. Yet they said that Charlie Parker was their Buddha. (Kelly 654)

Komunyakaa's acidic remark is on target, and the problem intensifies when those few blacks and women who were a part of the movement are given superficial treatment or are completely ignored.

The continual lack of a significant body of critical work on the poetry of Bob Kaufman is unconscionable. Kaufman, whose work has received high critical acclaim in Europe, but is missing from the Riverside and Norton anthologies on African American literature, was one of the most original poets to come out of the so-called beat movement. His contribution to jazz poetry certainly eclipses the work of Kerouac, whose use of bebop was often contrived. Not only did Bob Kaufman's poetry contain the rhythmic and improvisatory gestures of the music but so did his life. Kaufman's shamanistic vision and his refusal to compromise his reading of the American political and social landscape was heroic. He was a copacetic poet who, although quite capable of producing conventional verse, refused to do so and crafted work that reflected the chaos and brutality of his environment.[1] His experiments, which created a vocabulary that emphasized the abstract and tonal qualities of the music, as in the poem "Crootey Songo," foreshadowed the work of the language poets and other schools of the avant-garde. Assessing Kaufman's contributions to jazz poetry, Sascha Feinstein wrote that he "resculpted the muscular lines of bebop into verbal jazz imagery" (105). Kaufman's poetry also springs from a vocalese lineage established by musicians like Harry "the Hipster" Gibson, Slim Gaillard, Cab Calloway, Leo Watson, and others. By using language that reflected music, Kaufman demonstrated that the poem, whether heard aloud or read, could reclaim complex musical cadences deeply rooted in African American culture.

The innovative approach to jazz poetry expressed in the work of Stephen Jonas is strikingly similar to Kaufman's in terms of their shared interest in bebop. However, Jonas's contribution to the form entails a heightened, more "studied" sense of the tonal qualities of words. His attention to the musical cadences found in the African American vernacular and their rhythmical connection to jazz music makes his work exemplary. Like Kaufman, Jonas also lived his life as an outsider, improvising and negotiating his way through a society that sought to define him. Fortunately, writers like Joseph Torra and Aldon Lynn Nielsen have sought to reassert Jonas's importance as an innovator of American poetry. However, the continual lack of a substantive body of critical work that addresses the political and musical aspects of his poetry is appalling. Jonas's best poetry shows a writer willing to take risks by bringing, unfiltered and directly to the page, the language of the streets. His work has made a profound impact by expanding the musical possibilities of poetry. By making jazz such an integral part of his aesthetic, he directs our attention toward the musicality inherent in the African American vernacular. Armed with Williams's theory about the "variable foot" and Olson's emphasis on breath, Jonas wrote *Exercises for Ear,* which remains one of the most seminal works constructed in the jazz idiom. Jonas placed importance on the refrain in jazz poetry not just by simply using repetition but also by varying line breaks and spelling in order to bring out the subtleties of tone inherent in the music. Thus, his work articulates the African American cultural flow and enables listeners/readers to see and hear beyond the limitations of contemporary verse.

Jayne Cortez's reputation as a "performance poet" and her outstanding collaborative work with jazz musicians have continued to express the interconnectedness between music and poetry that was pioneered earlier by Langston Hughes. With the exception of D. H. Melhem's *Heroism in the New Black Poetry* and Aldon Lynn Nielsen's *Black Chant,* both of which contain a discussion of Cortez's work, it is disappointing that little has been written on Cortez's ability to synthesize her political agenda through the filters of jazz and poetry. Cortez uses jazz poetry as a vehicle to advocate resistance to political repression and racial injustice. Her familiarity with past and current musical trends have led to a body of work that displays an adept use of various rhythmical cadences to articulate the rich tapestry of the African diaspora.

Currently, Cortez is one of the few jazz poets to have recorded work on a major jazz label.[2] Her recordings and performances have won more audiences for poetry. Cortez has a musician's ear tuned to the intricacy of sound, and her poetry reflects a unique ability to draw attention to the rhythmic and historical legacies of jazz. It is her expansive vocabulary and strikingly visual imagery that infuse the genre with a tonal energy that veers it away from the clichéd and predictable narratives that is typical of most jazz poetry.

Although his poetry has been included in *The Norton Anthology of African American Literature* and is the subject of two special issues of the journals *Talisman* and *Callaloo,* Nathaniel Mackey has received less critical attention than his work deserves. The manner in which he uses jazz to inform his poetics is innovative and complex. Mackey's work reflects the continual change of the African American cultural landscape, and his work shows an engagement with several of the free jazz innovators who tend to avoid formal musical constraints. His use of disjunctive cadence and variable form that moves according to the rhythmic dictates of the poem creates a body of work that may at first appear inaccessible but yields "understanding" after several close readings. The esoteric imagery that Mackey infuses into his poetry instills in the reader a desire to explore other less familiar facets of African and African American culture. Additionally, it is the manner in which he uses jazz that adds to the cross-cultural mix of influences and brings out some of the most exciting experimental qualities of African American literature.

There continues to be a renewal of interest in jazz poetry, evidenced by the publication of three anthologies, *The Jazz Poetry Anthology, Moment's Notice,* and *The Second Set,* discussed earlier in this book. However, little critical effort has been made to examine how jazz has been used as a literary aesthetic.[3] There are two notable exceptions. Sascha Feinstein's *Jazz Poetry: From the 1920s to the Present* approaches the development of jazz poetry chronologically. Feinstein's historical survey is important because he introduces a fairly broad spectrum of American poets who have used the music. Aldon Lynn Nielsen's *Black Chant: Languages of African-American Postmodernism* focuses primarily on African American poetry from the 1950s to the present. The book highlights a variety of literary techniques employed by several significant African American postmodernists and shows how these writers made use of African American music. Both books have provided an insightful critical and historical view of how jazz has been used in poetry, thus laying down the necessary groundwork for further research.

Recent books like Michael Jarrett's *Drifting on a Read: Jazz as a Model for Writing* and Clark Coolidge's *Now It's Jazz: Writings on Kerouac and the Sounds* have approached literary criticism in interesting ways. Jarrett's book provides an insightful critique on how a jazz aesthetic has been applied to the writing of novels. Looking at prose sources, recordings, album covers, and liner notes, Jarrett incorporates all of these facets in his critical response, thus creating a musical and porous text that becomes improvisational as well as instructional and didactic. Coolidge's book works in a similar way but is more fragmented and personal in its response to the musical qualities of Jack Kerouac's prose. Thus, both books offer new ways of looking at and writing about jazz-inspired work.

More attention is being paid to younger poets like Harryette Mullen (Nathaniel Mackey's former student), who uses a jazz aesthetic to great effect. Her poetry has appeared in the canonical *Anthology of Modern American Poetry,* published by Oxford University Press. She has described her poetics as being a "traditional, eclectic, folksy, trashy, classical, avant-garde, worldly, naive, unorthodox, spiritual, polymorphously perverse, mammy-made, jig-rig, rube goldberg operation" (Mullen, "Telegraphs" 5). It is obvious from her description that Mullen is unsatisfied with one succinct definition of her poetry. She shares this commonality with several musicians who feel the same way about the word "jazz" as a terminal description of their work. Mullen has been influenced by the work of writers Gertrude Stein, M. B. Tolson, and Jean Toomer, and musicians Ma Rainey and Charles Mingus. The density and complexity of her work shows the influences from a wide variety of sources. From commercial jingles to song lyrics, from the language of the African American oratory to the vernacular of the street, Mullen blends and infuses her poetry with an energy that evokes the rich connection between pop and African American culture and shows how these distinctions become blurred. Her collection *Muse and Drudge* (1995), which she has described as a "praise song to women of the African Diaspora," is a verse poem composed in quatrains that uses unpredictable rhymes and rhythms. In doing so, Mullen has created a work that incorporates some of the aesthetic ideas of the free jazz movement in which time signatures become more spontaneous and therefore unpredictable. In the essay "Telegraphs from a Distracted Sibyl," Mullen discusses the collection.

> *Muse & Drudge* (also known as "Mules and Drugs") seems to be an attempt on my part to return to a more-or-less recognizably "colored," "negro," "black," or "african-american" base of folk-street-blues-based riffs, rap, and rhetoric, without returning to the specifically located subjectivity of my earlier work. I wanted to use all that I've learned since I strayed from the beaten to the off-beat path, while still keeping my promise to meet the devil at the crossroads, and walk a mile in some other body's down-or-upbeat sneakers, as the case may be, with plenty of word-play along the way. (5)

With her emphasis on "riffs" and "off-beat," Mullen uses language that is particular to jazz. Using a style similar to "quoting," in which a musician may musically allude to several pieces during the performance of one composition, Mullen skillfully alludes to several African American cultural sources in the following strophes.

> I dream a world
> and then what
> my soul is resting
> but my feet are tired
>
> half the night gone
> I'm holding my own
> some half forgotten tune
> casual funk from a darker back room
>
> handful of gimme
> myself when I am real
> how would you know
> if you've never tasted
>
> a ramble in brambles
> the blacker more sweeter juicer
> pores sweat into blackberry tangles
> going back native natural country wild briers (3)

By infusing references from African American texts by Langston Hughes ("I dream a world"), Wallace Thurman ("blacker more sweeter juicer"), Charles Mingus ("myself when I am real"), and blues lyrics,

Mullen creates a poem in which Gates's theory of the "talking book," discussed earlier, occur in a single text. Due to Mullen's attention to the rhythmical and tonal qualities of alliteration, there is an unmistakable lyrical quality that lends the poem to a musical setting.[4] It is obvious that Mullen has continued to further the form by paying close attention to the methods of her literary and musical predecessors.

The jazz-influenced poetry of Bob Kaufman, Stephen Jonas, Jayne Cortez, and Nathaniel Mackey are worthy of critical study because they are writers who have not entered mainstream American literature, a canon of works that tend to be more accessible and less complex. That these writers choose to veer away from the conventional linear narrative makes their work all the more challenging. Although I have addressed the key concerns of the jazz poets studied here, I have on the whole given more attention to how jazz is used as a technique in the writing of poetry. Hopefully this brings literature closer to the music. I remember spending one hot summer day with my family in Boston's Franklin Park, listening to the Duke Ellington orchestra perform a benefit concert for the Elma Lewis School of Fine Arts. The tenor saxophonist Paul Gonsalvez rose up and played a particularly beautiful rendition of "Prelude to a Kiss." When he finished, there was a moment of silence, and Duke leaned over and said into his mike, "now that's poetry." And so it was.

Notes

Chapter 1: The Jazz Impulse in Poetry

1. The influence of the drum is also prevalent in hip-hop performance. XCLAN rapper Professor X (Lumumba Carson) talks about the continual importance of the drum in popular culture by remarking that "the drum connects our African genes whether we are conscious of our connection or not. . . . So what is not heard through the written word can be attached or completed by the drum" (Perkins, *Droppin' Science,* 23).

2. See my discussion of Jayne Cortez's poem "If the Drum Is a Woman," in chapter 5.

3. The image of the "talking book" and literacy has been dealt with in several slave narratives. See John Marrant, *Narrative of the Lord's Wonderful Dealings with John Marrant, A Black* (London: Gilbert and Plummer, 1785), and Olaudah Equiano, *The Interesting Narrative of the Life of Olaudah Equiano, or Gustavus Vassa, the African. Written by Himself* (London: by the author, 1789). For particularly insightful discussions about this topic, see Houston A. Baker Jr., *Blues, Ideology, and Afro-American Literature: A Vernacular Theory* (Chicago: University of Chicago Press, 1985), and Henry Louis Gates Jr., *The Signifying Monkey: A Theory of African-American Literary Criticism* (New York: Oxford University Press, 1988).

4. Although there are several instrumental and vocal versions that infer various sensual readings of Ellington's 1938 ballad, I am referring specifically to the recording *Braggin' in Brass—The Immortal 1938 Year,* Columbia 465464. In *The Swing Era,* Gunther Schuller writes that Ellington's instrumental version featured "typically sentimental celloistic trombone statements" along with "Ellington's fluttery arpeggio piano clichés" (102). I am implying that it is exactly these orchestral colors that evoke sensual imagery.

Chapter 2: Voices Crossing Over

1. For a detailed account and an insightful discussion of the political and social implications of Mamie Smith's song, see Adam Gussow, "Shoot Myself a Cop": Mamie Smith's 'Crazy Blues' as Social Text," *Callaloo* 25,

no. 1, Jazz Poetry Issue. For more general information on women jazz and blues vocalists, see Linda Dahl, *Stormy Weather: The Music and Lives of a Century of Jazz Women* (New York: Pantheon, 1984), and Derrick Stewart-Baxter, *Ma Rainey and the Classic Blues Singers* (New York: Stein & Day, 1970).

2. By opening my discussion on jazz poetry in this fashion, I hope to show how the music was viewed in the popular imagination. Approaching the music from this angle is significant because it demonstrates, like the notoriety of ODJB, how several writers made jazz poetry popular by linking the music to "black depravity." Of course several historical antecedents followed, particularly in regards to the way rock-and-roll was viewed by the American middle class in the late 1950s and early 1960s.

3. My use of the phrase "the music" occurs frequently throughout this book. I am using it in the same manner as most African American musicians, in that it refers not only to jazz but also to other African American musical genres. I agree with Ingrid Monson, who writes in *Saying Something: Jazz Improvisation and Interaction* (Chicago: University of Chicago Press, 1996) that "its usage inverts the hegemonic presupposition that Western classical music can stand for all music, setting African American varieties on an equal footing with other forms and asserting pride in an aesthetics of improvisation that expects those who come within its orbit to interact on its terms" (101).

4. I am referring to Langston Hughes, *The Weary Blues and Other Poems* (MGM, 3697, 1958), with music by Leonard Feather and Charles Mingus.

5. For further discussion on Reed's use of "Jes Grew," see Robert Elliot Fox, *Conscientious Sorcerers: The Black Postmodernist Fiction of LeRoi Jones/Amiri Baraka, Ishmael Reed, and Samuel R. Delany* (New York: Greenwood, 1987).

6. There are about three additional anthologies that include a significant amount of jazz-influenced contributions by women beats. They are Ann Charters, *Portable Beat Reader* (New York: Viking Penguin, 1992), Anne Waldman, *The Beat Book: Poems and Fiction from the Beat Generation* (Boston: Shambhala, 1996), and Richard Peabody, *A Different Beat: Writings by Women of the Beat Generation* (New York: Serpent's Tail/High Risk, 1997).

7. Two particularly insightful studies of Baraka's use of jazz are William J. Harris, *The Jazz Aesthetic: The Poetry and Poetics of Amiri Baraka* (Columbia: University of Missouri Press, 1985), and Frank Kofsky, *Black Nationalism and the Revolution in Music* (New York: Pathfinder, 1970).

8. Ras Baraka's poem "In the Tradition Too," dedicated to his parents Amiri and Amina Baraka, is similar in its approach to black literary and political figures as sources of strength. The work contains several references to the various styles of African American music but pays particular attention to the contributions of early rap artists like Public Enemy and Big Daddy Kane and of reggae musicians like Bob Marley and Steel Pulse. See Ras Baraka and Kevin Powell's excellent anthology, *In the Tradition: An Anthology of Young Black Writers* (New York: Writers & Readers, 1992).

9. For further discussion of the theoretical concepts of the black arts movement, see Larry Neal, *Visions of a Liberated Future: Black Arts Movement Writings* (New York: Thunder's Mouth, 1989), and Addison Gayle Jr., ed., *The Black Aesthetic* (New York: Doubleday, 1971). Carolyn Fowler has self-published an extensive bibliography of the movement. See Carolyn Fowler, *Black Arts and Black Aesthetics: A Bibliography* (Atlanta: Carolyn Fowler, 1973).

10. For an excellent interpretation of black cultural expression and the numerous poems written in response to the music of John Coltrane, the reader should consult Kimberly W. Benston's *Performing Blackness: Enactments of African-American Modernism* (London and New York: Routledge, 2000).

11. For further discussion, see Sascha Feinstein, "John Coltrane and Poetics: An Interview with Michael S. Harper," *Indiana Review* 12 (spring 1989): 1–12.

12. Although Sascha Feinstein and Aldon Lynn Nielsen briefly discuss the poetry of these musicians, further research needs to be done. For a list of noteworthy jazz poetry recordings, see the discography.

Chapter 3: Body and Soul

1. A similar appropriation has occurred in poetry as well, where writers like Kenneth Rexroth and Jack Kerouac have received more notoriety for their jazz-inspired verse than innovators like Bob Kaufman, Amiri Baraka, or Ted Joans. Why have there been several documentaries on Jack Kerouac that highlight the importance of jazz to his writing, but few on Amiri Baraka? Even a recent compilation by Rhino Records called *The Beat Generation* fails to include any work by these three African American innovators.

2. Kaufman's poem also echoes the importance of water as a continuing trope in African American literature. Similar imagery has appeared in the work of Olaudah Equiano, Frederick Douglass, Langston Hughes, and

Paule Marshall. For further discussion, see Houston A. Baker, *Blues, Ideology, and Afro-American Literature: A Vernacular Theory* (Chicago: University of Chicago Press, 1984) and Paul Gilroy, *The Black Atlantic: Modernity and Double Consciousness* (Cambridge: Harvard University Press, 1993).

3. For several years Eileen Kaufman has been responsible for keeping the poet's legacy alive. Selections from her memoir, *Who Wouldn't Walk with Tigers?*, has been published in various anthologies of beat writing. Bob Kaufman's protégé Tony Seymor has also been instrumental in pushing for recognition of the poet, encouraging former San Francisco mayor Dianne Feinstein to proclaim "Bob Kaufman Day" in 1987 and to have a street named in the poet's honor.

4. This poem, with its opening line "Derrat slegelations, flo goof babereo," was revised and published as "Crootey Songo" in the collection *Golden Sardine*. The poem is discussed in further detail later on in this chapter.

5. Kaufman uses a language and literary technique similar to recordings made by bop vocalist Babs Gonzales and comedian Richard "Lord" Buckley, who was famous for retelling Shakespeare and the New Testament in jive talk.

6. Maria Damon discusses in further detail how Kaufman evokes various historical references by manipulating the spelling of Caryl Chessman's name. See *The Dark End of the Street: Margins in American Vanguard Poetry* (Minneapolis: University of Minnesota Press, 1993), 41. See also Caryl Chessman's autobiography, *Cell 2455 Death Row* (New York: Prentice-Hall, 1954); and Milton Machlin and William Reid Woodfield, *Ninth Life* (New York: Putnam, 1961).

7. Refer to the recording Carmen McRae, *Carmen Sings Monk* (RCA 3086–4-N, 1990).

8. Perhaps Kaufman was also familiar with Dizzy Gillespie's humorous bebop rendition of the spiritual, "Swing Low Sweet Cadillac," in which Gillespie employs images of earthly wealth as a means of salvation.

Chapter 4: Now's the Time

1. Aldon Lynn Nielsen analyzes Jonas's poem "Cante Jondo for Soul Brother Jack Spicer, His Beloved California and Andalusia of Lorca" and briefly discusses the aesthetic and social connections between the two writers. See Aldon Lynn Nielsen, "No Saints in Three Acts," *Impercipient Lecture Series* 1, no. 6 (July 1997): 15.

2. Jonas's jazz-influenced poem "One of Three Musicians" appears in

Sascha Feinstein and Yusef Komunyakaa's *The Jazz Poetry Anthology* (Bloomington: Indiana University Press, 1991), thus assuring him a place in the developing jazz poetry canon.

3. Jonas's poem "The Music Master" (after a Mozart divertimento) shows how he adapts classical music to poetic form. For a further discussion of Jonas's use of classical music, see Joseph Torra's introduction to *Stephen Jonas: Selected Poems* (Hoboken: Talisman, 1994), 9.

4. The manner in which music and voice are measured in oral poetry is discussed in great detail in chapter 6 ("Songs and Chants") of Isidore Okpewho's *African Oral Literature: Backgrounds, Character, and Continuity* (Bloomington: Indiana University Press, 1992). Okpewho discusses a "musical ladder," of which the lowest level happens when narrators use "normal speech" and seldom break "into passages in which they consciously alter their tone of voice." The second level occurs when there is a "conscious twist to the voice all through performance" (131). This has particular relevance in the oral delivery of jazz poetry in which there is no musical accompaniment. Thus, the various levels of this musical ladder can be applied to specific jazz poetry performances. For further discussion of the relevance of breath and voice to measure line breaks and gauge the musicality of a poem, see Dennis Tedlock's *The Spoken Word and the Work of Interpretation* (Philadelphia: University of Pennsylvania Press, 1983) and his article "Toward an Oral Poetics," *New Literary History* 8 (1977): 507–9.

5. Paul Lawrence Dunbar's use of dialect was problematic. In his 1939 landmark study of African American poetry, J. Saunders Redding observed that Dunbar's dialect was not representative of several of the black communities in the American South, and there was doubt his poetry would have been understood. Redding writes that he had "scant knowledge of many dialects, [and] made a language, a synthetic dialect that could be read with ease and pleasure by northern whites to whom dialect meant only an amusing burlesque of Yankee English" (J. Saunders Redding, *To Make a Poet Black* [Ithaca: Cornell University Press, 1988], 63). Although this may be true, Dunbar did have a strong sense of the rhythmic qualities of black speech, as evidenced in several of his poems.

Chapter 5: Hot House

1. For further discussion of Cortez's performative qualities, see D. H. Melhem's *Heroism in the New Black Poetry* (Lexington: University Press of Kentucky, 1990), 181–94.

2. Black arts theorists such as Haki Madhubuti (Don L. Lee), Maulana Karenga, Larry Neal, Hoyt Fuller, Amiri Baraka, and Addison Gayle Jr.

rejected the Western standards that were applied to literature by African Americans and demanded that a black criterion be established for judging the beauty and validity of art. Thus, the "black aesthetic" became a new way to critique African American culture and to move the black community closer to "liberation" and self-definition. For additional discussion, see Darwin T. Turner's "Afro-American Literary Critics: An Introduction," in *The Black Aesthetic,* ed. Addison Gayle Jr. (New York: Doubleday, 1971), 59–77. In chapter 2 of this book, I discuss the importance of the black arts movement and its connection to jazz poetry. In addition, I highly recommend Lorenzo Thomas's article "Ascension: Music and the Black Arts Movement," in *Jazz among the Discourses,* ed. Krin Gabbard (Durham: Duke University Press, 1995), 256–74, for an excellent overview of the role music played in the movement. For an insightful discussion comparing the theoretical concepts of the black arts movement and the Harlem Renaissance, see Houston A. Baker Jr., *Afro-American Poetics: Revisions of Harlem and the Black Aesthetic* (Madison: Wisconsin University Press, 1988). See also Madhu Dubey's *Black Women Novelists and the Nationalist Aesthetic* (Bloomington: Indiana University Press, 1994); Phillip Brian Harper's "Nationalism and Social Division in Black Arts Poetry of the 1960s," *Critical Inquiry* 19 (winter 1993): 234–55; Abby Arthur Johnson and Ronald Maberry Johnson, *Propaganda and Aesthetics: The Literary Politics of Afro-American Magazines in the Twentieth Century* (Amherst: University of Massachusetts Press, 1979); and Larry Neal, *Visions of a Liberated Future: Black Arts Movement Writings* (New York: Thunder's Mouth Press, 1989).

3. The fact that Cortez makes the "lonely woman" black is significant. Her use of the phrase "dark like me" appears to echo the title of the book *Black Like Me* (Boston: Houghton Mifflin, 1961) that was subsequently made into a film in 1964. The story related the true experiences of a white reporter, John Howard Griffin, who used a chemical to turn his skin black in order to experience racial prejudice firsthand. By appropriating the phrase, Cortez implies that her character is no interlocutor, but one who has experienced racism firsthand. When I was a high school student in the 1970s, *Black Like Me* and Claude McKay's *Manchild and the Promised Land* were often used as the standard texts in English classes to introduce students to issues of racism. Once, on the television show *Saturday Night Live,* African American comedian Eddie Murphy inverted the idea by altering his appearance in order to lampoon white racial privilege, cleverly calling his skit, "White Like Me."

4. Albert Murray discusses this further in chapter 12 ("The Blues as Statement") in *Stomping the Blues* (New York: Da Capo Press, 1976). Murray shows how Louis Armstrong, Miles Davis, Lester Young, and Jelly

Roll Morton all developed a public persona that helped to articulate similar qualities found in their music. For further discussion concerning how the media manipulates jazz imagery, see Arthur Knight's "Jammin' the Blues, or the Sight of Jazz, 1944" and Krin Gabbard's "Signifyin(g) the Phallus: Mo' Better Blues and Representations of the Jazz Trumpet," in *Representing Jazz,* ed. Krin Gabbard (Durham: Duke University Press, 1995).

5. In *The Swing Era: The Development of Jazz, 1930–1945* (New York: Oxford University Press, 1989), Gunther Schuller describes the importance of Ellington's composition "Cotton Tail." He writes that it is a piece that "both in its conception and performance was an important precursor of the big-band style of modern jazz. Typically it did so years before anyone had heard of 'modern jazz.' The jazz avant-garde of the mid-forties all drew upon the ideas in this seminal record: Gillespie in evolving his big-band style, Woody Herman for his catalytic band of 1945" (126). The connection I see to Jayne Cortez's poem is that the poet wants to get beyond the simplistic images of Ellington as mere "ballroom entertainer" and reveal the complexity of his music.

6. The surrealist journal *Arsenal* had a special issue that included poems by African American musicians Joseph Jarman and Cecil Taylor. Also included was an essay by Franklin Rosemont, "Black Music and the Surrealist Revolution," that dealt with the affinity between surrealist subversion and black revolution. See *Surrealist Subversions: The Surrealist Movement in the United States,* ed. Ron Sakolsky (Brooklyn: Autonomedia, 2002), 630–39.

7. The opening lyrics to Duke Ellington's 1956 composition are "A drum is a woman / Who won't stay out of your blood. / A drum is a woman / Its beat is like the quickening of a heart in love." Jayne Cortez uses these opening lines in her poem, "If the Drum is a Woman / why are you pounding your drum into an insane babble / why are you pistol whipping your drum at dawn / why are you shooting through the head of your drum" to indicate that she is using "beating on the drum" as a metaphor for sexual abuse and physical abuse. However, during an interview when drummer Michael Carvin asked drummer Kenny Clarke about the phrase, Clarke responded by saying that the drum has a coordinating and nurturing role and is responsible for enabling the soloist to "stay on track." This view is obviously opposed to Cortez's imagery that uses the phrase as a vehicle to speak out against domestic violence. For further discussion, see Ingrid Monson, *Saying Something: Jazz Improvisation and Interaction* (Chicago: University of Chicago Press, 1996), 64–66.

8. For what continues to be one of the most elegant discussions of the effect the railroad had on African American music, see Albert Murray, *Stomping the Blues* (New York: Da Capo, 1976), 118–26.

9. Although "Oop-Bop Sh-Bam" was recorded by Gillespie in 1946, six months later another, even more popular version was performed by bebop drummer Kenny Clarke & His 52nd Street Boys on the recording *The Bebop Era* (RCA #519; rec.9/5.46).

10. The eminent scholar of African poetry's oral tradition, Dr. Isidore Okpewho, has informed me that "oriki" is a Yoruba word for a poetic phrase conveying a salute, an homage, or a descriptive epithet. Cortez's inclusion of the word is obviously important because it places Babs Gonzalez and bebop phrasing in a distinctly African context.

Chapter 6: Interstellar Space

1. Although black arts poets like Amiri Baraka, Haki Madhubuti (Don L. Lee), Ebon, and Sonia Sanchez were viewed as being avant-garde by conservative black and white literary critics, their work did have firm grounding in African oral traditions. Using Isidore Okpewho's *African Oral Literature: Backgrounds, Character, and Continuity* (Bloomington: Indiana University Press, 1992) as a key reference, Joyce Ann Joyce has argued convincingly that poet Sonia Sanchez and other black arts poets' work stems directly from the longstanding tradition of African praise poetry. For further discussion, see Joyce Ann Joyce, *Ijala: Sonia Sanchez and the African Poetic Tradition* (Chicago: Third World Press, 1996).

2. Richard Quinn's "The Creak of Categories: Nathaniel Mackey's *Strick: Song of the Andoumboulou 16–25,*" in *Callaloo* 23, no. 2 (spring 2000): 608–20, offers profound insight on how Mackey works with musicians.

3. Readers interested in a wide range and multifaceted critique of Mackey's work are encouraged to read the special issue of *Callaloo: A Journal of African-American and African Arts and Letters* that was guest edited by Paul Naylor (vol. 23, no. 2, spring 2000), which is entirely devoted to Mackey's work.

4. Sascha Feinstein devotes an entire chapter to poetry that responds to the music of *John Coltrane in Jazz Poetry: From the 1920s to the Present* (Westport, Conn.: Greenwood Press, 1997), 115–42. Feinstein argues that Coltrane as a musician/philosopher had particular relevance for writers like Amiri Baraka, Michael Harper, Ebon, John Sinclair, Sonia Sanchez, Carolyn M. Rodgers, and several poets of the sixties who shared the anger and social political frustration Coltrane's work often articulated. Gunter H. Lenz's "Black Poetry and Black Music: History and Tradition: Michael Harper and John Coltrane," in *History and Tradition in Afro-American Culture* (Frankfurt and New York: Campus Verlag, 1984), is another important study that examines Coltrane's influence on American poetics,

with particular focus on Michael Harper's work. For further discussion, see Kimberly W. Benston's essay "Late Coltrane: A Re-membering of Orpheus," *Massachusetts Review* (winter 1977): 770–81. Benston correctly observes that "passages in Trane's music become so bright and so piercing that the sounds seemed to be words" (770).

5. A superb example of what I am referring to can be can be heard on John Coltrane's recording *Crescent* (Impulse! MCAD 5889 CD). Recorded in 1964 with McCoy Tyner on piano, Jimmy Garrison on bass, and Elvin Jones on drums, Coltrane brings a hesitant quality to his musical phrasing as he pushes himself further into spiritual exploration.

6. "Capricorn Rising" was later revised and retitled "Sweet Mystic Beast" and included in the collection *School of Udhra* (San Francisco: City Lights Books, 1993), 34–37. In the revised poem, more attention is given to the importance of the ram as a symbolic animal that represents creativity, particularly the music that emanates through the ram's horn. However, conspicuously missing are any direct references to Haiti and the music of Pharoah Sanders.

Coda: The Mixtery of Jazz Poetry

1. *Copacetic* is an adjective that was often used by jazz musicians in the 1920s and 1960s to describe an exceptionally fine musical performance. My use of it here is meant to connect Kaufman's poetry to its musical origins. For further discussion, see Neil Leonard's "The Jazzman's Verbal Usage," *Black American Literature Forum* 20 (1986): 151–60.

2. For a complete list of recordings by Jayne Cortez, please refer to the discography at the end of this book.

3. See also Robert Peter Gaspar's "Everyone and I Stopped Breathing: Jazz in American Poetry" (Ph.D. diss., University of Connecticut, 1992); Patrick James Brown's "Jazz Poetry: Definition, Analysis, and Performance" (Ph.D. diss., University of Southern California, 1972); and David Chinitz's "Jazz and Jazz Discourse in Modernist Poetry: T. S. Eliot and Langston Hughes" (Ph.D. diss., Columbia University, 1993). Each of these dissertations discusses jazz influences on modern American poetry and provides historical overviews.

4. The musicality of the poem has not gone unnoticed by my father, T. J. Anderson Jr., who set portions of *Muse and Drudge* to music in his composition *Seven Cabaret Songs*. The work premiered on September 16, 1995, at Wright State University in Dayton, Ohio, and was performed by jazz vocalist Nnena Freelon and the Mallarme Chamber Players.

Works Cited

Allen, Donald, ed. *The New American Poetry.* New York: Grove, 1960.

Allen, Donald, and Warren Tallman, eds. *The Poetics of New American Poetry.* New York: Grove, 1973.

Bacon, Paul. "Two Notes on Modern Jazzmen." In *The Art of Jazz: Ragtime to Bebop,* ed. Martin Williams, 216–18. New York: Da Capo, 1980.

Baker, Houston A. *Afro-American Poetics: Revisions of Harlem and the Black Aesthetic.* Madison: University of Wisconsin Press, 1988.

———. *Modernism and the Harlem Renaissance.* Chicago: University of Chicago Press, 1987.

Baraka, Amiri [LeRoi Jones]. "Amiri Baraka: John Coltrane, Jazz and Poetry." With Joel Lewis. *The Black Nation: Journal of African American Thought* 5 (summer/fall 1986): 73–79.

———. *The Autobiography of LeRoi Jones / Amiri Baraka.* New York: Freundlich, 1984.

———. *Black Magic: Collected Poetry, 1961–1967.* Indianapolis: Bobbs, 1969.

———. *Black Music.* New York: Quill, 1967.

———. *Blues People: Negro Music in White America.* New York: Morrow, 1963.

———. *Funk Lore: New Poems (1984–1995).* Los Angles: Littoral, 1996.

———. *Transbluesency: The Selected Poems, 1961–1995.* New York: Marsilio, 1995.

Basie, Count. *Goodmorning Blues: The Autobiography of Count Basie.* As told to Albert Murray. New York: Random House, 1985.

Benston, Kimberly W. "Late Coltrane: A Re-membering of Orpheus." *Massachusetts Review* (winter 1977): 770–81.

———. *Performing Blackness: Enactments of African-American Modernism.* New York: Routledge, 2000.

Berliner, Paul F. *Thinking in Jazz: The Infinite Art of Improvisation.* Chicago: University of Chicago Press, 1994.

Bremser, Ray. *Blowing Mouth: The Jazz Poems, 1958–1970.* Cherry Valley, N.Y.: Cherry Valley Editions, 1978.

Brown, Sterling A. *The Collected Poems.* New York: Harper, 1983.

Carruth, Hayden. *Sitting In: Selected Writings on Jazz, Blues, and Related Topics*. Iowa City: University of Iowa Press, 1986.

Cerulli, Dom, Burt Korall, and Mort Nasatir, eds. *The Jazz Word*. New York: Ballantine, 1960.

Clay, Mel. *Jazz, Jail, and God. Bob Kaufman: An Impressionistic Biography*. San Francisco: Androgyne Books, 1987.

Coolidge, Clark. *Now It's Jazz: Writings on Kerouac and the Sounds*. Albuquerque: Living Batch Press, 1999.

Cortez, Jayne. *Coagulations: New and Selected Poems*. New York: Thunder's Mouth, 1984.

———. *Firespitter*. New York: Bola, 1982.

———. *Jazz Fan Looks Back*. Brooklyn: Hanging Loose Press, 2002.

———. *Mouth on Paper*. New York: Bola, 1977.

———. *Pisstained Stairs and the Monkey Man's Wares*. New York: Phase Text, 1969.

———. *Somewhere in Advance of Nowhere*. New York: Serpent's Tail, 1996.

Crouch, Stanley. "Big Star Calling." *Yardbird Reader* 5 (1976): 99.

Damon, Maria. *The Dark End of the Street: Margins in American Vanguard Poetry*. Minneapolis: University of Minnesota Press, 1993.

Deren, Maya. *Divine Horsemen: The Living Gods of Haiti*. New York: McPherson, 1953.

Dillard, J. L. *Lexicon of Black English*. New York: Seabury Press, 1977.

Douglass, Frederick. *Life and Times*. New York: Collier, 1962.

Dubois, W.E.B. *The Souls of Black Folks*. 1903. New York: New American Library, 1969.

Dumas, Henry. *Play Ebony, Play Ivory*. Ed. Eugene Redmond. New York: Random, 1974.

Dunbar, Paul Laurence. *The Complete Poems*. 1913. New York: Dodd, 1980.

Duncan, Robert. *Fictive Certainties*. New York: New Direction, 1985.

Ellison, Ralph. *Invisible Man*. New York: Vintage, 1952.

———. *Shadow and Act*. New York: Vintage, 1964.

Farnsworth, Robert M. *Melvin B. Tolson, 1898–1966: Plain Talk and Poetic Prophecy*. Columbia: University of Missouri Press, 1984.

Feinstein, Sascha. *Jazz Poetry: From the 1920s to the Present*. Westport, Conn.: Greenwood Press, 1997.

Feinstein, Sascha, and Yusef Komunyakaa, eds. *The Jazz Poetry Anthology*. Bloomington: Indiana University Press, 1991.

———. *The Second Set: The Jazz Poetry Anthology*. Vol. 2. Bloomington: Indiana University Press, 1996.

Fernett, Gene. *Swing Out.* Midland, Mich.: V. Pindell, 1970.

Floyd, Samuel A., Jr. *The Power of Black Music: Interpreting Its History from Africa to the United States.* New York: Oxford University Press, 1995.

Foster, Edward. "An Interview with Nathaniel Mackey." *Talisman: A Journal of Contemporary Poetry and Poetics* 9 (fall 1992): 48–61.

Funkhouser, Gary. "Interview with Cecil Taylor." *Hambone* (n.d.): 18–39.

Garber, Frederick. "Fabulating Jazz." In *Representing Jazz,* ed. Krin Gabbard, 70–103. Durham: Duke University Press, 1995.

Gates, Henry Louis, Jr. *The Signifying Monkey: A Theory of African-American Literary Criticism.* New York: Oxford University Press, 1988.

Gates, Henry Louis, Jr., and Nellie Y. McKay, eds. *The Norton Anthology of African American Literature.* New York: W. W. Norton, 1997.

Gillespie, Dizzy. *To BE, or Not . . . to BOP.* With Al Fraser. Garden City, N.Y.: Doubleday, 1979.

Giovanni, Nikki. "Pisstained Stairs and the Monkey Man's Wares." *Negro Digest* 19 (December 1969): 35.

Grant, Barry Keith. "Purple Passages or Fiestas in Blue? Notes Toward an Aesthetic of Vocalese." In *Representing Jazz,* ed. Krin Gabbard, 285–303. Durham: Duke University Press, 1995.

Gruttola, Raffael de. "A Reminiscence." In *The Poetry of Stephen Jonas,* 29–30. Somerville, Mass.: Lift, 1992.

Gussow, Adam. "Shoot Myself a Cop": Mamie Smith's 'Crazy Blues' as Social Text." *Callaloo* 25, no. 1 (winter 2002): 8–44.

Harper, Michael S. *Healing Song for the Inner Ear.* Urbana: University of Illinois Press, 1985.

———. *Songlines in Michael Tree: New and Collected Poems.* Urbana: University of Illinois Press, 2000.

Harris, William J. *The Poetry and Poetics of Amiri Baraka: The Jazz Aesthetic.* Columbia: University of Missouri Press, 1985.

Hartman, Charles O. *Jazz Text: Voice and Improvisation in Poetry, Jazz, and Song.* Princeton: Princeton University Press, 1991.

Henderson, Stephen, ed. *Understanding the New Black Poetry: Black Speech and Black Music as Poetic References.* New York: Morrow, 1973.

Hill, Patricia Liggins, and Bernard W. Bell, eds. *Call and Response: The Riverside Anthology of the African American Literary Tradition.* Boston: Houghton, 1998.

Hughes, Langston. *The Collected Poems.* New York: Knopf, 1994.

Jarrett, Michael. *Drifting on a Read: Jazz as a Model for Writing.* Albany: SUNY Press, 1999.

Joans, Ted. "Jazz and Poetry." University of California at Berkeley, May 14, 1980.

———. *Teducation: Selected Poems, 1949–1999.* Minneapolis: Coffee House Press, 1999.

Johnston, Devin. "Nathaniel Mackey and Lost Time." *Callaloo* 23, no. 2 (spring 2000): 563–70.

Jonas, Stephen. *Exercises for Ear: Being a Primer for the Beginner in the American Idiom.* London: Ferry, 1968.

———. "Stephen Jonas: Four Letters." Ed. Stephen Dignazio. *:that: short sets of writing* 23 (July 1994): 1–16.

———. "The Poetry of Stephen Jonas." Ed. Joseph Torra. *Lift* 10–11 (1992).

———. *Selected Poems.* Ed. Joseph Torra. Hoboken, N.J.: Talisman, 1994.

Jost, Ekkehard. *free jazz.* New York: Da Capo, 1981.

Joyce, Joyce Ann. *Ijala: Sonia Sanchez and the African Poetic Tradition.* Chicago: Third World, 1996.

Kaufman, Bob. *The Ancient Rain.* New York: New Directions, 1981.

———. *Cranial Guitar: Selected Poems.* Minneapolis: Coffee House, 1996.

———. *Golden Sardine.* San Francisco: City Lights, 1967.

———. *Solitudes Crowded with Loneliness.* New York: New Directions, 1965.

Kelley, Robin D. G. *Yo' Mama's Disfunktional! Fighting the Culture Wars in Urban America.* Boston: Beacon Press, 1997.

Kelly, Robert, moderator. "Jazz Poetry: A Conversation." Interview with Yusef Komunyakaa and William Matthews. *Georgia Review* 46, no. 4 (winter 1992): 645–61.

Kerouac, Jack. *Mexico City Blues (242 Choruses).* New York: Grove, 1959.

———. *San Francisco Blues.* New York: Penguin, 1995.

Knight, Brenda, ed. *Women of the Beat Generation: The Writers, Artists, and Muses at the Heart of a Revolution.* Berkeley: Conari, 1996.

Lange, Art, and Nathaniel Mackey, eds. *Moment's Notice: Jazz in Poetry and Prose.* Minneapolis: Coffee House, 1993.

Last Poets. *Vibes from the Scribes.* Trenton: Africa World, 1992.

Lenz, Gunter H. *History and Tradition in Afro-American Culture.* Frankfurt and New York: Campus Verlag, 1984.

Lindsay, Vachel. *Collected Poems.* New York: Macmillan, 1949.

———. *Letters of Vachel Lindsay.* Ed. Marc Chenetier. New York: Burt Franklin, 1979.

Litweiler, John. *Ornette Coleman: A Harmolodic Life.* New York: William Morrow and Co., 1992.

Lock, Graham, ed. *Mixtery: A Festschrift for Anthony Braxton.* Devon, U.K.: Stride Publications, 1995.

Mackey, Nathaniel. *Atet A.D.* San Francisco: City Lights, 2001.

———. *Bedouin Hornbook.* In *From a Broken Bottle Traces of Perfume Still Emanate.* Vol. 1. Lexington: *Calalloo* Fiction Series, University of Kentucky Press, 1986.

———. "Cante Moro." In *Disembodied Poetics: Annals of the Jack Kerouac School,* ed. Anne Waldman and Andrew Schelling, 71–94. Albuquerque: University of New Mexico Press, 1994.

———. *Discrepant Engagement: Dissonance, Cross-Culturality, and Experimental Writing.* New York: Cambridge Press, 1993.

———. *Djbot Baghostus's Run.* In *From a Broken Bottle Traces of Perfume Still Emanate.* Vol. 2. Los Angeles: Sun and Moon, 1993.

———. *Eroding Witness.* Urbana: University of Illinois Press, 1985.

———. *School of Udhra.* San Francisco: City Lights, 1983.

———. *Whatsaid Serif.* San Francisco: City Lights, 1998.

Madhubuti, Haki R. [Don L. Lee] *Don't Cry, Scream.* Chicago: Third World Press, 1969.

———. *Dynamite Voices: Black Poets of the 1960s.* Detroit: Broadside, 1971.

Major, Clarence, ed. *Juba to Jive: A Dictionary of African-American Slang.* New York: Penguin, 1994.

Melhem, D. H. *Heroism in the New Black Poetry: Introductions and Interviews.* Lexington: University Press of Kentucky, 1990.

———. "A Melus Profile and Interview: Jayne Cortez." *Melus* 21 (spring 1996): 71–79.

Meltzer, David, ed. *Reading Jazz.* San Francisco: Mercury House, 1993.

Mullen, Harryette. *Muse and Drudge.* Philadelphia: Singing Horse, 1995.

———. "Telegraphs from a Distracted Sibyl." *American Book Review* 13, no. 3 (February–March 1996): 5.

Murray, Albert. *Stomping the Blues.* New York: McGraw-Hill, 1976.

Natambu, Kofi. "Words and Music in America." In *Moment's Notice: Jazz in Poetry and Prose,* ed. Art Lange and Nathaniel Mackey, 342. Minneapolis: Coffee House, 1993.

Naylor, Paul. "An Interview with Nathaniel Mackey." *Callaloo* 23, no. 2 (spring 2000): 645–63.

Neal, Larry. "Some Reflections on the Black Aesthetic." In *Black Aesthetic,* ed. Addison Gayle Jr., 12–15. New York: Doubleday, 1971.

Nelson, Cary, ed. *Anthology of Modern American Poetry.* New York: Oxford University Press, 2000.

Nielsen, Aldon Lynn. *Black Chant: Languages of African-American Postmodernism.* Cambridge: Cambridge University Press, 1997.

———. "No Saints in Three Acts." *Impercipient Lecture Series* 1, no. 6 (July 1997): 1–40.

O'Hara, Frank. *Lunch Poems.* San Francisco: City Lights, 1964.

Okpewho, Isidore. *African Oral Literature: Backgrounds, Character, and Continuity.* Bloomington: Indiana University Press, 1992.

O'Leary, Peter. "Deep Trouble/Deep Treble: Nathaniel Mackey's Gnostic Rasp." *Callaloo* 23, no. 2 (spring 2000): 516–37.

Olson, Charles. "Human Universe. In *Selected Writings,* ed. Robert Creeley, 53–66. New York: New Directions.

———. *The Maximus Poems.* Ed. George Butterick. Berkeley: University of California Press, 1979.

———. *Muthulogos: The Collected Lectures and Interviews.* Vol. 2. Ed. George F. Butterick. Bolinas, Calif.: Four Seasons Foundation, 1978.

———. "Projective Verse." In *Selected Writings,* ed. Robert Creeley, 15–30. New York: New Directions, 1966.

O'Malley, Robert G., ed. *The Jazz Cadence of American Culture.* New York: Columbia University Press, 1998.

Peabody, Richard. ed. *A Different Beat: Writings by Women of the Beat Generation.* New York: High Risk Books, 1997.

Porter, Lewis. *John Coltrane. His Life and Music.* Ann Arbor: University of Michigan Press, 1999.

Pound, Ezra. *Selected Poems.* New York: New Directions, 1926.

Quinn, Richard. "The Creak of Categories: Nathaniel Mackey's *Strick: Song of the Andoumboulou 16–25.*" *Callaloo* 23, no. 2 (spring 2000): 608–20.

Radano, Ronald M. "Jazzin' the Classics: The AACM's Challenge to Mainstream Aesthetic." *Black Music Research Journal* 12, no. 1 (1992): 79–95.

———. *New Musical Figurations: Anthony Braxton's Cultural Critique.* Chicago: University of Chicago Press, 1992.

Rampersad, Arnold. *The Life of Langston Hughes.* Vol. 1. New York: Oxford University Press, 1986.

Redmond, Eugene B. *Drumvoices: The Mission of Afro-American Poetry.* Garden City: Doubleday, 1976.

Reed, Ishmael. *Mumbo Jumbo.* Garden City: Doubleday, 1972.

Rexroth, Kenneth. *World Outside the Window: The Selected Essays of*

Kenneth Rexroth. Ed. Bradford Morrow. New York: New Directions, 1987.

Rosemont, Franklin. "Black Music and the Surrealist Revolution." *Surrealist Subversions: The Surrealist Movement in the United States*, ed. Ron Sakolsky, 630–39. Brooklyn: Autonomedia, 2002.

Rosemont, Penelope, ed. *Surrealist Women: An International Anthology*. Austin: University of Texas Press, 1998.

Rowe, Mike. *Chicago Blues: The Music and the City*. New York: Da Capo, 1981.

Rowell, Charles. "An Interview with Nathaniel Mackey." *Callaloo* 23, no. 2 (spring 2000): 703–15.

Sales, Grover. *Jazz: America's Classical Music*. New York: Prentice, 1984.

Sanchez, Sonia. *I've Been a Woman: New and Selected Poems*. Chicago: Third World, 1978.

Sandberg, Carl. *Complete Poems*. New York: Harcourt, 1950.

Schuller, Gunther. *Early Jazz*. New York: Oxford University Press, 1968.

———. *The Swing Era: The Development of Jazz, 1930–1945*. New York: Oxford University Press.

Scroggins, Mark. "Nathaniel Mackey." *Dictionary of Literary Biography*. Vol. 169, *American Poets since World War II*. Detroit: Gale Research, 1996.

Seymour, Tony. "A Be-Bop History of the Original Be-Bop Man." *Berkeley Barb*, May 6–12, 1977, 6–7.

———. "Don't Forget Bob Kaufman." *California Living. San Francisco Sunday Examiner and Chronicle*, April 25, 1976.

Taylor, Cecil. "Garden." In *Moment's Notice: Jazz in Poetry and Prose*, ed. Art Lange and Nathaniel Mackey, 116–37. Minneapolis: Coffee House, 1993.

Tolson, M. B. *Harlem Gallery: Book I, The Curator*. New York: Twayne, 1965.

Torra, Joseph. Introduction. *Stephen Jonas: Selected Poems*, ed. Joseph Torra, 1–12. Hoboken: Talisman, 1994.

Tracy, Steven C. *Langston Hughes and the Blues*. Urbana: University of Illinois Press, 1988.

Troupe, Quincy. "The Poetry of Jayne Cortez as Ritualized Passage." *Yardbird Reader* 5 (1976): 91–92.

Wallenstein, Barry. "Poetry and Jazz: A Twentieth-Century Wedding." *Black American Literature Forum* 25 (fall 1991): 595–620.

Werner, Craig Hansen. *Playing the Changes: From Afro-Modernism to the Jazz Impulse*. Urbana: University of Illinois Press, 1994.

Williams, Martin T. *Jazz Heritage*. New York: Oxford University Press, 1985.

Williams, William Carlos. *Interviews with William Carlos Williams: "Speaking Straight Ahead."* Ed. Linda Welshimer Wagner. New York: New Directions, 1976.

———. *Selected Essays*. New York: New Directions, 1969.

Woodson, Jon. "Jayne Cortez." *Dictionary of Literary Biography*. Vol. 41, *Afro-American Poets since 1955*. Detroit: Gale Research, 1985.

Discography

Armstrong, Louis. *Heebie Jeebies*. Okeh, 8300-A, 1926.

———. *The Louis Armstrong Story*. Vol. 2. Columbia, CL 852, 1957.

Austin, James, ed. *The Beat Generation*. Rhino, R4 70281, 1992.

Baraka, Amiri. *New Music—New Poetry*. India Navigation, 1048, 1981.

Calloway, Cab. *Hotcha Razz-Ma-Tazz*. Victor, 24690, 1934.

———. *Minnie the Moocher*. RCA, INTS 5121, 1981.

Coleman, Ornette. *The Empty Foxhole*. Blue Note, 1967.

———. *The Shape of Jazz to Come*. Atlantic, 781339–2, 1960.

Coltrane, John. *Crescent*. Impulse!, MCAD 5889, 1964.

———. *Giant Steps*. Atlantic, SD 1311, 1959.

———. *Kulu Se Mama*. Impulse!, AS-9106, 1966.

———. *A Love Supreme*. Impulse!, 77, 1964.

Cortez, Jayne. *Celebrations and Solitudes*. Strata-East, SES 7418, 1974.

———. *Cheerful and Optimistic*. Bola, BP-9401, 1994.

———. *Maintain Control*. Bola, BP-8601, 1986.

———. *Taking the Blues Back Home*. Verve, 314 531 918–2, 1996.

———. *There It Is*. Bola, BP-8201, 1982.

———. *Unsubmissive Blues*. Bola, BP-8001, 1980.

Davis, Miles. *Birth of the Cool*. Capital, T762, 1950.

Eckstine, Billy. *Jelly, Jelly*. Bluebird, B-11065, 1940.

Ellington, Duke. *A Drum Is a Woman*. Columbia, CL 951, 1957.

———. *At His Very Best*. RCA, LPM 1715, 1959.

Gillespie, Dizzy. *Oop-Bop-Sh'Bam*. Musicraft, 383, 1946.

Ginsberg, Allen. *First Blues*. John Hammond Records, 3905, 1982.

Gonzales, Babs. *Tales of Manhattan*. Jaro, JAM 5000, 1959.

Holiday, Billie. *Lady in Autumn*. Verve, 849434–2, 1959.

Hughes, Langston. *The Weary Blues and Other Poems*. Verve, 841 600-2, 1990.

Kerouac, Jack. *Blues and Haikus*. Hanover, 5006, 1958.

———. *Poetry for the Beat Generation*. Hanover, HML 500, 1958.

Kubernick, Harvey, ed. *JazzSpeak: A Word Collection*. New Alliance, NAR CD 054, 1991.

The Last Poets. *Chastisement*. Blue Thumb, BTS 39, 1972.

Lowenfels, Walter, ed. *New Jazz Poets*, Smithsonian, Cassette Series: 09751, 1967.

Mackey, Nathaniel. *Strick: Song of the Andoumboulou 16–25*. Memphis: Spoken Engine Co., 1995.

McRae, Carmen. *Carmen Sings Monk*. RCA, 83086, 1988.

Mingus, Charles. *A Modern Jazz Symposium of Music and Poetry with Charles Mingus*. Bethlehem, 3041, 1957.

———. *Thirteen Pictures: The Charles Mingus Anthology*. Rhino, R2 71402, 1977.

Monk, Thelonious. *The Composer*. Columbia, 463338, 1968.

Nordine, Ken. *Word Jazz*. Vol. 1. Rhino, R2 70773, 1990.

Patchen, Kenneth. *Poetry and Jazz at the Blackhawk*. Fantasy, 7008, 1958.

———. *Reads with the Chamber Jazz Sextet*. Cadence, CLP 3004, 1960.

Planets, Digable. *Reachin' (A New Refutation of Time and Space)*. Pendulum, 61414, 1993.

Rexroth, Kenneth, and Lawrence Ferlinghetti. *Poetry Readings in the Cellar*. Fantasy, 7002, 1957.

Sanders, Pharoah. *Journey to the One*. Evidence, 22016, 1967.

Shepp, Archie. *Fire Music*. ABC Records, A-86, 1965.

Smith, Bessie. *The World's Greatest Blues Singer*. Columbia, GP33, 1970.

Sun Ra and Henry Dumas. *The Ark and the Ankh in Conversation 1966*. Slug's Saloon, NYC. CD-1Ket02, 2001.

Taylor, Cecil. *Chinampas*. Leo Records, CDLR 153, 1991.

United Future Organization (Tadashi Yabe, Toshio Matsuura, Raphael Sebbag). *Loud Talkin*. Verve, 314 518 166–2, 1994.

Us3. *Hand on the Torch*. Blue Note, B000005HB8, 1993.

Index